THE

FOUR CIVILIZATIONS OF THE WORLD.

THE FOUR CIVILIZATIONS

OF

THE WORLD.

AN HISTORICAL RETROSPECT.

By HENRY WIKOFF,

AUTHOR OF "A VISIT TO PRINCE LOUIS NAPOLEON AT HAM," "POLITICAL ESSAYS," ETC., ETC.

PHILADELPHIA:
J. B. LIPPINCOTT & CO.
1874.

TO THE READER.

It has often struck me that a book was wanted that would give a concise and intelligible exposition of the history of France, England, and the United States. In this country especially, men, for the most part, are too busy to ransack ponderous volumes and grope their way through misty disquisitions. Furthermore, the history of these countries is often written with so much bias that it is indispensable to read more than one to acquire an accurate knowledge of their various phases during the vicissitudes that have befallen them. I have attempted, however inadequately, to supply this desideratum. The present volume contains a condensed sketch of the countries above named; and I may venture to challenge the most rigid criticism on the score of its perfect independence and impartiality; for without these history is but a delusion and a snare.

It is not a mere chronicle of facts and dates I have aimed at, but rather such an interpretation of the events of history and the actions of men as to show the effect of one and the influence of the other. In order that the distinctive features of the fourth civilization, under which we are now living, might be the more readily discerned, I have given, with extreme brevity, a *résumé* of the three ancient civilizations. I lingered for a moment over the marvels of the third one, not merely because it so completely eclipsed all that preceded it, but that it has left its impress on the world even to this very day.

Whoever seeks to understand the actual condition of France, England, and the United States, must penetrate into the mysteries of their past. The best guide to a knowledge of an individual is an investigation of his antecedents. So with a nation, which, through its infancy, youth, and maturity, undergoes various transformations, according to the circumstances which have accompanied its development. "A nation," said Jean Lemoine recently, speaking of France, "a nation, especially a great nation like ours, consists of its past, of its traditions, of an accumulated heritage of laws and customs, which are a part of its being." We must go back then to the origin of a country, and follow it, however rapidly, through its career if we would appreciate its actual position. To spare the reader the bewildering mass of details that usually forms the staple of history, I have discarded all irrelevant matter, all romantic incident, and sought to fix his attention on the important links in the long chain of cause and effect that constitute the story of the world. Without aspiring to the rank of those fortunate few alluded to by the poet—"*Felix qui potuit rerum cognoscere causas*"—still I entertain the hope that no one who peruses this retrospect will lay it down without a more just conception of the mysterious designs of Providence, which, after suffering mankind to endure for long centuries the deceptions and oppression of the three ancient civilizations, suddenly gave a new direction to their destiny by ordaining the advent of Christianity, the fourth civilization, which has brought in its train such amazing results.

It will be observed that this book, beginning at three thousand years before Christ, closes about the year eighteen hundred and thirty; and should its reception be at all encouraging, I propose to follow it up with one or more volumes, depicting the events of my own time, and the men who have figured in them.

THE AUTHOR.

CONTENTS.

FIRST CIVILIZATION.

SECOND CIVILIZATION.

A MYSTERY.

THIRD CIVILIZATION.

FOURTH CIVILIZATION.

THE PAPACY.

THE UNITED STATES.

AN HISTORICAL RETROSPECT.

FIRST CIVILIZATION.

ASIA.

THE first civilization on record is that of Hindostan, more familiarly known as India. Its origin is wrapped in fable, but the first dynasty may be traced to 3200 years before Christ. The date of the sacred books entitled the "Vedas" is put down at fifteen centuries before the same period. The "Institutes of Menu," a compilation of moral and political laws, are said to have appeared some twelve centuries before the Christian era.

The most remarkable feature in this civilization is, that it remains to this day nearly what it was five thousand years ago: that is to say, the vast majority of the population now, as then, are sunk in poverty and slavery; whilst the Upper Classes monopolize all the wealth and power, political and social.

The singular duration of this ill-balanced system is due to causes not difficult to discover. Chief among these must be placed the climate of the country. The heat makes the soil fertile, and food abundant and cheap. The excess of population, which is the natural result, produces an overstocked labor market, and makes wages so low as barely to sustain life.* The entire product of the industry of the masses, constituting the wealth of the country, is and has ever been, in the hands of the Upper Classes; and they, possessing the wealth, are able to engross all the knowledge, for wealth gives leisure, and leisure yields knowledge. Wealth and knowledge always command power, and thus it has come to pass that in India the Upper Classes are tyrants, and the people all slaves. This state of things, which owed its origin to physical causes, the laws and the religions of the country have from the remotest periods sought to perpetuate. The code attributed to Menu, already alluded to, rigidly forbids the people, under the cruellest penalties, to acquire knowledge. For instance, one of these native laws says:—"If, moved by the desire of instruction, any one listen to the reading of the sacred books, burning oil is to be poured into his ears. If, however, any one commit them to memory, he is to be killed." These and similar enactments are levelled especially at the Sudras—that is, the laboring population.

The Sudras are estimated by various writers at three-fourths of the Hindoos. The remaining fourth is divided into three *castes*. The first consists of the priests and the learned, and from this class all the functionaries are taken; the second *caste* consists of

* It is beyond dispute that wages are determined by the supply of labor in the long run. Labor may sometimes increase, it is true, without affecting wages, but this can take place only up to a certain point. When labor becomes redundant, wages must fall.

the army; the third, of the merchants and agriculturists. Below the fourth and lowest *caste*—the Sudras already mentioned—is still another order: those known as Pariahs—persons who have been expelled from the other *castes*, and from whom all Hindoos shrink with horror.

The oldest religion in India, and in the world, is Brahminism. It recognizes a Supreme Deity, who manifests himself in three forms and under three names, constituting a trinity, but who is worshipped as one god. The first manifestation is Brahma, the creator, who represents the past. His emblem is the sun. The second is Vishnu, the conservative principle, who represents the present. His emblem is water. The third is Siva, the principle of destruction, who represents the future. His emblem is fire. There are, besides, a number of subaltern gods, who execute the mandates of these three. The followers of Brahminism believe in the immortality of the soul in the form of metempsychosis; and their rites consist in ablutions, abstinences, &c. Brahminism is full of superstitions, some of which are of a revolting character. At the *fête* of the Juggernaut, the car of the god crushed under its iron wheels the fanatics who believed such a death ensured eternal happiness. Other zealots inflicted on themselves the most cruel tortures. Widows, for example, burned themselves on the bodies of their dead husbands.* It numbers about 100,000,000 of believers, and is still in many respects the dominant religion of Hindostan.

Another religion of Asia, which counts a still greater

* The English Government has humanely suppressed these odious customs.

following, having some 200,000,000 of adherents, is Buddhism, which was founded some 600 years before Christ, and was first preached in the north of India. It differs from Brahminism in one essential point: it admits all *castes* within its fold, and foreigners as well as natives. This religion is purely spiritual, and the chief deity, Buddha, represents supreme reason and absolute intelligence. It declares our present existence to be imperfect and perishable; that the world is an illusion of the senses; and that the soul should be detached from material things, and prepared for entrance into the true and imperishable world, where Buddha reigns supreme in a region eternal and indestructible. This religion appeared in China in the first century of our era, and continued to overspread various parts of Asia. It has been furiously persecuted by Brahminism, which in the fourteenth century expelled it from India; though its followers are now twice as numerous as those of the persecuting faith. Its sacred books are called "Commandments," and copies exist in the Great Library of Paris.

From this rapid sketch it will be seen that the laws and religion of the oldest empire in the world combined to maintain the ascendency of the Upper Classes, and to perpetuate the subjection of the masses. Historians note as a phenomenon that the people have never made an effort to throw off the yoke by insurrection. Whilst wars between Kings and Dynasties, whilst conspiracies and revolutions among the Upper Classes, have been common enough, the laboring population have tamely submitted to their fate, as if conscious that it was ordained of nature and nature's God.

A conclusive proof that it is to physical causes, such as climate, food, and soil, the condition of Asia is to be ascribed, is the fact that all tropical countries are in a similar condition. "There is no instance on record of any tropical country," says a learned writer, "where wealth having been extensively accumulated, the people have escaped their fate; no instance in which the heat of the climate has not caused abundance of food, and the abundance of food caused an unequal distribution, first of wealth, and then of political and social power. Among nations subjected to these conditions the people have counted for nothing; they have had no voice in the management of the State, no control over the wealth their own industry created; their only business has been to labor, their only duty to obey."

Thus much of Asia, usually called the cradle of the human race, since its history began there. It is declared by some writers that the *authentic* history of this continent hardly begins before the end of the tenth century A.D.

SECOND CIVILIZATION.

AFRICA

WHETHER we are to look for the first traces of civilization on the continent of Africa in Egypt or Ethiopia is uncertain; but it is beyond question that the former country ultimately attained the highest development. The history of Egypt may be dated from 2450 before Christ, when its first King, Menes, reigned. Before that all is fabulous.

The main features of Asiatic and African civilization were identical, and the same causes are assigned. In Egypt, the masses were poor and enslaved, whilst the Upper Classes possessed all the wealth and power. "The civilization of Egypt being, like that of India, caused by the fertility of the soil," says Buckle, "and the climate being also very hot, there were in both countries brought into play the same laws, and then naturally followed the same results. In both countries we find the national food cheap and abundant: hence the labor market oversupplied; hence a very unequal division of wealth and power; and hence all the consequences which such inequality will inevitably produce." In Asia, the ordinary food of the people was rice; in Egypt, and other parts of Africa, it was composed of dates, the fruit of the palm-tree. This fruit, which was abundantly produced with little labor, not only fed the millions of human beings that crowded Egypt in ancient times, but was likewise the food of animals of all kinds.

We have an excellent proof of the redundance of population produced by the cheapness of food in the statement of Herodotus, that there were said to be twenty thousand inhabited cities in Egypt when, nearly five centuries before Christ, he was travelling through the country.

The Egyptians were originally divided, like the Hindoos, into four *castes*—the priests, the army, the artisans, and the peasants, called *fellahs.* The Government at first was theocratic, and the sacerdotal was higher than the royal power. The land was divided among the Clergy, the Army, and the King, each of whom owned a third.

The same care was shown in Egypt as in India to keep the masses in profound subjection. They were forbidden to change the condition in which fate had placed them, every man being required to follow the pursuit of his father. All knowledge was confined to the Upper Classes; and severe penalties were inflicted, as in India, on those of the lower who sought for information.

The religion of ancient Egypt was a sort of Pantheism, in which all the forces and forms of nature were deified. Above all the rest was a god without name, eternal, infinite, and the source of all things. Then came a series of subaltern gods, as in India, with emblems almost similar. Lastly, animals, plants, and vegetables were worshipped in different portions of the country. The Egyptians believed in the immortality of the soul, and in metempsychosis. They had also great respect for the dead, and carefully embalmed the bodies of their parents.

The Mathematical and Physical Sciences, especially Astronomy and Geometry, were well known in ancient Egypt. Alchymy and Astrology were held in honour. Sculpture was highly developed; and Architecture soared into immense proportions, of which abundant evidence survives in those colossal pyramids and obelisks that still astonish travellers. Diodorus, the Greek historian, mentions that it took 360,000 men for twenty years to build one of the pyramids—a conclusive proof of the absolute manner in which the Government disposed of the masses.

This is a brief epitome of the ancient civilization of Egypt, the second on record. It seems evident that its character and duration must, as in the case of Asia, be attributed to physical causes; for it endures to this day almost the same as it was twenty centuries and more before our era.

A MYSTERY.

AMERICA.

THE occupants of the American continent are much given to fancy that, however inscrutable the origin of other parts of the world may be, they, at least, can boast of living in a land whose history is of yesterday. It should not be forgotten, however, that for unknown centuries before Columbus and his successors arrived, America was inhabited, not merely by wandering and savage tribes, but by a settled and civilized people. Two nations—Mexico and Peru—the one north and the other south of the equator, but under exactly the same physical conditions as regards climate and soil, were found by the astonished Europeans in possession of a civilization little inferior to their own.

It is a very remarkable fact that the religious, political, and social features of both these countries were almost identical with those of India and Egypt. In America, as in Asia and Africa, all the wealth and power were monopolized by the Upper Classes, whilst the lower were in a state of helpless subjection; the authority of the Priest was higher than that of the King; and the Government was despotic. In both continents, too, we find the same gods and idols worshipped; in both we find the people divided into *castes*, the lower classes performing all the labor, and subject to rigorous restraints against any attempt to better their condition. "The lower classes in Mexico and

Peru," says Prescott, "could follow no craft, engage in no labor or amusement, save such as the law prescribed. They could not change their residence or their dress, or even marry without the consent of the Government."

Mexico and Peru also resembled Egypt and India in the progress they had made in the Arts. In Architecture, Sculpture, Painting, and Music, these American communities were fully as advanced as those of Asia and Africa. In Astronomy also, and some other Sciences, Mexico and Peru had made some progress; and we are told by Prescott that they were skilled in Manufacture and Agriculture, and distinguished by much social refinement. Various authors bear testimony to the splendour of their temples and palaces; the extent of their fortifications, roads, and canals; the beauty of their arms, ornaments, vases, tapestry, and costumes. The pyramids in Mexico are compared by M'Culloch to those of Egypt; and Prescott tells us that the royal residence in Peru occupied twenty thousand men for fifty years, and that two hundred thousand men were employed on the royal residence in Mexico. He adds that the Mexican Monarchs, like those of ancient Asia and Egypt, had control of immense masses of men, and would sometimes turn the whole population of a conquered city, including the women, into the public works.

Various thinkers, and none more than Buckle, attribute the condition of Mexico and Peru, just as they attribute the condition of India and Egypt, almost wholly to physical causes. They maintain that the subjection of the lower classes in Mexico and Peru was due to the fact that food was cheap and labor redundant—the banana, potato, and maize being as plentiful in these countries as rice in India and dates in Egypt. It is both singular and striking that not merely the physical features, but the social condition of the two countries, remain to-day pretty much what they were before Cortes or Pizarro visited their shores. It would seem that neither Christianity, nor the Republican Institutions which have been since introduced there, have done much towards ameliorating the condition of the great mass of the population.

THIRD CIVILIZATION.

EUROPE.

The civilization which followed those already recorded in Asia and Africa, and which soared far beyond them, appeared in Europe some 2000 years before Christ. This may be considered as the third civilization, for no date can be assigned to that found existing in Mexico and Peru.

It will be seen that the startling development of intellect, which gradually arose in Europe, utterly eclipsed all that had gone before; but it cannot be denied that, in Religion and Government, the models bequeathed by Asia and Africa were, in the main, reproduced. Political power, wealth, and education, were, as hitherto, monopolized by the Upper Classes; and the masses still continued in the same condition of ignorance, poverty, and dependence. Religion, though stripped of many of the features which in Asia made it hideous, and in Africa degrading, was in nowise better calculated to exalt and advance Humanity. In this respect, the third civilization, though so far superior in its intellectual progress, was really no improvement on the first and second. All these civilizations must be regarded alike, and denominated alike. They were all Heathen, all Pagan: that is, all were founded on the theory that the Majority of mankind were slaves, and the Minority their natural masters. Consequently, the

Religions and Governments of each were created and constituted with the sole view of maintaining this state of things.

In the third civilization, it is true, we meet for the first time new words of grave import—we hear of Republics and Democracies. But, on close inspection, we discover that they had no reference to any Government in which the masses had any share: they were but new names for the only Government ever known in the world—a Government directed not merely by the intellect of the few, but one in which the interests of the many were unrecognized and disregarded.

It was not till the fourth civilization appeared that a new principle was born, a new doctrine was taught, and a new element introduced into the world—destined inevitably, in process of time, to change entirely the face of things, and to verify the words of St. Paul:—"Old things are passed away; behold, all things are become new."

This, however, shall be considered under its appropriate head. Meantime, the rise and growth of two great communities will be concisely reviewed as illustrative of the character of the third civilization.

GREECE.

THE first occupation of the peninsula afterwards known as Greece, was by barbarous tribes—the Pelasgians from Asia. Emigrants from Egypt and Phœnicia followed with the germs of civilization. Then came the Hellenic tribes from Caucasus about 1700 B.C., who seized on the country, which was named after one of them, Greece. The Caucasians are said to be the first white men who entered Europe. More Egyptians and Phœnicians followed; amongst whom were Cecrops, who founded Athens 1643 B.C., and Cadmus, who is supposed to have brought the alphabet of Phœnicia into Greece. During this period, Agriculture and the Arts made advances; Laws and Institutions were established; and a Religion modelled on those of Egypt and Phœnicia was founded. Then succeeded the "Heroic Age," from 1500 to 1200 B.C., signalized by the fabulous exploits of Hercules, Theseus, and Jason, the foundation of the Olympian Games, the establishment of the Amphictyonic Council (a Congress of the Confederacy), and ending with the Trojan War. Next followed the "Middle Age," when for two centuries constant wars prevailed, throwing back the progress of the country.

To this succeeded the rise of that famous civilization which is still the wonder of the world. About 900 B.C. the marvellous poems of Homer appeared; and about this time, too, manners began to grow milder, religion more esteemed. Lycurgus appeared in 898

B.C. in Sparta, and established some wise principles of legislation.

The renown of Greece, however, is chiefly identified with Athens, the capital of Attica. The earliest Government of this famous city was Monarchical. After a period of some 500 years came the Aristocratic regime, divided into three periods: in the first period the Archons (magistrates) being elected for life, in the second for ten years, and in the third for one year. This lasted some 562 years.

It was near the close of this period, in the year 593 B.C., that Solon, who was then sole Archon, made a Constitution, which, considering the epoch, is a marvellous production. By this Constitution, Sovereign Power was vested in an assembly of citizens, classified according to income. As a check upon this body, he created a Senate, with which he associated in political power the Areopagus, or Supreme Court. This remarkable structure skilfully blended the Democratic and Aristocratic elements, but ignored the Monarchical—an omission which led to its ruin. Solon also repealed the cruel laws of Draco, and substituted a milder code. All these beneficent institutions were overthrown in ten years by Pisistratus, and Solon died of patriotic grief.

For the fifty years following, Pisistratus first, and afterwards his sons, exercised dictatorial power.* Then began the Democratic epoch, or what was called the Republic, which existed for 364 years.

The Athenian Republic, which all the other republics in Greece resembled, was somewhat singular in its organization. The inhabitants were divided into

* The first hospital for wounded soldiers in the world was founded at Athens by Pisistratus. Louis the XIV. founded the first in France, over 2000 years later—the *Hôpital des Invalides* at Paris.

three classes—the citizens, the freedmen, and the slaves. The citizens only had the franchise. Their vote elected the nine Archons, or executive magistrates, made the laws, and decided on peace and war. This looks like the Universal Suffrage of our days; but when we compare the number entitled to vote with those not so privileged, it will be seen how far it was from a Democracy as now understood. At no time in Athens were there more than 20,000 citizens or voters to some 350,000 non-voters. The latter were mostly slaves, and were occupied in the avocations now followed by our middle and lower classes. These slaves were all of the same colour and race as their masters. Thus it was the Minority who governed. "Athens," says De Tocqueville, "with her universal suffrage, was after all merely an aristocratic republic, in which all the nobles had an equal right to the government." *

Soon after the so-called Republic had been instituted, the wars against the Persians began, and lasted some forty years. Happily the Greeks came forth victorious from this conflict, else the dawning civilization of Europe would have been submerged in Asiatic barbarism.

The culmination of Athenian glory and power was reached on the close of these hostilities. Then appeared that wonderful galaxy of great men whose fame has never been eclipsed—to select only a few—Socrates, Plato, Aristotle, in Philosophy; Herodotus, the father of History, followed by Xenophon and Thucydides; Æschylus, Sophocles, Euripides, and Aristophanes, in the Drama; Phidias and Apelles, in the Arts; Hippocrates, the father of Medicine.

* See vol. ii. p. 73.

The three greatest intellects of Greece, and whose influence over succeeding ages was permanent, were Socrates, Plato, and Aristotle. A single word of these profound thinkers, who lived in an epoch no less than 400 years before Christ.

Socrates was the author of the first code of Morals that appeared in Europe.* In this he admirably defined the different virtues. He declared the practice of good was the only means to happiness; proved by new arguments the existence of a God, and the immortality of the soul; denounced the frivolous philosophy of his time, chiefly aiming at the Sophists; and laid down that the true study of mankind was man. His boldness alarmed the Government, and he was condemned to death, on the charge of attacking the Established Religion, and promulgating New Divinities. His escape from prison was planned by his friends; but he declared that "the laws should not be disobeyed," and drank the poison whilst discoursing calmly on the soul.†

His disciple, Plato, whether alarmed at the fate of his master, or from the constitution of his mind, gave himself up to abstract speculations. He was the father of Metaphysics; and sought to prove that man was the mere product of "ideas." He declared in one of his discourses that "reason was the true principle of man's nature, although in the present existence there is mingled with it a foreign element—matter, which, by obstructing its development, becomes the cause of man's falling short of perfection." His most famous

* Confucius, who died in China, 479 B.C., just before the birth of Socrates, is regarded by some as the first writer on Morals.

† "Virtue," said Socrates, "was the intelligent performance of duties, whose scope man may arrive at by a study both of his own nature, and of the laws of an all-wise Creator discoverable in the system of the Universe. In this pursuit happiness is inseparable from virtue."

book was a description of the "Ideal Republic," in which he launched many crude theories that have become the source of modern Socialism. His writings are remarkable for sublime conceptions, moral purity, and a style never surpassed. Hence his appellations of the "Homer of philosophy," the "Divine Plato." In his "Republic" he uses these striking words:—"That as an individual cannot be at peace with himself except by the harmonious adjustment of all his faculties, wherein each is allowed its due weight; so in the whole world happiness is proportionate to justice; and each individual derives the greater benefit from the community the more complete the harmony is in which he lives with all his fellow-citizens."

Beyond a doubt, the master-mind of antiquity was Aristotle. All the knowledge then existing he possessed, and vastly augmented it. For many centuries his works constituted the limit of all learning, and no one questioned his authority. Though the disciple of Plato, he rejected his master's ideal doctrines, and endeavoured to establish science on the solid ground of facts rather than on mere ideas. Philosophy, he said, was the science of cause and effect. He is attacked by the moderns for having employed the deductive method by reasoning from hypotheses; but it must be remembered how much easier it was for Bacon in the seventeenth century of our era to use the inductive method by reasoning from experiment than it was for Aristotle some three centuries before Christ, when so few facts were known. His work on Logic he called "*Organon*," as Logic was the *organ* of all science: it was the first complete code on that topic. His works are too numerous to detail; but they embrace essays on Rhetoric, Poetry, Art, Morals, Politics, Natural

History, Anatomy, Astronomy, Physics, Psychology, Metaphysics, Theology. In Psychology, he endeavoured to classify the faculties of the soul, which, he said, was the hidden power that gave life, and which he called intellect. In Theology, he demonstrated the Divine existence on the continuity of movement, and said God was the supreme goal or end of all things, to which all tended, all aspired. In Art, he said the beautiful was only found in the imitation of nature. In Morals, he declared virtue was to be found in the equilibrium of the passions. In Politics, he asserted that the final aim of society was utility—a bold doctrine in those days. His works on Zoology and Comparative Anatomy are declared by Cuvier never to have been exceeded for accuracy and depth.

This is but a brief and superficial sketch of this stupendous intellect.* If Bacon is considered a phenomenon in the seventeenth century, what must we think of Aristotle, who lived upwards of nineteen centuries before him? Philip, King of Macedonia, paid him a just compliment when he asked him to superintend the education of his son, afterwards Alexander the Great, declaring that "he was not so proud of having a son as he was of having Aristotle for his tutor." The philosopher afterwards accompanied Alexander in his Asiatic conquests, and gathered new materials of knowledge. He finally established himself at Athens; but being accused of impiety, he abandoned the city, saying "he wished to spare the Athenians a new crime, already guilty of the death of Socrates."

A conspicuous feature is apparent alike in the

* The works of Aristotle were not published till nearly two centuries after his death, having been concealed by his admirers. Apellicon discovered and published them about a hundred years before Christ.

writings of each of these great thinkers. They all believed in the progress of mankind; but they were compelled, from fear of death, to discuss the moral perfection of man rather than his political elevation. In commenting on Grecian philosophy, Macaulay says sneeringly:—"The ancient philosophy dwelt largely in theories of moral perfection, which were so sublime that they could never be more than theories; in attempts to solve insoluble enigmas; in exhortations to the attainment of unattainable frames of mind. It disdained to be useful, and was content to be stationary." The reproach is unjust; for in those days, as for long centuries after, thinkers who ventured to enlighten mankind as to their political debasement simply challenged martyrdom. All they could do was to declare that man was capable of the highest moral development. It is clear, I think, that these Greek philosophers believed in man's future political regeneration. It was more than two thousand years later before it could be safely declared that "all men were born free and equal."*

Fearing to fatigue the reader, I will but add that the theories of these three great masters created a profound intellectual movement. Several of their pupils founded Schools of Philosophy. I can only notice the Stoics, who asserted that reason alone should govern man, and the Epicureans, who retorted that the passions were better guides than mere reason. In a note will be found a tabular statement of these doctrines and their application.†

* American Declaration of Independence, July 4, 1776.

† Stoical system made reason supreme over the passions.

Love of	money,	subdued by	reason,	produces	prodigality.
,,	war,	,,	,,	,,	cowardice
,,	women,	,,	,,	,,	celibacy.

The rule of Pericles, which lasted some thirty years, witnessed the last bright page of Grecian civilization.* Civil wars then broke out between the rival states, and these enabled the ambitious Philip, King of Macedonia, to subject the whole of Greece to his sway. Demosthenes, the Athenian orator, launched his thunderbolts in vain. In spite of his furious *Philippics*, Grecian independence fell. Alexander the Great maintained the supremacy his father had won. The efforts made by the Greeks to recover their freedom were constantly baffled by civil discords, until the Romans attacked them, and converted Greece into a Roman province under the name of Achaia, in 146 B.C.

The religion of Greece was imported from Asia Minor and Egypt, but it was greatly modified and refined. Polytheism prevailed; but the gods were not mere hideous creations to inspire terror, as in India; nor were they worshipped in the forms of animals and

Love of knowledge,	subdued by reason,	produces	credulity.
,, religion,	,,	,,	,, atheism.

Epicurean system made passions supreme over reason.

Love of money,	uncontrolled by reason,	produces	avarice.
,, war,	,,	,,	,, anarchy.
,, women,	,,	,,	,, licentiousness.
,, knowledge,	,,	,,	,, utopias.
,, religion,	,,	,,	,, fanaticism.

In contrast to the above systems might be added a table where reason and the passions are balanced.

Reason	and love of	money	produce	prudence.
,,	,,	war,	,,	courage.
,,	,,	women,	,,	marriage.
,,	,,	knowledge,		common sense.
,,	,,	religion,	,,	worship.

* During this epoch, more than in any previous one, Greek colonies sprang up in Italy, Gaul, and Hispania. At Nismes, in the south of France, Grecian busts and statues of great beauty are frequently dug up, which prove that the colonists brought their native love of art with them. Nismes was afterwards occupied by the Romans, but the relics of Roman art are far inferior to those of their predecessors.

plants, as in Egypt. The Greek religion was a sort of protest against the monstrous inventions of the Asiatic imagination; and their deities were but a higher type of humanity, endowed with supernatural attributes, greater knowledge, strength, and beauty, but appealing rather to the love than fear of their worshippers. The religion of the Greeks, like their drapery, was easy-fitting and graceful, and neither incommoded their pursuits nor disturbed their consciences.

It must be seen at a glance how much all succeeding nations owe to the intellect of Greece. Various authors account in various ways for the amazing development to which it attained in form, variety, and depth.

It should be observed that the two civilizations that preceded were both the products of tropical countries; where, as already shown, abundant food led to excess of population, to poverty and ignorance. Furthermore, tropical countries are characterized by certain material phenomena, such as earthquakes, pestilences, hurricanes, which inspire wonder and terror, and thus encourage superstition. Besides these dangers incidental to tropical climates, there was a sublime grandeur in the aspects of nature in all those countries where civilization began, that impressed on their populations a sense of awe and helplessness. The vast mountains, mighty rivers, endless forests, interminable jungles, scorching deserts, together with the multitudes of animals and reptiles destructive to life, could not fail to indicate to man his feebleness and inability to cope with natural forces. In this way the mind was filled with images of the grand and terrible, and reduced to a timid and anxious state. Surrounded by dangers they could neither understand nor avoid, the imagination of man became inflamed; and a belief in supernatural intervention grew up. The mysterious and the invisible were thought to be present; and the emotions of fear and weakness thus engendered, laid the foundation of that superstition which was the basis of the religion, literature, and arts of those ancient countries.

The influence of the external world on the mind cannot be questioned. If it be sublime and terrific, as in the tropical countries referred to, it makes the imagination predominate over the reason; it inspires a spirit of reverence instead of one of inquiry, and, therefore, creates a disposition to neglect the investigation of natural causes, and to ascribe events to supernatural ones. It is in this way, argues Buckle, whose reasoning I have almost textually adopted, that the whole tropical civilization had to struggle with innumerable difficulties unknown to the temperate zones where European civilization first appeared. In all the civilizations exterior to Europe, nature conspired to increase the power of the imagination, and weaken the authority of the reason.

In Greece, where European civilization began, we see a country altogether the reverse of India. The works of nature, which in India are of startling magnitude, are in Greece far smaller, feebler, and less threatening to man. In Greece the aspects of nature are so entirely different that the very conditions of existence are changed. Dangers of all kinds were far less numerous than in the tropical countries. The climate was more healthy; earthquakes, hurricanes, wild beasts, more rare. This striking difference in the natural phenomena of the two countries gave rise to corresponding differences in the mental associations. The tendency of the surrounding phenomena was, in India, to inspire fear; in Greece, to give confidence. In India, man was intimidated; in Greece, he was encouraged. In India, obstacles of every sort were so numerous, so alarming, so inexplicable, that the difficulties of life could only be solved by appealing to the direct agency of supernatural causes. In Greece, nature was less dangerous, less intrusive, and less mysterious than in India: consequently, the human mind was less appalled and less superstitious. Natural causes began to be studied; and man, gradually waking to a sense of his own power, sought to investigate events with a boldness and success previously unknown.

The effect of these different habits of thought on the religion, literature, and arts of these two countries must be apparent. The works of nature in Greece being so much smaller and feebler, became more accessible—easier to experiment on, and to observe with minuteness. Thus an inquisitive and analytic spirit was encouraged; and the Grecian mind was tempted to generalize the appearances of nature, and refer them to the laws by which they were governed. In Greece, therefore, everything tended to exalt the dignity of man, while in India all tended to debase it.

To sum up the whole, it may be said the Greeks had more respect for human powers, and the Hindoos more for superhuman. The first dealt more with the known and available, the second with the unknown and mysterious. In Greece, for the first time in the history of the world, the imagination was tempered and confined by the understanding: and the gain was complete; for the inquiring and sceptical faculties of the understanding were cultivated, and the exuberance of the imagination checked. Whether or not the balance was accurately adjusted is another question; but it is certain the adjustment was more nearly arrived at in Greece than in any other previous civilization. Greek literature was, therefore, the first in which there was a deliberate and systematic attempt to test all opinions by their consonance with human reason, and thus vindicate the right of man to judge for himself on all matters which are of supreme importance.

From the pages of Buckle,* who investigated all authorities on the subject, I have abridged the foregoing explanation of the marvellous contrast between the civilization that sprang up in Europe and those that preceded it in Asia and Africa. The summary of this great writer's line of argument has, I hope, been of sufficient length to enable the reader to form some general idea why it was that the human mind, freed from the shackles that cramped it in Asia and Africa, expanded so suddenly in Greece, and rose to such wonderful altitudes. There may have been strong and sagacious intellects among the Priests and Kings of ancient India and Egypt; but the reasoning and the authorities of Buckle prove that the tropical civilizations, however productive they might have been of Poets and Artists, never could have produced a mind so acute, powerful, and profound as that of Aristotle.

* It is evident that Buckle, in his analysis of the civilizations of Asia, Africa, and Europe, adopted the theories of Montesquieu, who, in his *l'Esprit des Lois* (1748), was the first to point out how radically the institutions and character of a nation are influenced by its climate, soil, and food.

ROME.

My chief purpose is accomplished in having shown the birth and prominent features of European civilization; which was destined never wholly to die, though submerged in a deluge of barbarism. I will not, therefore, weary the reader with any details of Roman civilization, since it was nothing more than an inferior reproduction of what was borrowed from Greece. Rome produced Jurisconsults, Historians, Orators, Dramatists, and Poets—all of great eminence, but none that eclipsed their masters. The conspicuous feature of Roman history was her warlike spirit, which was only satiated by the conquest of the then known world. In legislation or philosophy, however, Rome begot nothing new, and added nothing to the knowledge the genius of Greece had created.

Two of the most remarkable intellects perhaps of the Latin world were Cicero, the Orator, and Tacitus, the Historian. Cicero was born in 107 B.C., and went to Athens in his twenty-sixth year to study his art. His greatest triumphs were achieved in oratory, but many of his writings prove that he was also a profound thinker. His work on Government, of which fragments only survive, displays a wonderful comprehension of the subject. I will quote one of its most striking passages, which I shall refer to hereafter, when I come to speak of the Constitution of the United States. "In my judgment," wrote Cicero, "that is the best constituted government which, in moderation, is composed of these three original elements—the Royal, the Aristocratic, the Popular." * Of course no such model form of government had ever existed; but it is none the less impressive that Cicero gave the weight of his authority in favour of the blending of the three elements in all good government.†

Hardly less remarkable, though written some 161 years later, was the opinion pronounced by Tacitus, the greatest of Roman historians, born 54 years after Christ. In his "Annals," which extend from the death of the Emperor Augustus to that of Nero, he remarks —"All nations and cities must be governed either by the People, the First men, or a Single ruler. A form of government constituted of these three it is easier to admire than to believe possible. If it should ever exist, it will be of short duration." ‡—The fate of the American Constitution will decide the accuracy of this confident prediction.

Roman Jurisprudence has left enduring monuments. Three codes of law were compiled, the last of which is the most celebrated. This Code was drawn up after

* "Statuo esse optime constitutam rempublicam quæ ex tribus generibus illis, regali, optimo, et populari, modice confusa."—*Cic. Fragm.*

† There were before Cicero several Greek writers of eminence, Plato, Aristotle, and notably Polybius, who discussed the conjunction of the three original elements as necessary for good government. Even as far back as 884 B.C., Lycurgus, in his marvellous Constitution of Sparta, attempted to combine these three elements. The opinion of Cicero, however, is entitled to special deference, not merely for his genius and learning, but that it was also founded on the experience and reflections of all the greatest writers and legislators who had preceded him.

‡ "Nam cunctas nationes et urbes populus, aut primores aut singuli regunt, delecta ex his et constituta reipublicæ forma, laudari facilius quam evenire, vel, si evenit, haud diuturna esse potest."—*Tac. Ann.* iv.

the Empire had been divided, by order of Justinian, Emperor of the East, in 529 A.D. The Justinian Code was a digest of all the laws and statutes of Justinian's predecessors, and received the name of *Corpus Juris Civilis*—the body of the civil law—and has maintained its ascendency down even to our own times.

Three different forms of government succeeded each other in Roman history: the first Monarchical, the second Consular, the last Imperial.

Rome was founded 753 B.C., and began with a Monarchical regime, which lasted 244 years.

Then arose what is called the Republic, if such a term can be applied to a Government wholly Aristocratic. Two magistrates, called Consuls, were charged with the Executive power; and these were elected by the citizens assembled in *Centuries*—electoral bodies consisting of 100 citizens each. There were originally 193 Centuries, of which 188 were composed of those who possessed more or less income. Consequently the election of the Consuls was in the hands of those only who had property. Besides, none but a Senator could be elected Consul. Furthermore, in Rome, as in Athens, the citizens who had the franchise were but a Minority of the population; as the Majority consisted of those who were free but not citizens, and of the slaves. The citizens were divided into Patricians and Plebeians, or those who were noble and those who were not; but De Tocqueville, a great authority, remarks that "all the citizens belonged, in fact, to the aristocracy, and partook of its character." Speaking of the struggles between the Patricians and the Plebeians, he adds, "they were simply intestine feuds between the elder and the younger branches of the same family." During the whole period of the Consulate, the Sovereign Power was really in the hands of the Senate, a purely aristocratic body.

The Consular Government lasted 480 years, when the Monarchy was restored under Augustus Cæsar, the first Emperor, 29 B.C. At this time the Roman power was at its height. The frontiers extended to Britain, the Elbe, the Rhine, the Danube, the Black Sea, the Euphrates, the Desert of Africa, and the Atlantic.

The Roman Empire was divided in 364 A.D. into East and West. The Empire of the West was overthrown by the barbarians under Odoacer, 476 A.D., after an existence of 505 years. Odoacer took the title of King of Italy.

FOURTH CIVILIZATION.

CHRISTIANITY.

THAT the rise of Christianity gave a new direction to the history of the world is incontestable; and I am, therefore, fully justified in dating from this period the fourth civilization. It was the ideas which were born of Christianity that eventually prostrated the Roman Empire—the most powerful of all pagan civilizations. Surrounded by ruins, and resisted by savage hordes, the fourth civilization struggled on successfully through the wild anarchy of the Dark Ages, the chivalric splendour and lawless society of the Middle Ages, until, in modern times, it is acquiring a strength and preponderance quite irresistible. Even by the unbeliever, Christianity cannot be regarded otherwise than as a "divine revelation;" for, whilst proclaiming the immortality of the soul, and the hope of future happiness, it leads inevitably to the moral and physical regeneration of man on earth. In a word, it is the conflict between Pagan principles and Christian doctrine that has agitated the world for so many centuries; and though we may raise the cry of "Peace! peace!" as did the false prophets in the days of Jeremiah, there will be no peace till all nations are organized on the basis of the fourth civilization. What that basis is, its character and solidity, will become clearer as this book advances.

In the 29th year of the reign of Augustus Cæsar, Christ the Saviour appeared on earth. The doctrines He propagated were wholly different from those of any religion then existing or previously known. My object is not to enter on any spiritual discussion of the new faith; but simply to notice some of its important effects on the condition of mankind, and the history of the world. Whatever sceptics may say of its saving power hereafter, they cannot deny that Christianity brought into the world a principle till then not only never heard of, but utterly repugnant to the policy and interests of the Governments and Upper Classes of that period—I mean the principle of *Equality*. Christ was the first to preach that all men were equal in the sight of God.

"The most profound and capacious minds of Greece and Rome," says De Tocqueville, "were never able to reach the idea, at once so general and so simple, of the common likeness of men, and of the common birthright of each to freedom: they strove to prove that slavery was in the order of nature, and that it would always exist. Nay more, everything shows that those of the ancients who had passed from the servile to the free condition, many of whom have left excellent writings,* did themselves regard servitude in no other light. All the great writers of antiquity belonged to the aristocracy of masters, or at least they saw that aristocracy established and uncontested before their eyes. Their mind, after it had expanded itself in every direction, was barred from further progress in this one; and the *advent of Jesus*

* Æsop, the Grecian fabulist, and Terence, the Roman dramatist, were both slaves who had been given their freedom.

Christ upon earth was required to teach that all the members of the human race are by nature equal and alike."

It was evidently the mission of the Messiah, not only to prepare the Souls of men for Redemption, but to bring about their Material Regeneration in this world. In every line and precept He rebuked the powerful and rich, and manifested profound sympathy for the poor and the lowly. He constantly promised the reward of eternal bliss hereafter to the weary and afflicted. "The last shall be first, and the first shall be last," He said; and albeit this had reference to a future state, still the effect on the popular mind of His time was none the less infectious and stirring. Christianity has been called the religion of Democracy; and, assuredly, no Creed had ever before appeared that displayed such deep solicitude for the poor and oppressed. Justice and Benevolence were its corner-stones. Whilst it enjoined on all to do unto others as they would have others do unto them, it also inculcated forbearance and submission; for the followers of Christ were told to love their enemies, and to do good to them that did them evil: if a man smote them on one cheek, they were to turn to him the other. The new Gospel ensured to believers the Beatitude of Paradise, but it also sought to promote Peace on Earth and Good-will amongst men.

A Religion so full of consolation, charity, and love, was indeed a Revelation; and was destined to inspire Humanity with new and more exalted aspirations both as to Earth and Heaven. It is no wonder the new Church spread rapidly amongst the masses, nor that it was resisted and persecuted by the defenders of the old beliefs. Up to this period all the religious

Creeds that had prevailed were propagated by men belonging to the Governing Class, and used to maintain the subjection of the lower orders. The Christian religion was the first that was preached by men of the humblest condition; and its precepts not only opened to the weary and oppressed believer the portals of Heaven, but were calculated to effect his emancipation on Earth.

Christianity appeared in a Roman province of Asia Minor, and thence spread onwards till it attacked Paganism in its stronghold, the great metropolis of Rome. An eloquent writer* gives an interesting sketch of the enthusiasm of the early Christian converts in Rome. Speaking of the Imperial city after midnight, he says—"And at such an hour there were men and women who stole forth from their various houses, and with mantles covering their faces, hastened to a lonely spot in the suburbs, and entered the mouth of a dark cave. They passed through long galleries, moist with damp and odorous of death, for coffins were ranged on either side in tiers one above the other. But soon sweet music sounded from the depth of the abyss; an open chamber came to view, and a tomb covered with flowers, laid out with a repast, encircled by men and women, who were apparelled in white robes, and who sang a psalm of joy. It was in the Catacombs of Rome where the dead had been buried in the ancient times that the Christians met to discourse on the progress of the faith; to recount the trials which they suffered in their homes; to confess to one another their sins and doubts, their carnal presumption, or their lack of faith; and also to relate their sweet visions of the night, the answers to their

* Winwood Reade.

earnest prayers. They listened to the exhortations of their elders, and perhaps to a letter from one of the apostles. They then supped together as Jesus had supped with His disciples, and kissed one another when the love feast was concluded. At these meetings there was no distinction of rank; the high-born lady embraced the slave whom she had once scarcely regarded as a man.* Humility and submission were the cardinal virtues of the early Christians; slavery had not been forbidden by the apostles, because it was the doctrine of Jesus that those who were the lowest in this world would be the highest in the next. Slavery was therefore esteemed a state of grace, and some Christians appear to have rejected the freedman's cap on religious grounds, for Paul exhorts such persons to become free if they can."

The above extract refers to the period succeeding the death of the Saviour, and whilst the Apostles were still preaching the new tidings in the different Roman provinces. "In that age," says my authority, "every Christian was a missionary. The soldier sought to win recruits for the heavenly host; the prisoner of war discoursed to his Persian jailor; the slave girl whispered the gospel in the ears of her mistress as she built up the mass of towered hair; there stood men in cloak and beard at street corners, who, when the people, according to the manners of the day, invited them to speak, preached, not the doctrines of the Painted Porch"—the Grecian Schools—"but the words of a new and strange philosophy; the young wife threw her arms around her husband's neck, and made him agree to be

* The slaves of Rome, like those of Greece, were mainly of the same colour and race as their masters.

baptized, that their souls might not be parted after death. The disconsolate woman, whose age of beauty and triumph had passed away, was taught if she became a Christian her body in all the splendour of its youth would rise again. The poor slave, who sickened from weariness of a life in which there was for him no hope, received the assurance of another life in which he would find luxury and pleasure when death released him from his woe."

The same writer then goes on to say, "Soon it was whispered there was in Rome a secret society which worshipped an unknown God. Its members wore no garlands on their brows; they never entered the temples; they were governed by laws which strange and fearful oaths bound them ever to obey; their speech was not as the speech of ordinary men; they buried instead of burning the bodies of the dead; they married; they educated their children after a manner of their own. The politicians who regarded the Established Church as essential to the safety of the State became alarmed. Secret societies were forbidden by the law, and here was a society in which the tutelary gods of Rome were denounced as rebels and usurpers. The Christians, it is true, preached passive obedience and the divine right of kings; but they *proclaimed that all men were equal before God*—a very dangerous doctrine in a community where more than half the men were slaves. The idle and superstitious lazzaroni did not love the gods, but they believed in them; and they feared lest the 'atheists,' as they called the Christians, would provoke the vengeance of the whole divine federation against the city, and that all would be involved in the common ruin. Soon there came a time when every public calamity—an epidemic, a fire, a famine, or a flood—was ascribed to the anger of the offended gods. And then arose imperial edicts, popular commotions, and the terrible street-cry of '*Christiani ad leones*'—to the lions with the Christians." *

But these persecutions only served to fan the flame; for to those who believed in the New Religion, death was merely a surgical operation, with the certainty of entering into eternal happiness. The Christians, therefore, encountered it with joy; and the sight of their cheerful countenances as they were led to execution induced many to inquire what this belief could be that seemed to rob death of its terrors.

The same writer remarks that the advancing Creed had no success among the great moralists and thinkers of the Roman Empire, who looked upon it as a new and noisy form of superstition, and rejected it with contempt. They knew the Pagan gods were only an idle fable, but they were none the less disposed to deride these strange "tales of a God who took upon Him the semblance of a Jew, and suffered death upon the gallows for the redemption of mankind." "In the Latin world, therefore," continues he, "the new belief was never the religion of a scholar and a gentleman. It was the creed of the uneducated people who flung themselves into it with passion. It was something which belonged to them, and to them alone. They knew nothing of their own great writers; they had never tasted intellectual delights, for the philosophers scorned to instruct the vulgar crowd. And now the vulgar crowd found teachers who interpreted to them the Jewish books, who com-

* I owe it to the author to say, that I may have occasion to modify or abridge hereafter certain passages from his book.

posed for them a magnificent literature of sermons and epistles, a literature of enthusiasts and martyrs, written in blood and fire. The lower classes had no share in the politics of the Empire, but now they had politics of their own which all could discuss—the people, women, and slaves. The barbers gossipped theologically. Children played at church in the streets. The Christians were no longer citizens of Rome. God was their Emperor: Heaven was their fatherland. They despised the pleasures of this life; they were as emigrants gathered on the shore, waiting for a wind to waft them to another world. They rendered unto Cæsar the things that were Cæsar's, for so it was written they should do. They honoured the king, for such had been the teaching of St Paul. They regarded the Emperor as God's vicegerent upon earth, and disobeyed him only when his commands were contrary to those of God. But this limitation, which it was the business of the Bishops to define, made the Christians a dangerous party in the State."

Christianity, whose rise and growth are so vividly described in these extracts, continued to spread, until at last, in the year 313 A.D., the Emperor Constantine accepted it as the Religion of the State. But Paganism was still all-powerful; for though the Emperors were baptized as Christians, they continued to be invested, like their heathen predecessors, with the office of *Pontifex Maximus*, or High Pontiff of the old religion. In the reign of Valentinian, 364 A.D., Toleration was enforced, and the professors of either Faith were forbidden to molest each other. The Emperor Theodosius, who died 396 A.D., went a step further, and ordered that the sacrifices to the old gods should not be paid by the State as hitherto. Yet as late as 410 A.D., when Alaric was battering at the gates of Rome, the Senate went up to the Capitol, and made sacrifices to their ancient gods, which the Bishop of Rome, Innocent I., doubtless witnessed. The fall of the Roman Empire, 476 A.D., may be regarded as the end of Paganism, for Christianity then finally superseded it.

The growth of the New Faith would have been certainly more rapid, but for the disputes that broke out among its professors. The most celebrated, but not the first of these disputes, was that of Arius, who, in 312 A.D., declared his disbelief in the Divinity of Christ, as do the Unitarians of our day. It was to extinguish this heresy that the first Christian Assembly took place. At the Council of Nice, in Asia Minor, 325 A.D., the various Bishops met,* under the Presidency of the Emperor Constantine, when the subversive doctrines of Arius were denounced. It was some three hundred years before the Sect disappeared, and during this interval other heresies sprung up.†

One more quotation will be made from the author already cited. "In the first age of Christianity," he says, "the Church was a republic. There was no distinction between clergymen and laymen. Each member of the congregation had a right to

* The number of Bishops at this time was estimated at 1800—1000 in Greece, and 800 in Roman provinces.

† From the year 264 A.D., when Sabellius and the Sabellians were denounced at the Council of Alexandria, down to 1843, when the "Free Church of Scotland" was founded by Chalmers, no less than fifty-five different leading sects have arisen, all professing Christianity, but each with some new modification of its own. Joe Smith, the Mormon, is the only one who got up another bible, written, as St Joe declared 1830, by Mormon, a Jewish prophet, 600 years before Christ.

preach, and each consulted God on his own account. A committee of presbyters, or elders, with a Bishop, or chairman, administered the affairs of the community.

"The second period was marked by an important change. The Bishop and presbyters, though still elected by the congregation, had begun to monopolize the pulpit; the distinction of clergy and laity was already made. The Bishops of the various Churches met together at councils or synods to discuss questions of discipline and dogma, and to pass laws; but they went as representatives of their respective congregations.

"In the third period the change was more important still. The congregation might now be appropriately termed a flock. The priests were possessed of traditions which they did not communicate to the laymen. The Water of Life was kept, as it were, in a sealed vessel. There was no salvation outside the Church; no man could have God for a Father unless he had also the Church for a mother; excommunication was a sentence of eternal death. From this time disputes were only between Bishops and Bishops; the laymen followed their spiritual leaders, and often took up material weapons on their behalf. In the synods the Bishops now met as princes of their congregations; and under the influence of the Holy Ghost (*Spiritu Sancto suggerente*) issued imperial decrees. The penalties inflicted were of the most alarming nature to those who believed that purgatory and hell-fire were at the disposal of the priesthood; but those who had doubts on the subject allowed themselves to be damned with equanimity. When the Church, however, was united to the State, the secular arm was then at its disposal, and was rigorously used."

These three periods of the primitive Church cover the interval from the rise of Christianity down to the conversion of Constantine—over 300 years. The same writer remarks that the Bishops of that day were all of them ignorant and superstitious men: but they did not all of them think alike; and as if to insure dissent, they set to work to define that which many believed had never existed, and which, if it had, could never be defined. They described the topography of Heaven. They dissected the Godhead, and expounded the Immaculate Conception. They not only said that three was one, and that one was three, but they undertook to explain how this combination had been brought about.

After the adoption of Christianity by Constantine, when it became the State religion, the Church is said to have lost much of its early Democratic character; and the Bishops, who had formerly been the Tribunes of the people, became the creatures of the Crown. Just as in Asia and Africa; just as in Greece and Rome in the days of Paganism, the heads of the Christian Church were no sooner recognized by the State than they were obliged to give it their support. It was in 313 A.D. that Constantine, by his edict at Milan, made Christianity the religion of the Empire, and at the Council of Nice, 325 A.D., as stated, the New Faith was formally inaugurated.* Henceforward the Church made rapid

* It was Constantine who first created ecclesiastical distinctions, and made Archbishops and Patriarchs, each with large jurisdictions and superior powers. The Patriarchate of Alexandria became the most powerful, but was swept away in the seventh century by the Mohammedans.

advances, and devoted itself to the accomplishment of three great works—the conversion of the barbarians, the overthrow of heresies, and the preservation and diffusion of civilization.

The Goths, the Vandals, the Lombards knew the name of Christ at the close of the fourth century; but they first embraced Arianism, afterwards returning to the true Faith. The Franks were converted under Clovis, the founder of the French Monarchy, in 496; the Anglo-Saxons at the end of the sixth century; the Germans in the eighth century. The more distant populations of Northern Europe—the Danes, Swedes, Russians, Poles, and Hungarians—were converted one after another from the ninth to the fifteenth centuries.

In Asia and Africa, Christianity made slower progress; and in the seventh century, the followers of Mahomet nearly blotted it out altogether. The new Church had also to contend with internal dissensions. In the ninth century, a Schism broke out which separated the Church in the East, called the Greek Church, from the Church in the West, called the Latin or Roman Church. Almost at the same period, during the eighth and ninth centuries, raged the Iconoclastic Controversy, as to whether images of Christ and the saints should be exposed in the churches or not.

DARK AGES.

The Roman Empire of the West fell to pieces, as already stated, at the close of the fifth century. Probably Constantine foresaw its fate when he removed the political Capital from Rome to Constantinople. During the fifth century, the Empire had been repeatedly assailed by the Goths, Huns, and Vandals; and finally the Herules under Odoacer in 476 A.D., the Ostrogoths in 493, and the Lombards in 568, became masters of the whole of Italy. During the same period, the most of Roman Britain was occupied by the Saxons and other northern tribes; whilst the Franks took possession of Gaul. Thus the old Roman Empire of the West became the prey of the various German tribes.

The new religion, unquestionably, precipitated the fall of this once great power. Proclaiming the equality of all men before God, Christianity overthrew Paganism by alienating the masses held in slavery. Bereft of religious and moral support, the Imperial Government sought to maintain itself by a crushing despotism, till at last the barbarians were welcomed as liberators.

The ensuing three centuries were a period of frightful anarchy, and are fitly described as the Dark Ages. The various barbarous tribes who possessed Italy and France were engaged in constant wars, and all traces of former civilization disappeared.

The zeal and courage of the followers of the Cross never faltered. They struggled to propagate the Faith, and to mitigate the ferocity of the times. To the Christian Priests, also, the world is indebted for the preservation of the literary relics of antiquity. Devoting portions of their time to cultivation of the earth, and to religious instruction, they gave their leisure to copying the ancient manuscripts, which they hid away in the recesses of their abodes. Accordingly, it is not surprising to find that the Monasteries, which began to spring up in the sixth century, were respected even by the ruthless Chiefs of that epoch.*

The advent of Charlemagne towards the end of the eighth century, changed the face of Europe. It was he who put an end to the invasions of the barbarians from the North and of the Mohammedans from the South, and thus saved the West of Europe. One after the other hė overthrew all the barbarous Chieftains, and restored peace and order in France, Italy, Germany, and a portion of Spain. He then endeavoured to revive Learning and the Arts. He called over Alcuin, a humble Priest of Yorkshire (780), remarkable for his great knowledge, and with his aid founded numerous schools at Paris, Tours, and Aix-la-Chapelle, where Grammar, Arithmetic, Theology, and the Humanities were taught. He founded an Academy, or University, the first in France; of which he was a member, and Alcuin the head. He built numerous harbours which initiated Commerce, and stimulated Agriculture: above all, he

*** Saint Benoit founded in 529, in the south of Italy, the first religious residence or monastery, and gave to his disciples who followed him thither the name of Benedictines, after his own appellation of Benedictus.**

made the wise laws which are known under the title of "Capitularies." Among these 1151 ordinances may be found precepts, moral advice, and religious exhortation. As, for instance, "We must practise hospitality." "If any man meets a beggar who will not labor with his hands, let him beware of giving anything to him." "Let no man think that he can only pray God in three languages, for God can be worshipped in every tongue; and the prayer of every man is answered if he asks for those things that are right."

Appearing in the midst of a barbaric and lawless age, Charlemagne achieved every kind of greatness — military, political, and intellectual. Out of a chaos of nations and institutions not only foreign but hostile to each other, he created a vast and powerful Monarchy which he governed with rare administrative skill and marvellous wisdom. His conquests vastly aided Christianity, for he introduced the New Religion among various wild tribes. He restored Leo III. to his Papacy, and was crowned by him "Emperor of the West" in the year 800.* Measured by the age in which he lived, and by his services to civilization, Charlemagne of France may be considered as one of the greatest men of any epoch.

His Empire crumbled to pieces in the hands of his descendants; and from the fragments grew up three distinct Nationalities—France, Germany, and Italy. In each of these States, now so well defined, the population at that time differed widely in race,

* After Constantine had removed to Constantinople, 330 A.D., the Roman Empire was divided into East and West, each governed by an Emperor. The title of "Emperor of the West" was revived by Leo III., and bestowed on Charlemagne, who was really master of all the territory once tributary to the Roman Empire.

language, manners, and usages. Many centuries and various events were necessary to weld and mould them into that national unity they now possess.

Although the great work of Charlemagne seemed to perish with himself; though lawlessness and bloodshed appeared once more to resume their sway; yet, from his advent we must date the Birth of Modern Society. "From the time of Charlemagne," writes M. Guizot, "the face of things changes; decay is arrested, progress recommences. Yet, for a long time, the disorder will be enormous; the progress partial, often hardly visible, and frequently suspended. This matters not. We shall no longer encounter those long ages of disorganization, of ever-increasing intellectual sterility; and, through a thousand sufferings, a thousand interruptions, we shall see power and life revive in man and society. Charlemagne marks the limit at which the dissolution of the ancient Roman world is consummated, and where the formation of modern Europe, of the new world, really begins. It was under his reign, and, as it were, under his hand, that the shock took place by which European society, turning right round, left the paths of destruction to enter those of creation."

Before dismissing this dreary epoch known as the Dark Ages, it is worth remarking that the moral inundation which swept over Europe at the end of the fifth century, was composed entirely of the Teutonic element. The Saxons who seized on Britain; the Franks, or "free men" of the Rhine, who occupied Gaul; the Herules and Lombards who appropriated Italy; the Goths who dashed into Spain, were all German tribes.

The conquering Teutons, it must be remembered,

in addition to Roman colonies and Roman civilization, found a strong Celtic element in nearly all the countries which fell into their hands. For a time, the two elements, Teuton and Celtic, remained separate and hostile—the one in the pride of complete domination, the other in the despair of complete subjection. But these distinctions gradually ceased, and were almost wholly lost sight of. The Frank and the Gaul, the Saxon and the Briton amalgamated, and together formed new nations neither Teutonic nor Celtic. The supremacy of the conquerors, however, did not wholly pass away. They still constituted the Upper Classes, and owned all the land; whilst the conquered tilled the soil, and endured all the toil and humiliations of serfdom.

THE NEW POLITY.

I HAVE now done with general history. Hereafter I propose to call attention more especially to the career of the three countries—France, England, and the United States—which have marched in the van of the fourth civilization. Their struggles and sacrifices have contributed to undermine the political and social structure bequeathed by the ancient world, and to lay the foundations of a New Polity. This modern organization has taken deep root in all of the countries named, and each has assisted in its development. The salient features of this new condition are Religious Toleration, Political Liberty, and Legal Equality. These are the fruits of that fourth civilization which communicated a new impulse to Humanity by declaring the Equality of all men before God.

We observed, under the first, second, and third civilizations, that the various religions of each sustained the laws which vested all the power in the hands of the few, and consigned the many to eternal thraldom. The doctrines of Christianity, on the contrary, imparted to the masses strong hopes of redemption, both here and hereafter; and from that day to this, they have, blindly but earnestly, groped onwards, as if under divine impulsion, through endless vicissitudes, until they have emerged, as it were, on a plateau in each of the three countries in question, where no right, no privilege, no benefit is denied to any member of the community. All are guaranteed against wrong; and none can be refused what his Intelligence commands: Property is divided; Power is held in common; and the Capacities of all classes are unrestricted.

Such a condition of things rectifies the injustice and cruelty of the ancient civilizations, and approaches as near an ideal state as the infirmities of human nature admit. It is simply utopian to imagine that any human society can endure, where ignorance and vice shall share the advantages achieved by intelligence and virtue.

It cannot be without interest to contemplate the panoramic progress of France and England as, issuing from the mists of the Dark Ages, they entered upon their tempestuous voyage across the Middle Ages. As they advance, it will be remarked that the striking feature of each century is the gradual Rise of the Democracy. Under the ancient civilizations, wars and convulsions left society where they found it—the Minority monopolizing power and wealth; the Majority vegetating in endless bondage. In the six hundred years which comprise the Middle Ages, we shall see the men who under the old civilizations would have died slaves, begin to rise higher and higher in the political and social scale. In France we shall remark that the Crown appealed to the Democracy in its struggles with the Feudal Nobles; whilst in England it was the Aristocracy which allied itself to the People to check the tyranny of the Monarchy. If such combinations ever occurred in the ages preceding Christianity, the Masses derived no advantage; for they seemed unconscious that any change in their condition was possible. It was not until the tidings went forth that all men were equal in the sight of

God that the oppressed began to weary of their fetters.

At the dawn of the Middle Ages but two classes existed in France—the Nobility and the serfs. The more intelligent of the latter by degrees created an intermediate position for themselves, and so reduced the inequality which had prevailed. From this Middle Class arose those various categories of men that gradually acquired importance in the State, and took position by the side of their former masters. From this Middle Class were recruited the members of that Christian Church which opened its ranks alike to poor and rich; and the being who as a serf would have languished in perpetual servitude, claimed his place as a Priest in the midst of Nobles. From this class, too, emerged the Legal Functionary who, as society became more civilized, and the relations of men more complicated, was required to interpret the laws and direct their application. From this class, also, sprang the Capitalist, who, profiting by the prodigality of the feudal Lords, accumulated wealth which opened the way to influence and power. From this class, likewise, was born the Minstrel, who, as years rolled on, was transformed into the Chronicler, and who finally became the Man of Letters and of Science whose magic wand, in the end, dispelled the France of the Middle Ages with its distinctions and its privileges, and established a community where Intellect alone predominates.

In every century from the Christian era to the present, a contest has gone on to bridge the Gulf which existed in the ancient world between the minority and the multitude—in other words, to diminish the distance and increase the equality between them. This fact is commented on by De Tocqueville, who says :—"In perusing the pages of our history we shall scarcely meet with a single great event in the lapse of seven hundred years, which has not turned to the advantage of equality. The Crusades and the wars of the English decimated the nobles and divided their possessions; the erection of the *communes* introduced an element of democratic liberty into the bosom of feudal monarchy; the invention of fire-arms equalized the villain and the noble on the field of battle; printing opened the same resources to the minds of all classes; the post was organized so as to bring the same information to the door of the poor man's cottage and to the gate of the palace; and Protestantism proclaimed that all men are alike able to find the road to heaven. The discovery of America offered a thousand new paths to fortune, and placed riches and power within the reach of the adventurous and the obscure."

So uniform has been this tendency, so irresistible the continuous rise of this popular tide, that De Tocqueville calls it a "providential fact," as it has "all the characteristics of a divine decree: it is universal, it is durable, it eludes all human interference, and all events, as well as all men, contribute to its progress." Nor is this phenomenon peculiar to one country, for it is alike manifest throughout Christendom. The same author, not more conscientious than profound, declares that "in the Christian countries of the present day, the equality of conditions is more complete than it has ever been in any time or in any part of the world." It is only necessary to contrast Christendom and its moral and material progress, with the Heathen Nations and their benighted and inert condition, to prove that the World's Renovation dates from Christianity, the origin of the New Polity.

The discovery of America yielded more than mere wealth, as suggested by De Tocqueville, to the adventurer. It served a higher purpose. It provided a wilderness where the representative of the Middle Class, putting his faith in the equality before God the Messiah taught, could go and found a Polity based on the same principle applied to earth. There, at least, no obstructions would be raised by the cunning of the few to the welfare of the many. There neither Monarchies, nor Feudal Systems, nor Established Creeds, would prevent the deliberate essay of an experiment wholly untried. To this desolate region the Puritan, with the New Testament in his hand, wended his solitary way, and piously proceeded to lay the cornerstone of a political and social Fabric, where all men might dwell together, enjoying the benefits of willing Co-operation, but where none would be suffered to use his intellect, power, or wealth to the injury of the rest. Over the portals of this novel Edifice, since grown to stately proportions, was inscribed the comprehensive doctrine to which it was dedicated:—"*And as ye would that men should do to you, do ye also to them likewise.*"

This *Hegira* of the Puritans was the grandest event of the seventeenth century, so prolific of marvels; and in due course of this Retrospect we shall cross the Atlantic with that devoted band of fanatics who, regardless of danger, and indifferent to wealth or power, sought the shores of an unknown world to plant an Idea which they believed had come of God.

FRANCE.

FRANCE.

MIDDLE AGES.

THE epoch known as the Middle Ages dates from the tenth to the sixteenth centuries. The most prominent feature of this period was the FEUDAL SYSTEM, which may require a word or two of preliminary explanation.

The Feudal system is regarded by some as a Military, by others as an Aristocratic institution. It may be fairly regarded as both, for while it was Military in its origin, it became Aristocratic in its development.

The rise of Feudalism dates from the parcelling out of the conquered territory of the Roman Empire amongst the invading tribes, whose King or Chief first chose his portion, and divided the rest among his captains. These, in their turn, made concessions of land—first called *benefices*, and afterwards *fiefs**—to their soldiers, on condition that they and their

* *Fiefs.*—In modern Latin, *feodum;* from the Saxon *fee,* salary; and *od,* property—whence *feudality* or feudalism. This word designated the land given in recompense for military service by a chief to his soldiers. The word *fief* was employed for the first time in a chart of Charles le Gros, in 884, to designate the concessions described, which, up to the ninth century, had been called *benefices*—in Latin, *beneficium.* The fiefs were divided into the *great fiefs,* or feudal peerages; then into *single fiefs,* which derived directly from the crown; and *double fiefs,* whose owners did not derive from the crown, but from his first suzerain or lord, who was himself most likely the vassal or feudatory of some other suzerain or lord more powerful. The number of fiefs in France varied in this way to an endless extent.

heirs should do military service, and make payments of money or produce.

Thus every tenant, it will be seen, was bound to render military and pecuniary service to his landlord, and became in fact a slave, as his life and labor were at the command of the landowner. The recipient of the land was called a vassal, and the donor was styled the Suzerain or Lord. This same Suzerain was, in his turn, the vassal of the Crown for the land conferred on him, and bound to render "faith and homage."

All the land, both that of the great vassals of the Crown, who in the sixth century took the name of Barons, as well as that of their tenants, was held under a certain tenure or condition, which is familiarly known as the feudal tenure. This mode of holding land, which lasted during most of the Middle Ages, is the very opposite of the freehold system; for the former is held on a condition, and the latter is free from all condition. The feudal and the freehold tenures are therefore just the reverse of each other.

The gift of lands for military service may be traced to the time of the two Roman Emperors, Severus and Probus, 222 and 276 A.D. It was the immemorial usage of the German tribes. When, therefore, the Roman Empire fell into the hands of the victorious barbarians, Europe was organized on this territorial basis.

The feudal tenure was first introduced into Gaul by the Franks, who under their King, Clovis, 481 A.D., became the dominant people of Europe. * In the

* Clovis drove the Romans, the Visigoths, &c., out of Gaul, which was thereafter called France, and founded the French monarchy, the first strong government that emerged from the ruins of the Roman Empire. It broke up after his death in 511 A.D.

course of two centuries many of these great landowners in France became so rich and powerful as to threaten the Monarchy. They were constantly engaged in wars with each other: and the stronger seizing on the land of the vanquished, so added to his possessions and to the number of his retainers or vassals. In 715 A.D., Charles Martel, one of these territorial Lords, actually governed France under the name of "Mayor of the Palace;" and his son, Pepin the Short, in 752 A.D., deposed the King, Childeric III., and had himself proclaimed in his place, becoming the Founder of the second French dynasty.

From the time of Clovis, the Royal Power became constantly weaker from the usage of dividing the Kingdom among the various heirs, until, as just related, one of the feudal Lords was able easily to seize on the Monarchy. Charlemagne, one of the sons of Pepin, raised the Monarchy by his genius to such a height as utterly to eclipse the rivalry of the great feudal Chiefs; but on his death, his Kingdom was again split up, and the Royal Power once more declined. The successors of Charlemagne were all weak men, on whom the feudal Chiefs were able to impose their own terms. About 876 A.D., they forced Charles the Bald, grandson of Charlemagne, to declare their estates hereditary. They even went further, and succeeded in causing the government of the various provinces of the Kingdom, which were all in their hands, to be also declared hereditary.

We now enter the Middle Ages in France, the subject of this chapter. From this time the power of the leading Barons became so great that they treated the Royal Authority with contempt. In 987 A.D., one of the feudal Chiefs, Hugh Capet, got himself declared King by his vassals, on the death of Louis V., the Feeble, the last King of the second dynasty. But Hugh Capet also found his Sovereignty almost as limited as that of the dynasty which he had dispossessed. He was nominally King of France, but beyond his own domains his supremacy was ignored.

At this period France was divided into numerous territories called Duchies and Counties, at the head of which was one of these feudal Barons; who was styled Duke or Count according as his territory was either a Duchy or County. These titles were of Roman origin, but the Kings of the Franks adopted them with a different signification. They were now applied to territory, and denoted its extent; for a Duchy was usually larger than a County. At the beginning of the tenth century, then, the whole of France was owned by various Dukes and Counts,* who were the hereditary possessors of their lands, wholly independent in their jurisdiction, and exercising, by consent of the Crown, the rights of Sovereignty. They coined money, levied taxes, and, when interest or passion dictated, made war on each other.† Finally, to guarantee their power and wealth, they established Primogeniture towards the end of the tenth century, so that their

* The title of Marquis was rare at this period, and was chiefly honorary. It was given to the owners of land presented by the King with letters patent.

† With a view to check the barbarous hostilities constantly raging between the feudal nobles, the Church induced them to consent to a suspension of arms during the days dedicated to religious services. This was called *La Paix de Dieu*, and began in 1041. Louis IX., in his reign, 1226-1270, issued an ordinance that forty days must elapse after the offence was given before any conflict should begin. This was called *La Quarantaine du Roi*. These "private wars" between the feudal barons went on up to the fourteenth century, when they were gradually checked by the progress of civilization and the growth of the royal power.

lands and dignities might descend unimpaired to their eldest sons.

No such organization had ever existed before. The Roman law created the rank of *nobiles*, or *known men*, but Primogeniture was never recognized. In Greece, Egypt, and India, such a class as this feudal Aristocracy never appeared. It originated in France, as described, and spread over Europe, where it is still extant, though shorn of its ancient power and grandeur. Strange that France which first inaugurated an Hereditary Aristocracy in Europe should be the first to abolish it!

These feudal Nobles, in order to enhance their prestige, began, towards the close of the tenth century, to use family arms and crests to illustrate the exploits of themselves and their ancestors. Heraldry, which was simply the record of the pedigree of these families, came into fashion. Ceremonies, pageantries, and etiquette were gradually introduced to heighten the splendor and gratify the pride of the feudal Aristocracy.

The institution of Chivalry, or Knighthood, was created in the eleventh century, as a new means of adding lustre to the Nobility. No one could be a Knight but a Nobleman, and those who received the honor had special privileges conferred. They could carry a banner, appear at tournaments,* wear a gold

* The first tournament of the Middle Ages took place at Strasburg, in 842, at the interview between Louis of Germany and Charles I. (the Bald) of France. The Emperor Henry I., who died in 936, was very fond of this species of amusement, and made several laws for its regulation. Geoffrey II. of Brittany was killed in a tournament at Paris, August 19, 1186. Tournaments were introduced into England during the reign of Stephen, 1135–54. They were prohibited by Henry II., 1154–89, and were again established in the reign of Richard I., 1189–99. Edward III. held a tournament at Dartford in 1330, and another at Windsor, January 19, 1334, soon after the institution of the Order of

collar and gilded armor, assume the title of *Monseigneur*, while their wives were entitled to that of *Madame.* A Knight had to pass through three degrees of promotion—that of *varlet*, *page*, and *esquire*—and received his sword of Knighthood amid religious and military ceremonies, which were all meant to enhance the distinction.*

The object of this feudal institution was partly to stimulate military ardor in the Nobles, partly to soften and improve the manners of a rough and warlike age. To cultivate a spirit of chivalry or courtesy towards women, the weak, the defenceless, a Knight was bound by oath always to draw his sword against injustice, to defend the widow and orphan, and to obey implicitly the orders of his Lady and his King. The Knight who failed in these duties was declared in a Court of Chivalry to be a felon, and lost his privileges.† During the period of the Crusades, Chivalry

the Garter. Henry VIII. and the Duke of Suffolk maintained the field against all comers in May 1513. Henry II. of France lost his eye in a tilt with Count Montgomery, and died shortly afterwards of the wound, 1559. After this accident tournaments were discontinued in France.

A magnificent festivity, in imitation of the mediæval tournaments, was held by the Earl of Eglinton at his castle in Ayrshire, August 1839. The Marquis of Londonderry officiated as "King of the Tournament," and Lady Seymour as "Queen of Love and Beauty." Many of the guests were in ancient costumes, and the expense of the entertainment is said to have amounted to £40,000. The Emperor Napoleon III., then Prince Louis Napoleon, was one of the mimic warriors on this occasion.

* "The young man, the esquire," says Guizot, "who aspired to the title of knight, was first divested of his clothes and put into the bath —a symbol of purification. Upon coming out of the bath, they clothed him in a white tunic—a symbol of purity; in a red robe—a symbol of the blood which he was bound to shed in the service of the faith; in a saga, or close black coat—a symbol of the death which awaited him as well as all men."

It may be added, the modern practice of duelling grew out of the institution of chivalry.

† There were other classes of knights sworn to defend the Church against the infidels, as the Knights Hospitallers, founded in Jerusalem

was at its zenith, but declined with the Feudal System.*

The feudal Lords, who lived with all the pomp the age could furnish in their *chateaux* or castles, had no other occupation than warfare with each other from motives of rivalry or plunder. Their amusements were the chase, or festivities at the castle. A few facts from the lives of some of them will illustrate the character of the Middle Ages better than any description.

William I., Duke of Normandy, forced the Count of Bretagne to acknowledge himself his vassal in 928. He defeated the Count of Cotentin, who laid siege to Rouen, the capital of Normandy, in 933; defended King Charles the Simple against the Duke of Burgundy; aided in restoring Louis IV. to the throne; and, finally, was assassinated by the Count of Flanders in a conference proposed by the latter, in 943.

Another William of Normandy, in 1035, went into Italy with two of his brothers, and followed by three hundred Norman adventurers disguised as pilgrims. He first took service with the Prince of Salerno, and afterwards with the Greek Patriarch. He fought for six years to recover Sicily from the Infidels or Saracens. His last exploit was the capture of Calabria; of which he declared himself the sovereign Count, dividing a portion of his conquests with his followers.

in 1099, afterwards known as the Knights of Malta, who wore a white cloak with a red cross; also the Knights Templars, founded also in Jerusalem by some of the Crusaders in 1118. This last order became very powerful and rich. They were suppressed in France by Philip le Bel in 1307, and by the Pope Clement in 1312. Their number and wealth made them dangerous in the eyes of these rulers.

* In our days, the title of Knight or Chevalier is given to those admitted to any order of honor, as the Orders of the Garter and Bath in England, the Legion of Honour in France, the Golden Fleece in Spain, &c.

Roger, a brother of William, invaded Sicily, then occupied by the Saracens, in 1061, with a band of mercenaries; and, after fighting for twenty-eight years, conquered the whole island, and restored the Christian religion, obtaining in 1098 from the Pope Urbain, for himself and successors, the dignity of Apostolic Legate, with all the powers of that high function.

Simon de Montfort, Baron and Count, joined the Fourth Crusade in 1199, and distinguished himself in Palestine. On his return, he was elected by the Barons, Chief of the army against the Albigeois heretics, who were commanded by the Count of Toulouse. He signalized himself by his courage and cruelties, overthrew the Count of Toulouse, 1213, and seized his estates, which Pope Innocent III. bestowed on him. Montfort was killed, 1218, by a stone whilst besieging Toulouse, which had again revolted. He was called the "Maccabee" of his epoch.

Guy de Dampierre, Count of Flanders and Peer of France, accompanied Louis IX. to Africa in 1270. Having married his daughter to Edward of England without the permission of Philip III., his Suzerain, the King declared war against him, defeated him, and seized on his castle and estates. Dampierre came to Paris to beg forgiveness of the King, but was imprisoned at Compiègne, where he died.

The Counts of Flanders were vassals of the King of France; but in 1297, the Count Guy de Dampierre revolted against Philip IV., which led to the conquest of the County of Flanders, and its annexation to France. In 1302, however, the Flemish rebelled and defeated Philip, who was obliged to restore their feudal Counts. In 1337, the Flemish cities recognized Edward

III. of England as the King of France, which began a war of a hundred years between the English and French. The *Seigneurie* of Flanders afterwards passed over by marriage to the House of Austria, which led to long wars between France and Austria.*

John, Count of St. Pol and Luxemburg, was in the service of the French King, but in sympathy with the Duke of Burgundy and the English. He was Governor of Paris for two years in the name of Henry V. of England. It was he who took Jeanne d'Arc prisoner at Compiègne, 1430, and who sold her to the English for £10,000. He opposed the reconciliation of the French King and the Duke of Burgundy. His death occurred in 1446.

Louis, Count of St. Pol, his nephew, was in the service of Louis XI. of France, who made him *Connétable*, after giving him his sister-in-law as wife. Notwithstanding, he conspired with the Duke of Burgundy and the English against the King. Being convicted of this crime by the Parliament, he was beheaded.†

The Duke de Guise, of the House of Lorraine, took a leading part on the Catholic side against the Protestants, and gave the signal for the massacres of St Bartholomew, 1572, by ordering the assassination of Admiral Coligny. He was afterwards assassinated by the King's Guards at Blois, 1588.

The House of Montmorency, which took its name, as was the custom, from its estate near Paris, was

* Flanders next fell into the hands of Charles V. of Spain, who included it in the United Provinces; then it went back to Austria; then returned to the French under Napoleon. In 1814 it was ceded to the King of Holland, and in 1831 became the kingdom of Belgium.

† It was in the magnificent castle of Count St. Pol, built in 1470, that Prince Louis Napoleon was confined for six years—1840 to 1846. The wall of one of the towers of this castle is nine feet in thickness, and has these words engraved on it, "*Mon mieux*"—"My best."

founded in 950 by Bouchard, one of the great Feudatories * of the Duke of France, Hugh Capet, afterwards King. He had the title of "First Christian Baron, and First Baron of France." This family boasted of having produced six *Connétables* of France, twelve Marshals, four Admirals, several Cardinals, and a great number of Generals and Statesmen. It was also allied to most of the Royal Families of Europe. One of the Dukes of Montmorency, Henry II., born in 1595, was made Admiral at seventeen by Louis XIII. He inherited from his father the Government of Languedoc, one of the provinces of France. In the civil war between the Protestants and Catholics, 1620, he defeated the Duke de Rohan, the Protestant leader. As the victorious Commander of the French army in Piedmont, he was made a Marshal in 1629. Angry at not being made a *Connétable*, he conspired against Louis XIII., and raised a Revolution in Languedoc, but was defeated. Covered with wounds, he was made a prisoner, and executed at thirty-eight years of age. His wife retired to a convent.

The House of Rohan, descended from the ancient Kings of Brittany in the west of France, held the rank of Princes. For this reason they bore the well-known device on their arms, "*Roi ne puis, Duc*

* It was customary for one feudal noble to acknowledge himself the vassal of another, if he had received from him land called *fiefs*, by which he was bound to fealty. In those days, any one who obtained land on the usual feudal conditions could sub-grant it; so that the vassal to the first became suzerain to the last. This process of *subinfeudation*, as it was called, went on in France to a great extent, and, some writers say, created those habits of obedience or submission unknown in any other country. It is true that every vassal in his turn was bound to obedience. The great baron, vassal to the king, was pledged to obey him as his suzerain. The next, who received land from the baron, was equally bound. This system, which lasted several centuries in France, has affected the national character, and explains that submission to the Government of the day which is so remarkable.

ne daigne, Rohan suis"—"King I cannot be, Duke I disdain, Rohan I am." One of the Rohans, Henry, Prince de Léon, married the daughter of Sully, the celebrated Minister of Henry IV. At the death of this King, he became leader of the Protestants, and headed their wars against Louis XIII. He was defeated at the siege of La Rochelle by Cardinal Richelieu, 1628, and banished. He then went to Venice, and became a General of the Republic in a war with Spain. He afterwards commanded a French army in the north of Italy, being restored to the favor of Richelieu. Finally, he joined Bernard, Duke of Saxe-Weimar, as one of the Generals of the Protestant army of Germany, and was killed in battle, 1638.

The House of La Rochefoucauld, founded, as most of the preceding, in the eleventh century, produced many distinguished men. One of the best known is the Duke who figured in the War of the Fronde, 1648, and who was afterwards made Governor of the province of Poitou by Louis XIV. He was intimate in his latter years with Madame de Sévigne. He refused to enter the French Academy, as he shrank from speaking in public. He is best known by his book of "Maximes," published in 1665, a work remarkable for the *finesse* of its style, and the boldness of its paradoxes. He asserted that "Self-interest is the only motive of human actions."

The above sketches of some of the feudal Lords are taken at random from French Annals, and are not, perhaps, the most interesting, but they serve to illustrate the epoch. Similar portraits might be cited from the feudal history of the other countries of Europe, but would occupy too much space. The two following pictures of feudal life in Italy are striking.

The House of Montferrat, in Lombardy, was founded by Alderame, created Marquis of Montferrat in 967 by Otho I. of Germany. This family reigned over the Marquisate of Montferrat for nearly six hundred years. William, the sixth Marquis, joined Charles of Anjou of France in his conquest of Naples, and afterwards fought against the French King when he attempted to subjugate Lombardy. He subsequently seized on numerous Italian towns in the north, and added them to the possessions of his family. He was finally taken prisoner by the inhabitants of Alexandria, who revolted against him, and was shut up in an iron cage, where he died, after seventeen months of captivity, in 1292. Perpetually at war with various feudal Lords, especially the Visconti and the Sforza, Lords of Milan, the family of Montferrat gradually declined in the fifteenth and sixteenth centuries, and disappeared in the person of John George, 1533, who died without issue. His fiefs passed to Frederick II., Marquis of Mantua, who had married his niece.

In the fifteenth century, the feudal Barons of the Kingdom of Naples conspired against King Ferdinand, and endeavoured to put the Duke of Calabria on the throne; but afterwards they abandoned their design, and made their submission to the King as his loyal vassals. Twenty years afterwards, the Barons got up a new conspiracy, which Ferdinand discovered, and succeeded in defeating by inveigling the conspirators into his palace, and there assassinating them. One only, the Prince of Salerno, escaped. He took refuge at the Court of Charles V. of France, and promoted ardently the war against Naples, which ended in the overthrow of Ferdinand in 1495.

From the above extracts, the reader may form some notion of the condition of Europe for some five hundred years and upwards—say, from the tenth to the fifteenth centuries—whilst the Feudal System was in the plenitude of its power. I cannot forbear, however, making a quotation from a brilliant writer, whose graphic sketches convey a still more vivid idea of this interesting period—a period that gave birth to that Hereditary Aristocracy which even to the present day is so prominent and influential. The following extract from Mr Winwood Reade brings out in an impressive manner the notable features of the feudal regime, or "the Government of the Castle." The citation begins just at the moment when the Roman Empire was breaking up, and the German tribes were trying to force their entrance into the west of Europe, which hitherto had been under the subjection of the Romans:—

"*The Ancient Germans—The Castle Kings—The Castle a Home—The Castle an Academy—Chivalry—The Serfs—Tournament—The Town.*

"The province of Gaul"—now France—"was taxed to death, and then abandoned by the Romans. The Government could no longer afford to garrison the Rhine frontier; the legions were withdrawn, and the Germans entered.

"The invading armies were composed of free men, who, under their respective captain or heads of clans, had joined the standard of some noted warrior chief. The spoil of the army belonged to the army, and was divided according to stipulated rules. The king's share was large, but more than his share he might not have. When the Germans, instead of returning with their booty, remained upon the foreign soil, they partitioned the land in the same manner as they partitioned the cattle and the slaves, the gold crosses, the silver chalices, the vases, the tapestry, the fine linen, and the purple robes. An immense region was allotted to the king; other tracts of various sizes to the generals and captains (or chiefs and chieftains), according to the number of men whom they had brought into the field; and each private soldier received a piece of ground. But the army, although disbanded, was not extinct; its members remained under martial law; the barons or generals were bound to obey the King when he summoned them to war; the soldiers to obey their ancient chiefs. Sometimes the king and the great barons gave lands to favourites and friends on similar conditions; and at a later period money was paid instead of military service, thus originating rent.

"They surrounded themselves with a body-guard of personal retainers; their prisoners of war were made to till the ground as serfs, and soon they reduced to much the same condition the German soldiers, and seized their humble lands. In that troubled age none could hold property except by means of the strong arm. Men found it difficult to preserve their lives, and often presented their bodies to some powerful lords in return for protection, in return for daily bread. The power of the king was nominal; sovereignty was broken and dispersed. Europe was divided amongst castles; and in each castle was a prince who owned no authority above his own, who held a high court of justice in his hall, issued laws to his estates, lived by the court fees, by taxes levied on passing caravans, and by ransoms for prisoners, sometimes obtained in fair war, sometimes by falling upon peaceful travellers. Dark deeds were done within those ivy-covered towers which now exist for the pleasure of poets and pilgrims of the picturesque. Often from turret chambers and grated windows arose the shrieks of violated maidens and the yells of tortured Jews. Yet castle-life had also its brighter side. To cheer the solitude of the isolated house minstrels and poets and scholars were courted by the barons, and were offered a peaceful chamber, and a place of honour at the board. In the towns of ancient Italy and Greece there was no family; the home did not exist. The women and children dwelt together in secluded chambers; the men lived a club-life in the baths, the porticoes, and the gymnasia. But the castle lord had no companions of his own rank except the members of his own family. On stormy days, when he could not hunt, he found a pleasure in dancing his little ones on his knee, and in telling them tales of the wood and weald. Their tender fondlings, and their merry laughs, their half-formed voices, which attempted to pronounce his name—all these were sweet to him. And by the love of those in whom he saw his own image mirrored, in whom his own childhood appeared to live again, he was drawn closer and closer to his wife. She became his counsellor and friend; she softened his rugged manners; she soothed his fierce wrath; she pleaded for the prisoners and captives, and the men condemned to die. And when he was absent, she became the sovereign lady of the house, ruled the vassals, sat in the judgment-seat, and often defended the castle in a siege. A charge so august could not but elevate the female mind. Women became queens. The Lady was created. Within the castle was formed that grand manner of gentleness mingled with hauteur, which art can never simulate, and which ages of dignity can alone confer.

"The barons dwelt apart from one another, and were often engaged in private war. Yet they had sons to educate and daughters to marry; and so a singular kind of society arose. The king's house or court, and the houses of great barons, became academies to which the inferior barons sent their boys and girls to school. The young lady became the attendant of the Dame, and was instructed in the arts of playing on the virginals, of preparing simples, and of healing wounds; of spinning, sewing, and embroidery. The young gentleman was at first a Page. He was taught to manage a horse with grace and skill, to use bow and sword, to sound the notes of venerie upon the horn, to carve at table, to ride full tilt against the quintaine with his lance in rest, to brittle a deer, to find his way through the forest by the stars in the sky and by the moss upon the trees. It was also his duty to wait upon the ladies who tutored his youthful mind in other ways. He was trained to deport himself with elegance; he was nurtured in all the accomplishments of courtesy and love; he was encouraged to select a mistress among the dames or demoiselles; to adore her in his heart, to serve her with patience and fidelity, obeying her least command; to be modest in her presence; to be silent and discreet. The reward of all this devotion was of no ethereal kind, but it was not quickly or easily bestowed; and vice almost ceases to be vice when it can only be gratified by means of long discipline in virtue. When the page had arrived at a certain age, he was clad in a brown frock; a sword was fastened to his side, and he obtained the title of Esquire. He attended his patron knight on military expeditions, until he was old enough to be admitted to the order. Among the ancient Germans of the forest, when a young man came of age, he was solemnly invested with shield and spear. The ceremony of knighthood at first was nothing more. Every man of gentle birth became a knight, and then took an oath to be true to God, and to the ladies, and to his plighted word; to be honourable in all his actions, to succour the oppressed. Thus, within those castle-colleges arose the sentiment of Honour, the institution of Chivalry, which, as an old poet wrote, made women chaste and men brave. The women were worshipped as goddesses, the men were revered as heroes. Each sex aspired to possess those qualities which the other sex approved. Women admire, above all things, courage and truth; and so the men became courageous and true. Men admire modesty, virtue, and refinement; and so the women became modest, virtuous, and refined. A higher standard of propriety was required as time went on. The manners and customs of the dark ages became the vices of a later period; unchastity, which had once been regarded as the private wrong of the husband, was stigmatised as a sin against society, and society found a means of taking its revenge. At first the notorious woman was insulted to her face at tournament and banquet; or knights chalked an epithet upon her castle gates, and then rode on. In the next age she was shunned by her own sex; the discipline of social life was established as it exists at the present day. Though it might sometimes be relaxed in a vicious court, at least the ideal of right was preserved. But in the period of the Troubadours, the fair sinners resembled the pirates of the Homeric age. Their pursuits were of a dangerous, but not of a dishonourable nature; they might sometimes lose their lives; they never lost their reputation.

"We must now descend from ladies and gentlemen to the people in the field, who are sometimes forgotten by historians. The castle was built on the summit of a hill, and a village of serfs was clustered round its foot. These poor peasants were often hardly treated by their lords. Often they raised their brown and horny hands and cursed the cruel castle which scowled upon them from above. Humbly they made obeisance, and bitterly they gnawed their lips, as the baron rode down the narrow street on his great war-horse, which would always have its fill of corn, when they would starve, followed by his beef-fed varlets with faces red from beer, who gave them jeering looks, who called them by nicknames, who contemptuously caressed their daughters before their eyes. Yet it was not always thus: the lord was often a true nobleman, the parent of their village, the godfather of their children, the guardian of their happiness, the arbiter of their disputes. When there was sickness among them, the ladies of the castle came down, bringing them soups and spiced morsels with their own white hands; and the castle was the home of the good chaplain, who told them of the happier world beyond the grave. It was there also that they enjoyed such pleasure as they had. Sometimes they were called up to the castle to feast on beef and beer in commemoration of a happy anniversary or a Christian feast. Sometimes their lord brought home a caravan of merchants whom he had captured on the road; and while the strange guests were quaking for the safety of their bales, the people were being amused with the songs of the minstrels, and the tricks of the jugglers, and the antics of the dancing-bear. And sometimes a tournament was held: the lords and ladies of the neighbourhood rode over to the castle; turf banks were set for the serfs, and a gallery was erected for the ladies, above whom sat enthroned the one who was chosen as the Queen of Beauty and of Love. Then the heralds shouted, 'Love of ladies, splintering of lances, stand forth, gallant knights; fair eyes look upon your deed!' And the knights took up their position in two lines fronting one another, and sat motionless upon their horses like pillars of iron, with nothing to be seen but their flaming eyes. The trumpets flourished; '*laissez aller*,' cried a voice; and the knights, with their long spears in rest, dashed furiously against each other, and then plied battle-axe and sword, to the great delight and contentment of the populace.

"In times of war the castle was also the refuge of the poor, and the villagers fled behind its walls when the enemy drew near. They did not then reflect that it was the castle which had provoked the war; they viewed it only as an hospitable fortress which had saved their lives. It was, therefore, in many cases regarded by the people, not only with awe and veneration, but also with a sentiment of filial love. It was associated with their pleasures and their security. But in the course of time a rival arose to alienate the affections, or to strengthen the resentment of the castle serf. It was the town.

"In the days of the Roman Republic, and in the first days of the Empire, all kinds of skilled labour were in the hands of slaves: in every palace, whatever was required for the household was manufactured on the premises. But before the occupation by the Germans, a free class of artisans had sprung up, in what manner is not precisely known; they were probably the descendants of emancipated slaves. This class, divided into guilds and corporations, continued to inhabit the towns: they manufactured armour and clothes; they travelled as pedlars about the country, and thus acquired wealth, which they cautiously concealed, for they were in complete subservience to the castle lord. They could not leave their property by will, dispose of their daughters in marriage, or perform a single business transaction without the permission of their liege. But little by little their power increased. When war was being waged, it became needful to fortify the town—for the town was the baron's estate, and he did not wish his property to be destroyed. When once the burghers were armed and their town walled, they were able to defy their lord. They obtained charters, sometimes by revolt, sometimes by purchase, which gave them the town to do with it as they pleased; to elect their own magistrates, to make their own laws, and to pay their liege-lord a fixed rent by the year, instead of being subjected to loans, and benevolences, and loving contributions.* The Roman law, which had never quite died out, was now revived; the old municipal institutions of the Empire were restored. Unhappily the citizens often fought among themselves, and towns joined barons in destroying towns. Yet their influence rapidly increased, and the power of the castle was diminished. Whenever a town received privileges from its lord, other towns demanded that the same rights should be embodied in their charter, and rebelled if their request was refused. Trade and industry expanded; the products of the burgher enterprise and skill were offered in the castle halls for sale. The lady was tempted with silk and velvet; the lord with chains of gold, and Damascus blades, and suits of Milan steel; the children clamoured for the sweet white powder which was brought from the countries of the East. These new tastes and fancies impoverished the nobles. They reduced their establishments, and the discarded retainers, in no sweet temper, went over to the town.

"And there were others who went to the town as well. In classical times the slaves were unable to rebel with any prospect of success. In the cities of Greece every citizen was a soldier. In Rome an enormous army served as the

* Charters were granted to towns by the King only. Louis VI. was the first to give them, as related elsewhere.

slave-police. But in the scattered castle states of Europe the serfs could rise against their lords, and often did so with effect. And then the town was always a place of refuge : the runaway slave was there welcomed ; his pursuers were duped or defied ; the file was applied to his collar ; his blue blouse was taken off ; his hair was suffered to grow ; he was made a burgher and a free man. Thus the serfs had often the power to rebel, and always the power to escape ; in consequence of which, they ceased to be serfs and became tenants.

"The extinction of villeinage was not a donation, but a conquest: it did not descend from the court and the castle ; it ascended from the village and the town. The Church, however, may claim the merit of having mitigated slavery in its worst days, when its horrors were increased by the pride of conquest and the hostility of race. The clergy belonged to the conquered people, whom they protected from harsh usage to the best of their ability. They taught as the Moslem doctors also teach, and as even the pagan Africans believe, that it is a pious action to emancipate a slave. But there is no reason to suppose that they ever thought of abolishing slavery, and they could not have done so had they wished."

MONARCHY ASSAILS FEUDALITY.

MIDDLE AGES.

FROM the copious extract given, the reader can hardly fail to obtain a more familiar comprehension of the Feudal System. That system he will now have learned was nothing else than the exercise of arbitrary power by the great landowners called feudal Lords. During the greater part of the Middle Ages, these Noblemen were wholly independent and irresponsible, acknowledging no law but force, and wielding despotic sway over their fiefs or estates; masters equally of the property and lives of their tenants or vassals. "They were," says a distinguished writer, "isolated despots, each of whom was a sovereign in his own domains, doing what was right in his own eyes, giving no account of his actions, and asking no opinion as to the nature of his conduct towards his subjects. In the course of time this system met with greater popular detestation than others which had reduced the people to more monotonous and lasting servitude. The peasants led a precarious and uncertain life, involved in all the quarrels of their chief, and enduring all the vengeance of his enemies. In the eleventh and twelfth centuries there were numerous peasant insurrections, in which atrocious crimes were perpetrated upon the nobles, their families, and retainers.

These led to atrocious retaliations, and we see at this time the beginning of that fierce antagonism between class and class which existed for so long in France, and which culminated at the revolution of 1789."

There was only one authority in Europe that struggled steadily to check the supremacy of the feudal Nobility: that was the Royal Power. For several centuries in all the States of Europe a conflict was maintained between the Crown and the Barons. In France the Kings, in Germany the Emperors, in Italy the Popes, constantly sought by force or diplomacy to curtail the dictatorship of the Aristocracy; and in each of these countries the Aristocracy as fiercely defended their rights.

The nature of the contest which took place in England between the Crown and the Barons I will reserve for a future chapter, relating here what occurred in France. It was in the latter country that the feudal despots held larger possessions, exercised greater authority, and kept their vassals under better discipline than elsewhere.

When a weak man was on the throne of France, he shrank from any collision with the Barons, lest he might be deprived of his crown; for many of the more powerful carried their ambition so far as to aspire to the Regal Authority. There were many French Kings, however, of ability and courage, who made bold efforts to reduce the exorbitant power of these Lords of the soil.

One of the first who assailed them with success was Louis VI., whose reign, 1108–37, was memorable for the Rise of a Middle Class. At this time there was no such thing as a standing army, and the King had fewer retainers at his command than many of his powerful Nobles. Under these circumstances, Louis looked round for aid to carry out his purpose of strengthening the Royal Power, so utterly defied by the contumacious Barons. His eye fell on various small clusters of men, called *Communes*, scattered here and there over the country, composed chiefly of the serfs who had fled from the violence and exactions of their despotic landlords. Collecting in groups of a few hundred, more or less, these fugitive slaves had built walls round their habitations, and thus defied the power of their Suzerain.

Among the first of these *Communes* was *Le Mans*, which was established in 1066. Others followed; and at the beginning of the twelfth century several had grown to considerable size, and all of them had a Militia force trained by frequent contests with the vassals of some predatory Baron.

Louis VI. proposed to incorporate these *Communes** —to give them a Mayor and Municipal privileges, but on the condition that they put their Militia at his service. This condition the *Communes* gladly accepted, as the object of the King was to fight the common enemy. Thus fortified, the King began his attacks on the Barons.

It cost him a siege of three years before he took the castle of the Lord of Puiset. He afterwards assailed the Counts of Mantes, Montfort, Montmorency, &c., and demolished the castle of the Lord of Montlhery, who claimed jurisdiction over 133 fiefs or estates, and 300 parishes. Finally, he attempted to seize on Normandy, which then belonged to Henry I. of Eng-

* Louis VI. also gave charters to several old towns to make them independent of feudal and ecclesiastical pretensions, such as Soissons and Laon. Soissons was a flourishing city of Gaul at the time of the Roman invasion.

land, son of William the Conqueror, but was defeated, 1119.

His son, Louis VII., continued the war against the Aristocracy; and, among others, he attacked the Count of Champagne. Whilst engaged in the contest with this Nobleman, the King burnt the town of Vitry; and 1300 people perished who had taken refuge in the church. To expiate this crime, Louis put himself at the head of the Second Crusade, 1147, and performed prodigies of valor.*

Philip Augustus, his son, continued the struggle against Feudality, and vanquished the Count of Flanders and the Duke of Burgundy. He added to the domains of the Crown, the Duchy of Normandy, the Countships of Artois, Evreux, Meulan, and eight others. This remarkable man greatly increased the Royal Power in other ways also: he incorporated numerous *Communes*, and also created a Militia called the *Ribauds*, 1189.†

His grandson, Louis IX., subdued several of the Lords who had revolted, and amongst the rest the Count de la Marche, 1242.‡

* After his return from the East, Louis VII. repudiated his wife Eleonore, 1152, whom he suspected of adultery. She then married Henry II. of England, grandson of William the Conqueror, and brought to him as dowry her great possessions in France—Guenne, Poitou, Auvergne, Perigord, Limousin, &c. Louis VII., enraged at this marriage, sustained the sons of Henry II., who had revolted against their father, and welcomed to his court Thomas à Becket, Archbishop of Canterbury, after he had quarrelled with the English king.

† This king greatly embellished Paris. He was the first to pave some of the streets; commenced the markets, and the hospital known as *l'Hotel Dieu;* continued the building Notre Dame; protected the University of Paris; made excellent laws; and encouraged commerce.

‡ During the reign of Louis IX., in 1250, a band of marauders, called Pastoureaux, under the leadership of a Hungarian monk, wandered about the country committing great ravages. They declared themselves the enemies of the nobles and the clergy, attacking the castles and devastating the churches. They were overtaken and cut to pieces

The grandson of Louis, Philip IV.,* who died 1314, devoted himself to not only breaking down the Feudal Power, but also to diminishing the ascendency of the Church. He accomplished, besides, a great deal for the cause of Centralization—that is, increasing the Royal Power at the expense of feudal rights and privileges. He made considerable additions to the Royal domains, the most notable being the city of Lyons and the diocese of Viviers. With a view to replenish the Royal Treasury, he sold charters to the *Communes*. Philip IV. was also the first, some writers assert, to establish a permanent or standing army.

One of the earlier causes which contributed to weaken the feudal Nobles was the eagerness with which they threw themselves into those famous expeditions to Asia Minor against the Infidels. The motives of these Crusades will be considered in another place. Here it is sufficient to say, that in order to raise money to fit out their vassals for these expensive enterprises, many of them were obliged to mortgage their domains to the Crown, and were afterwards unable to redeem them.

Another cause, however, which was much more efficacious in reducing the power of the Nobles, and adding to that of the Kings, was the Invention of gunpowder.

The testimony is conflicting as to the date of this

in 1251. These were the forerunners of that revolution which five hundred years later swept over France.

* Louis VI., in 1130, was the first who called the representatives of the *Communes*, which he sought to develop, to sit in council with the clergy and the nobles; but these representatives were allowed no other *rôle* than that of spectators of the deliberations of the two great orders. Philip IV. was the first who called the three orders—the clergy, the nobles, and the delegates of the third class (that is, the middle class)—to assemble and deliberate on national affairs, in 1302. This assembly was called *Les Etats Généraux*—the States General.

event. By some it is attributed to Roger Bacon, an English Monk, and to the year 1250; by others to B. Schwartz, a German Monk, who lived nearly half a century later.* It is certain that gunpowder came

* Some authors pretend that gunpowder was used in battle against Alexander the Great, by some Hindoo tribes, 355 B.C. It is asserted by others that gunpowder artillery was employed by the Chinese in 85 A.D. Its exportation from England was prohibited by Henry V. in 1414.

The following dates showing its use in artillery may be found interesting:—

A.D.

1118 The Moors used artillery in an attack upon Saragopal.

1156 Abdelmumem, the Moorish king, takes Mahadia from the Sicilians by means of artillery.

1308 Guzman el Bueno takes Gibraltar from the Moors by means of artillery.

1327 Edward III. uses "crakeys of war" in his expedition against Scotland.

1331 Ibn Nason Ben Bia mentions that balls of iron thrown by means of fire were military weapons of the Moors.

1338 The French use artillery at the siege of Puy-Guillaume.

1347 Edward III. uses espringals and bombards at the siege of Calais.

1364 Small hand-cannon are constructed in large numbers at Perouse.

1366 The Venetians first used artillery at the siege of Chioggia.

1378 John of Gaunt uses 400 cannon night and day in a fruitless attack upon St Malo.

1381 Eleven pieces of ordnance are mentioned as existing in the Hotel de Ville, Bologna.

1382 Portable bombards, subsequently called culverines, are introduced in France. Field-guns are employed by the people of Ghent against Bruges.

1386 The English capture two French vessels armed with heavy artillery.

1394 The Turks use artillery at the siege of Constantinople.

1418 The English, under the Duke of Gloucester, fire red-hot balls at the siege of Cherbourg.

1460 James II. is killed by the accidental bursting of a cannon at the siege of Roxburgh Castle.

1477 Louis XI. causes twelve portable cannon to be cast to throw metal shot, and to be used as a siege train.

1488 Gun-carriages greatly improved are constructed in France.

1491 Charles VIII. of France attacks Rennes with an artillery force drawn by 3000 horses.

1498 The Portuguese find artillery much in use in India.

1521 Brass cannon are first cast in England. Pigafetta, the secretary of Magellan, states the walls of the town of Borneo are defended by six iron and fifty-six brass cannon.

1543 Large mortars to fire shells are made in England by Peter Bawd.

into use in Europe in the beginning of the fourteenth century, for we find that Gibraltar was taken from the Moors in 1308 by the employment of artillery.

The application of gunpowder to war led to extraordinary results, both political and social. "Up to this time," says Buckle, "it was considered the duty of nearly every man to be prepared to enter the military service, for the purpose of either defending his own country or attacking others. Standing armies were entirely unknown, and in their place there existed a rude and barbarous militia, always ready for battle, and always unwilling to engage in those peaceful pursuits which were then universally despised. Nearly every man being a soldier, the military profession, as such, had no separate existence; or, to speak more properly, the whole of Europe composed one great army, in which all other professions were merged.

"To this the only exception was the ecclesiastical profession, but even that was affected by the general tendency, and it was not at all uncommon to see large bodies of troops led to the field by bishops and abbots,

1545 The *Mary Rose*, man-of-war, sinks off the coast of France with 600 men on board owing to the weight of her artillery. Breech-loading cannon have been recovered from the wreck.
1547 Iron cannon are first cast in England about this year.
1554 At the battle of Remi, Charles V. employs light guns with limbers drawn by two horses, and called the Emperor's pistol.
1686 The colossal brass gun "Malick è Meidan," or "lord of the plain," cast at Bejapore in commemoration of the capture of the city this year by the Emperor. Arungzebe is the largest cast cannon in existence, measuring 14 feet 1 inch in length, with a bore of 2 feet 4 inches, and requiring an iron shot weighing 1600 lbs.
1847 Major Cavalli's rifled breech-loading cannon is introduced.
1854 Mr (afterwards Sir) William Armstrong's gun is introduced.
1855 The Horsfall gun is constructed
1860 Mr Whitworth's rifled artillery is tested.
1864 The Mackay gun is tested at Liverpool.

to most of whom the arts of war were, in those days, perfectly familiar. At all events, between these two pursuits men were all divided ; the only avocations were war and theology ; and if you refused to enter the Church, you were bound to do military duty.

"As a natural consequence, everything of real importance was altogether neglected. There were, indeed, many priests and many warriors, many sermons and many battles ; but on the other hand, there was neither trade, nor commerce, nor manufactures; there was no science, no literature ; the useful arts were entirely unknown, and even the highest ranks of society were unacquainted, not only with the most ordinary comforts, but with the commonest decencies of civilized life.

"But so soon as gunpowder came into use, there was laid the foundation of a great change. According to the old system, a man had only to possess what he generally inherited from his father, either a sword or a bow, and he was ready equipped for the field. According to the new system, very different weapons were required, and the equipment became more costly and more difficult.

"First, there was the supply of gunpowder, then there was the possession of muskets, which were expensive articles, and considered difficult to manage. Then, too, there were other contrivances to which gunpowder naturally gave rise, such as pistols, bombs, mortars, shells, mines, and the like. All these things, by increasing the complication of the military art, increased the necessity of discipline and practice, whilst, at the same time, the change that was effected in the ordinary weapons deprived a great majority of men of the possibility of procuring them.

"To suit the altered circumstances, a new system was organized, and it was found advisable to train up bodies of men for the sole purpose of war, and to separate them, as much as possible, from those other employments in which, previously, all soldiers occasionally engaged. Thus it was that there arose standing armies."

The above quotation is more applicable to the "Dark Ages" than even to the early part of the "Middle Ages." From the fifth to the tenth centuries, it is true enough that the only avocations were War and Theology; that all men were divided between these two professions; and that, if any one refused to enter the Church, he was enrolled in the rude and barbarous Militia. But the condition of men had improved by the end of the tenth and beginning of the eleventh centuries; for feudal life, with its baronial castles and gorgeous trappings, had rapidly developed; and it is hardly correct to say of this period that "the highest ranks were unacquainted, not only with the most ordinary comfort, but with the commonest decencies of civilized life."

There is a more important point, however, than this. What was the date of standing armies in Europe? On this point the statements of Buckle are contradictory. He begins by telling us that standing armies were formed almost immediately after gunpowder was invented. If this be so, it is easy to find the date when standing armies arose; for "cannons," says he, "were certainly used in war before the middle of the fourteenth century." If standing armies followed immediately the invention of gunpowder, then they must have come into existence by the middle of the fourteenth century, or soon after, for cannons were then in use. Yet we are informed by Buckle that the "first standing armies were formed in the middle of the fifteenth century"—a whole century, that is, after the invention of gunpowder. In fixing the rise of standing armies at this date, Buckle probably followed the authority of Hallam, who states that "Charles VII. of France raised the first standing army in Europe, and levied a poll-tax in 1444 to defray the expenditure." French authorities assert that Philip IV., who died in the beginning of the fourteenth century, was the first to raise a standing army; and that Charles VII., who lived over a century later, provided for its regular payment by creating a tax.

The object of this digression on gunpowder is to show the reader what an immense advantage was gained by the Kings of France in their struggle with the feudal Lords, when they had a standing army at their command.

Various causes—the victorious assaults of successive Kings, continual conflicts with each other, their expenditure in the Crusades—gradually weakened that powerful body of Nobles, who once exercised Sovereign Power in their respective domains, and brought them more and more under the control of the Royal Power. In 1465, a formidable League, with Charles the Bold of Burgundy and the Duke of Brittany at its head, was organized against Louis XI.; but this adroit and able Monarch managed to dissolve and overcome it. By stratagem and force Louis inflicted many damaging blows on the feudal Nobility, wresting from them, and adding to the Crown, numerous fiefs, such as Picardy, Burgundy, Franche-Comté, &c. Few did more than Louis XI. for the territorial unity of France.

The partiality he displayed to the Middle Class

—who at this time began to be called the *Bourgeoisie*, from living in *Bourgs*, or walled towns—was as remarkable as the hostility he displayed to the Nobility. He granted to various towns, as Bordeaux, Dijon, &c., *parlements*, that is, Courts of Justice of the highest jurisdiction.*

In 1484, during the Regency of Anne, the daughter of Louis XI., the States General were called together, when the Nobility revolted and took the field. They were beaten by the Royal troops in 1488.

From that period, for over a hundred years, down to Louis XIII. in 1610, there were frequent conflicts between the Royal Power and the feudal Nobility; which tended steadily to diminish the ascendency the latter once possessed. Their doom was sealed when Cardinal Richelieu was invested with supreme power in 1623.

This extraordinary man had early resolved on three great projects: to suppress the Protestant faction; to end the predominance of Austria; and, above all, to break down the feudal Nobility, destroy their factious spirit, and reduce them to subordination. He accomplished the first in taking La Rochelle, the headquarters of the Protestants, after a siege of thirteen months. He succeeded in the second by repeated victories over Austria, which ended in the Treaty of Westphalia, 1648. His greatest, and most difficult feat, however, was the overthrow of the great Nobles, who still wielded immense influence, though no longer at the head of armies of vassals as in the old days of Feudality two hundred years before.

Perceiving the purpose of Richelieu, the Nobles

* Louis XI. introduced printing into France from Mayence, where Guttenburg invented it in 1442.

resorted first to intrigue to deprive him of power. Uniting with the brother of the King, Gaston Duke of Orleans, they succeeded in inducing Louis to sign a decree ejecting Richelieu from office. The Cardinal, however, hearing of the conspiracy, flew to Versailles the same day, and regained his position with the King. To escape a similar danger, he resorted to the most rigorous measures. He seized all the conspirators within his reach: exiled some,* imprisoned others, and condemned Marshal Marillac to death.

The more powerful adopted the old tactics, and defied the stern Cardinal in the field. The Duke of Montmorency, Hereditary Governor of Languedoc, raised an insurrection; and having met the troops dispatched by Richelieu at Castelnaudary, 1632, was defeated, made prisoner, and executed. Rather than yield to their implacable enemy, some of the most resolute of the Nobility, *in utrumque parati*, had recourse to foreign aid, and applied to Austria and Spain. The Dukes of Bouillon and Guise, with the Count of Soissons, encountered the army of Richelieu at Mariée, 1641, and were defeated. The Count perished in the combat, but the others escaped.† The Marquis of Cinq Mars, who had, conjointly with the Duke of Orleans, negotiated with Spain to obtain troops and money, was arrested at Narbonne, tried and executed at Lyons with his accomplice De Thou, 1642. By this relentless policy Richelieu gave a deathblow to Feudality in France.

* Marie de Medicis, mother of the King, and the Duchess de Chevreuse, the confidant of the Queen, Anne of Austria, were among the exiled. Even the Queen herself was assigned for some time to a convent at Paris.

† The Duke de Bouillon was afterwards compelled, for this act of treason, to give up his principality of Sedan, which was annexed to the crown.

Not long after this, another effort was made by the discomfited Nobles to regain their supremacy. After the death of Louis XIII. in 1643—Richelieu having died in 1642—Anne of Austria became Regent during the minority of Louis XIV., and she appointed Cardinal Mazarin her Minister.* Thinking the opportunity favourable, the Nobles rose in insurrection; and in 1648 the struggle known as the War of the *Fronde* began.

For five years the result was uncertain. The Regent was compelled at one time to abandon Paris and make her headquarters at St Germain, where she ordered a siege to be opened against Paris. To conciliate this powerful League, Mazarin retired to Cologne, but discord breaking out among the Chiefs of the *Fronde*, he was recalled. A bloody combat took place at the gates of Paris between the Royal troops commanded by Turenne, and the forces of the *Fronde* led by the Prince of Condé. Desperate exertions were made by the Aristocracy to involve all France in this supreme effort to recover their waning power. The beautiful Duchess of Longueville† and her husband, the Dukes of

* Mazarin was an Italian, and the Pope's Legate at Paris. He entered the service of Richelieu, who recommended him as Minister after his death. He had not the genius or firmness of the French Cardinal, but, by subtlety and diplomatic skill, he achieved his ends none the less surely. He left a large fortune to his five nieces, who were all beautiful, and made grand alliances. The young king was greatly enamoured of one of them, but she was sent away from Paris by the cautious Mazarin. Two of these ladies afterwards separated from their husbands, and became noted for their romantic adventures. One of them had a *liaison* with Charles II. of England, and died in London.

† This lady, equally celebrated for her beauty and intelligence, was an ardent champion of the *Fronde*. She induced Marshal Turenne, and afterwards the Duke de La Rochefoucauld, to join it. The latter was greatly enamoured of the lovely Duchess, and commemorated it in the well-known lines—

"Pour mériter son cœur, pour plaire à ses beaux yeux,
J'ai fait la guerre aux rois, je l'aurais faite aux dieux."

Beaufort and La Rochefoucauld, and many other aristocratic leaders, made a tour of the provinces, calling on them to rise against the Throne. As in the days of Richelieu, the rebellious Nobles sought foreign as well as domestic aid—the Prince of Condé having made a secret alliance with Spain.

After numerous vicissitudes, Mazarin was again forced to resign his post; but on the arrest of several of the chief leaders of the *Fronde*, he was able to return to power and put an end to the Rebellion in 1653. With the fall of the *Fronde*, the Feudal System, which once exercised sovereign sway over the dismembered territory of France, sank into the tomb; and upon it was built the solid foundations of the Monarchy, now left without a rival to dispute its monopoly of power.

TRIUMPH OF THE MONARCHY.

SEVENTEENTH CENTURY.

LOUIS XIV. spoke truly when he declared, *l'état, c'est moi*—"the state, that's me"—for his will was law. *Quod principi placuit legis habet vigorem.* The Clergy who had dominated France during the Dark Ages, and the feudal Nobles who had held sway over it during the Middle Ages, were now both bereft of political influence; and the Monarchy, which had resisted the one and struggled against the other, emerged at last triumphant. The King was now more absolute than ever the Clergy or the Nobles had been, and the abuse of power was just as great. Though the Monarchy was thus omnipotent, the Nobles, however, still retained their estates and many important privileges; amongst others, exemption from taxation. The Feudal System, so far as the authority of the Crown was concerned, was broken down in 1653; but, for all the rest, it remained in force till the Revolution of 1789 blotted it out entirely. "The relations the nobles bore to the throne," says Buckle, "became entirely changed; that which they bore to the people remained almost the same. In England, slavery or villenage quickly diminished, and was extinct by the end of the sixteenth century, but in France it lingered two hundred years later."

It is certainly an astonishing fact that up to the

French Revolution of 1789 the Lower Class was divided into two categories—those who were free, and those who still remained in a servile condition. Cassagnac, in his work on the Révolution, states that "in 1789 there still existed in France one million and five hundred thousand serfs." It was only a short time before the Revolution that Louis XVI. abolished serfdom in the royal domains. These facts are conclusive proof that the Feudal System was only finally eradicated by the tremendous tornado which covered France with ruins in 1789.

The reader has now been presented with the conspicuous features of Feudality during the Middle Ages as they were revealed in France. It prevailed in all the countries of the Continent; but its aspect was everywhere the same, except in England, where its development received a check from causes that will be described. Gradually yielding to the pressure of events, Feudality has everywhere disappeared in Europe, save, as I have said, in Germany, where successive Emperors were not so successful in their struggles with the Barons as were the Kings of France. The consequence is, that up to our day Germany is still split up into a number of small baronial estates, where the heirs of feudal ancestors still retain the title and dignity of Sovereign over their hereditary domains; though the exercise of the old feudal rights has long been controlled by the growth of popular power.

In discussing the merits of the Feudal System, we may assert that, while it had little to recommend it, it would be illogical to condemn it as worthless; since it was the natural product of the state of things then existing, and must have had a *raison d'être*, some purpose to fulfil, some end to accomplish. It certainly tended to diminish the utter disorganization into which society was thrown by the irruption of the barbarians.

"The Feudal System," says Buckle, "was a vast scheme of policy, which, clumsy and imperfect as it was, supplied many of the wants of the rude people among whom it arose. The connection between it and the decline of the ecclesiastical spirit is very obvious; for the Feudal System was the first great secular plan that had been seen in Europe since the formation of the Roman civil law; it was the first comprehensive attempt which had been made during more than four hundred years to organise society according to temporal, and not according to spiritual circumstances." From the fifth to the tenth century, Europe was under the domination of the Ecclesiastics of the New Religion. During these Dark Ages their spiritual sway over the masses was unmolested, and even Charlemagne thought it expedient to conciliate the Clergy. Towards the end of the tenth century, however, the Lords of the soil thought themselves strong enough to defy clerical control; and they set up a Government which made them Sovereign each in their own domain, and equally independent of King or Pope. Up to this period the Priests of the young Christian Church enjoyed an undisputed supremacy; but when the Barons stepped into the field with a Government, not only temporal, but based on force, they encountered a rival they were not at first disposed to acknowledge. Hitherto the Clergy had been a privileged class. They were exempted from all the burdens of the State, and not called to do military service. They lost these immunities when Feudalism spread over Europe, and they ceased to be the sole controlling class. Instead of men looking up to the Church as hitherto, they began now to look up to the Nobles. It was natural enough the Clergy should chafe under this change of position. They discerned plainly that Feudalism was a Secular Government, and that, if it endured, Theocracy was at an end. They foresaw they should be forced to divide the power they had for several centuries monopolized. A struggle ensued between Feudality and the Church, which ended ere long in their reconciliation. The Church found itself weaker and the Barons stronger than was supposed. In fact the power of the Church was declining, because the masses were becoming less ignorant and superstitious.

The Feudal System, and the Birth of the Middle Class, were the two prominent features in France of the epoch known as the Middle Ages. The first I have treated perhaps too copiously; but I have little to relate of the latter, for the reason that their rise as an influential body met with a check which effectually stopped their political development.

It has been already mentioned that Louis VI., 1108, seeing that the inhabitants of the numerous *Communes* which were springing up all over France might be of service to the Monarchy in its duel with Feudality, purchased their support by the concession of Municipal rights. This policy, as I showed, was followed up by many of his Successors. When, however, the French Kings found that, with the aid of standing armies, they were strong enough to fight the feudal Nobles, and that they could dispense with the Militia hitherto supplied by the *Communes*, they lost no time in abrogating, one after another, all the privileges they had granted. Already from the fourteenth century they began curtailing the privileges of the *Communes;* and in the reign of Charles IX., 1560–74, all jurisdiction over their own affairs was taken from the Municipalities, and they fell under the government of the Crown. By the end of the reign of Henry IV., 1610, "it seemed to be quite forgotten," says a French authority, "that the towns of France had ever possessed any franchises at all."

The Middle Class in France steadily advanced in numbers and opulence, although thus cunningly stript of all political rights when too weak to resist; but they grew up under the domination both of the Crown and their old masters the Nobles, deprived of all Municipal freedom, ignorant of all Political usages; and, therefore, they were deficient in that love of liberty and independence which is inherited from free institutions.* The Middle Class of England, as we shall see, had a very different history; and it is owing to this that their political knowledge and influence guarantee to-day the tranquillity of that nation. Indeed, it may be said that the best interests of modern Europe, her repose, and material prosperity, are bound up with the moral and political authority the Middle Class is destined to wield. It is the Middle Class, placed between the upper and lower ranks, and closely connected with both, which is naturally called to exercise the *rôle* of arbitrator; obtaining for one all just concessions, and protecting the other from undue exactions.

The French Monarchy, as already stated, after the

* Down to 1870 the French towns were still under the tutelage of the Government, and the Republican party is as averse as the Monarchical to granting them independence.

struggles for centuries with the Papacy and the feudal Nobles, at last overcame both; and when Louis XIV. began in 1661 to govern, he was absolute master of the country. His despotism was above all control: no King of England, Saxon or Norman, ever wielded such arbitrary power. The reign of this Monarch, extending over fifty years, was brilliant: he was able, firm, laborious; skilful in administration; and a friend of letters and arts. He surrounded himself with sagacious Ministers, as Colbert, Louvois; and with great Generals, as Condé, Turenne, Vauban. A galaxy of illustrious writers adorned his epoch, as Racine, Corneille, Molière, Boileau, La Fontaine, Bossuet, Massillon, Fénélon; and the Arts flourished under such great masters as Lebrun and Lesueur. The military successes of Louis were numerous, and added greatly to the French territory. Amongst his other conquests was the province of Alsace, lately lost in the war of 1870. He vastly adorned Paris and its neighbourhood; built the *Hôpital des Invalides*, the Colonnade of the Louvre, the Palace of Versailles, the Trianons; and founded the manufacture of Gobelins tapestry. In his latter years he fell under Clerical influence, and was induced to revoke the Edict of Nantes, which recognized the Protestant worship. Louis XIV. was the most distinguished Potentate of his time, and was surnamed, *Le Grand Monarque.*

After his death the Monarchy fell into incompetent hands, and rapidly declined. Moreover, the events that had occurred in England began to reverberate in France, and to stimulate her *litterateurs* to assail a Despotism that regarded France as little better than a royal domain.

DECLINE OF THE MONARCHY.

EIGHTEENTH CENTURY.

THE heir to the throne, Louis XV., was but five years old at the death of his great-grandfather, and Philip, Duke of Orleans, was declared Regent, 1715, during his minority. The Regent was a man of brilliant talents, and obtained early distinction in arms. He afterwards occupied himself with Natural Science. While at the head of the Government he effected great reforms; reduced the army; and extinguished four hundred millions of debt. He allowed himself, however, to be dazzled by the seductive financial schemes of John Law, a Scotchman, who proposed to the Regent a plan to liquidate the National Debt.

Law was authorized, 1716, to establish a Bank of Discount, the first of the kind in France. This private bank was created in 1718 a public bank. The shares were eagerly sought after, and rose to 40 per cent. premium; and this may be regarded as the origin in France and Europe of stock-gambling. A Company was organized by Law soon afterwards, and allied to the Bank, which had the privilege to trade with the French possessions on the Mississippi, China, and the East Indies. An immense quantity of paper notes were issued by the Bank, far beyond its real assets; but in three years the bubble exploded, and great numbers were ruined. Law was obliged to leave France, and died in poverty in Venice, 1729.

The reign of Louis XV. began in 1723, and was the most discreditable France had ever known. He first engaged in a war against Austria; and afterwards, in 1756, supported by Austria and Russia, he began the "Seven Years' War" against Frederick the Great of Prussia and his ally, England. In this war France was deprived by England of Canada, and all her possessions in the East Indies.

The odious feature of this reign was the baneful influence exercised by two women, Madame de Pompadour, and, afterwards, Madame du Barry, mistresses at different periods of the King, who gave himself up so entirely to their sway, that they controlled the affairs of the State, making and overthrowing successive Cabinets. The scandalous debauchery of Louis brought the Monarchy into contempt; and a movement similar to what happened in England in the time of James I. began in France, headed by many remarkable men, to strip the Crown of its excessive prerogatives. Elizabeth and Louis XV. were the two last Sovereigns who, in England and France, wielded Absolute power.

The striking events which had occurred in England, ending in the substitution of Parliamentary Government for that of the King, had attracted the attention of thinking men in France; and during the reign of Louis XV. many eminent writers went over to London, studied the language, and set to work investigating the contest which had culminated in the downfall of Royal Authority, and the erection on solid foundations of Personal Liberty and Parliamentary Sovereignty. No Parliament existed in France in which to conduct a similar conflict. An appeal to the nation was therefore made through literary channels. A wonderful profusion of illustrious writers appeared at this epoch, nearly all of whom, as remarked, visited England, and made themselves masters of her literature, philosophy, and politics. Enlightened by these inquiries, they returned, and began a furious crusade against the doomed institutions in Church and State of their native land.

It would be tedious to cite the list of all these literary combatants, but some of them deserve special mention.

Baron Montesquieu, in 1748, published his "*Esprit des Lois*"—"The Spirit of Laws"—after twenty years of study; and this remarkable book attracted the attention of Europe. He passed in review all the legislation of the world, ancient and modern, and endeavoured to show how far it was adapted to human nature generally, and how far it could be ascribed to local causes. He was the first to point out that the civil and political laws of any nation can be distinctly traced to the peculiarities of its climate, soil, and food. This palpable truth is now generally accepted; and Buckle makes it the basis of his sketch of Asiatic and European civilization. The style as well as the matter of Montesquieu's book have secured it enduring popularity.

Diderot and D'Alembert united in publishing an Encyclopædia in twenty-eight volumes, 1751–72, which is regarded by all as one of the striking books of the eighteenth century. It contained contributions on Science and Art by all the great writers of the day.

The highest intellect of France began, unhappily, at this period to surrender itself to Atheism.

Condillac, a disciple of Locke, in 1754, published his "*Traité des Sensations*"—"Treatise on Sensations"—seeking to prove that all our ideas spring from sensation, or are the effect of the action of the external world upon us.

Helvetius, in 1758, wrote a book on "*L'Esprit*"—"The Mind"—to prove that man only differed from the brute by his external organization. He denied that he had any spiritual nature. All his faculties he asserted were created by physical impressions. He concluded that man in all his opinions and conduct was only guided by self-instinct. "Everything we have," says Helvetius, "everything we are, we owe to the external world; nor is man himself aught else except what he is made by the objects which surround him." These views were meant to overthrow every code of Morals hitherto known, and were hailed with applause.

The two writers, however, who made the most impression on their epoch were Rousseau and Voltaire.

J. J. Rousseau was a Swiss, born at Geneva in 1712; but his reputation was made in France, where he wrote nearly all his books. His celebrated romance "*La Nouvelle Heloise*"—"The New Heloise," 1759, fascinated the literary and fashionable world by its charms of style and passionate sensibility; but the book that followed this, "*Le Contrat Social*"—"The Social Contract," 1761, made a far more lasting impression. It was in this work that he expounded those principles of Absolute Equality that later became the keynote of the Revolution. He touched on the same topic in an essay, "*De l'Origine de l'Inégalité parmi les Hommes*"—"On the Origin of the Inequality amongst Men"—written previously, 1753. His well-known book, "*Mes Confessions*"—"My Confessions"—was published after his death, which occurred in 1778.

The most prolific and versatile writer of his epoch was Voltaire, born near Paris, 1694. Poet, dramatist, historian, and philosopher, his works constitute in themselves a library. Acquiring in England a thorough knowledge of the language, he made known in France, by translations, the astronomy of Newton, the philosophy of Locke, and the dramas of Shakespeare. Beyond doubt, he towered over all the literary giants of his time by the variety of his knowledge, the depth of his observation, the lucidity of his style, and, above all, by the gift of a sarcastic wit that accomplished more than solid argument could effect. Voltaire appeared at the very moment when France began to cast off, as it were, her vestments of the Middle Ages, and don the costume of modern times.

Of all the men who shared in the demolition going on, Voltaire cut the deepest. He seemed especially endowed for the work. His vast learning challenged all past knowledge, and his scathing wit destroyed all reverence for the present. The Monarchy, the Aristocracy, the Clergy, even Christianity itself, were all assailed in turn, and seemed to wither at his touch. He did more than all the rest to open the Gulf into which the France of the Middle Ages was destined to fall. He died in 1778, and must have foreseen the catastrophe that was hourly approaching. A striking proof of his comprehensive and penetrating mind may be seen in the fact that he was the first who ever suggested Universal Freedom of Trade. It was then regarded as a monstrous paradox.

Many other able thinkers appeared at this epoch;

and the object of them all was to concentrate the French mind on the Material world, and emancipate it from all sense of authority, religious and political.

This tendency to material views and interests led to an ardent culture of Physical Science.* Chemistry, Geology, Botany, and Zoology made immense progress, and brought forth Lavoisier, Cuvier, Bichat, and Jussieu. To this same tendency is due the birth of Political Economy, which is simply the Science of the Material welfare of Nations.

Beyond cavil the founder of the new study was Quesnay, who from his youth was remarked for his love of Agriculture, and his earnest desire to raise the condition of the peasantry. He wrote constantly on all topics connected with the Soil, declaring in 1758 that it was the sole Source of Wealth, and for that reason should bear the weight of all taxation. He also advocated Liberty of Labor and Free Trade. Gournay, who wrote on the same subjects, differed from his contemporary as to the Soil alone being productive of a Nation's Wealth, arguing that the Products of Industry were also a source of Income. Turgot, at the same period, devoted his great intellect to the material condition of France, and published, 1766, his "*Réflexions sur la Formation et la Distribution des Richesses*"—"Reflections on the Formation and Distribution of Wealth."

It was from these remarkable and practical men that Adam Smith of Scotland received his first

* Buckle remarks that in the eighteenth century each of the three leading nations of Europe had a separate part to play. England diffused a love of freedom; France, a knowledge of physical science; while Germany revived the study of metaphysics and created philosophic history.

lessons in Political Economy—lessons which he embodied with singular ability in his work on the "Wealth of Nations," 1776. Smith declared that the Wealth of a Nation is its Labor; and, further, that its Trade and Commerce should be Free.

It should be born in mind, however, that it was Descartes * who destroyed the intellectual structure of the Middle Ages, by proving that all authority was fictitious which was not based on human reason; as it was Richelieu who overthrew the political system of the Middle Ages, by suppressing Feudality and undermining Ecclesiastical power. These two men, by their writings and policy, put an end to the power of the Nobles and Priests, who controlled France for several centuries. The period which followed, when the Royal authority freed from the opposition of the Nobles and Clergy found itself Absolute, was only a resting-place as it were for the Nation. France during this interval was really maturing for the new phase of national existence on which she was about to enter. The thinkers of the time suspected this, and by reflection and travel were training for the *rôle* of Pioneers. Most of them, as related, hurried to England to study the nature of the Government best adapted for the coming epoch. There the authority of the King, and the authority of a Class, had disappeared. The New authority represented the Nation—its intellect, its interests, and its will. In England there was much for the political missionaries of France to contemplate, but nothing for them to export, as the history of their country was so dissimilar. In France for centuries two classes, the Aristocracy and the Clergy, had governed, and these gave way to an

*See chapter on the Papacy for summary of the labors of Descartes.

Absolute Monarchy. Moreover, the Middle Class that had grown up had neither political rights nor the knowledge to use them. If, then, the Monarchy were overthrown, where was the political power to go? What class or institution existed in France fit to wield it? The Aristocracy, the Clergy, the Monarchy, knew of but one kind of power—the most absolute; the Middle Class had conceived of none else; the masses were unfit for any other; yet the knell of Absolute Government in France had sounded. What was to succeed was the affair of other generations.

The French reformers of the eighteenth century had only one task, that of clearing the way for National emancipation. Arbitrary Monarchy was a relic of a bygone age: it was a solecism in the new one. Its sudden fall might lead to chaos, but with reckless ardour the axe was applied to its roots.

The cardinal feature of the reign of Louis XV. was universal Scepticism. Not only were the claims of the Church over the conscience denied, not only was the right of the State to obedience rejected, but Christianity itself was canvassed and repudiated. For centuries blind belief had prevailed in France. When it came to be regarded as only ignorance and superstition, a violent reaction ensued; and all authority, divine and human, was spurned.

The amazing activity of the French intellect during the latter part of the eighteenth century arose from its having broken through the fetters which Spiritual and Political tyranny had imposed on it for centuries; and its investigations took an exclusively Material direction, because it now doubted the truth of every theory in Science, Politics, and Religion that had been hitherto recognized. In a very short time the

Scepticism of the thinkers seized on the Nation; and the consequence was, the overthrow of the whole Fabric of Government, political, religious, and social, which had maintained itself in France for so many centuries.

Thus were the seeds of the tempest sown.

THE REVOLUTION.

EIGHTEENTH CENTURY.

In 1774, Louis XVI., grandson of Louis XV., ascended the throne at twenty years of age. He was both amiable and virtuous, but without the capacity to direct, much less to control the deep fermentation then pervading France. He singularly resembled the unfortunate Charles I. Like him, he was moral and kind-hearted, but weak and vacillating; and like him, he allowed his Queen to exercise over him a fatal ascendency. Both appeared at an epoch when their faults, however venial, could have no other result than Death for themselves and Revolution for their respective countries.

The King called to his aid the leading men of the day—Turgot, Malesherbes, and Necker. Many abuses were abolished, and many useful institutions were established.*

In 1778, Louis gave assistance in men and money to the English Colonies in North America against the Mother-country, and guaranteed their Independence by the Treaty of Versailles, 1782.

The dilapidated state of the Finances compelled the King to call two Assemblies of the Notables, consisting

* The *Mont de Piété*—State pawnbrokers—and the *Caisse d'Escompte*—a bank of discount, the origin of the Bank of France—were two of the most useful institutions founded at this time.

of the heads of the Nobility, Clergy, and Magistracy, 1787–88. They quarrelled, and decided nothing. He then convoked the States General, May, 1789, which had not met since 1614, and which, as already seen, was composed of the three Orders, the Nobility, Clergy, and *Tiers-Etat*—Third Estate, or Middle Class.* When the States assembled, the Nobility and Clergy refused to deliberate in common with the *Tiers-Etat.* The Deputies of the Middle Class thereupon withdrew in June, and met separately in a hall at Versailles used as a tennis court, and assumed the name of the National Assembly. This incident caused agitation in Paris; but it augmented greatly when, soon afterwards, the *Tiers-Etat* were ordered to disperse. They defied the Government, and swore never to adjourn till they had given a Constitution to France. The excitement in Paris became so alarming that troops were ordered to concentrate on Versailles, the residence of the King.

On the 11th of July, the Prime Minister, Necker, the idol of the people, was dismissed. This spark caused an explosion which shook all Europe to its centre. On the 14th of July the people of Paris rose in insurrection, and captured the *Bastille.*† The National Assembly or *Tiers-Etat*, regardless of the co-operation of the Representatives of the Nobility and Clergy sitting at Versailles, began legislating with extraordinary boldness. In August, 1789, they voted the abolition of all Feudal privileges. Then followed a Decree proclaiming Religious Liberty and Freedom of

* Convoked for the first time in 1369.

† The *Bastille* was a large fortress built in 1343. Like the Tower of London, it was meant either to defend or menace Paris. It was used latterly as a prison of State. The mistresses of Louis XV., by *lettres de cachet*, sent any one there who gave them umbrage.

the Press. In October, the people of Paris went to Versailles *en masse*, and demanded the King's return to the Capital. The National Assembly then removed to Paris. In November, they voted that the property of the Church belonged to the Nation. In January, 1790, the old territorial division of France into Provinces was superseded by breaking up the Kingdom into eighty-three Departments. In March, the sale of the church property was voted to the extent of 400 millions of francs; in April, paper money, called *assignats* *—from the church lands being assigned as security—was created; and in June, all Titles of Nobility were abolished. In 1791, the King's Right of Pardon was suppressed.

It was in June of this same year that the King and his family were discovered endeavoring to escape from France, and brought back to Paris. In July, all Orders of Knighthood were abolished: and in September, a Constitution was voted and accepted by the King.

The Constitution gave the Executive power to the King, and the Legislative power to a single Chamber called the Legislative Assembly—to be elected by the people, and to consist of seven hundred and forty-five Members.

The leading man of the National or *Tiers-Etat* Assembly was Mirabeau. Though a Nobleman of ancient descent, he threw himself with ardor into the Revolutionary movement; and, by his energy and unrivalled eloquence, gave it an impetus which soon outran his wishes. Whether from sympathy with

* The emission of *assignats* or paper notes went on increasing till they reached, in 1796, the sum of 45 millions of francs, which then became worthless.

the Royal Family, or because he was bribed, he abandoned his violent opposition to the Government, and thereby endangered his immense popularity. He died April, 1791.

Another man as prominent, but far inferior in oratory, was the Abbé Sieyès.* It was he who proposed that the deputies of the *Tiers-Etat* should organize as the National Assembly. He acquired great importance by a *brochure* in 1789 entitled—"*What is the Tiers-Etat? Everything. What has it hitherto been? Nothing. What does it demand? To become something.*"

The Legislative Assembly met in October, 1791. In November, they declared all emigrants condemned to death, with the confiscation of their property, who did not return to France within two months. In April, 1792, they declared war against Austria; in May, they condemned to transportation all Ecclesiastics who did not acknowledge the Constitution; and in July, they decreed "*The Country in Danger*," and held Permanent Sessions—ordering all the Municipalities to do the same, and the National Guard to rise *en masse*. In August, they suspended the functions of the King, and voted that a new Assembly, to be called the National Convention, should be convoked.

In this Legislative Assembly, were organized two parties, which soon began struggling for the supremacy. The first was known as *la Montagne*—the

* This extraordinary man, after figuring in all the sanguinary phases of the revolution, a member of the National Assembly, and afterwards of the Convention, in which he voted the King's execution, became at last the colleague of General Bonaparte as one of the three Consuls. Later, he was transformed into a Count of the Empire. After the fall of Napoleon, he retired to Brussels; but after the revolution of 1830, he returned to Paris, where he died in 1836.

Mountain—from its members occupying the upper benches of the Assembly. It was headed by violent and unscrupulous men, whose aim was to seize on the Government. The second was called *la Gironde*, as its leaders, the Girondists, were Deputies from the Department of the *Gironde.* They were eloquent and patriotic men, who desired the political regeneration of France, but were opposed to sanguinary excesses.

COMMITTEE OF PUBLIC SAFETY.

After the capture of the *Bastille* in July, 1789, the old Municipal government of Paris with its Prévot and Assessors was overthrown, and a new organization called the COMMUNE was substituted. Paris was divided into forty-eight Sections, with an Administration at their head; and over all was placed a Mayor with two Councils. The object of this scheme was to concentrate in the hands of the central power complete control over Paris and its populace. The first two Mayors were Bailly and Pétion.

During the administration of the latter, the *Tuileries*, where the Royal Family resided, was sacked by the mob, August, 1792; and in September, several thousand persons who had been imprisoned on suspicion of being Royalists were brutally massacred.* Pétion made no opposition to these atrocities, yet was soon thrown aside as too moderate. The Municipal government, or *Commune*, was then administered by the most bloodthirsty leaders of the populace.

The National Convention—the most violent of the

* The monsters who murdered these unhappy people, estimated at eight thousand, were paid 24 sous each per day by the *Commune.* Thiers relates that the life of a young girl was granted her, on the condition of her drinking a bowl of the blood of a fellow-prisoner.

three Assemblies which had appeared since July, 1789—met in September, 1792, in the Palace of the Tuileries. The parties of the *Montagne* and the *Gironde*, who had only engaged in skirmishes in the Legislative Assembly, were destined in this to come into conflict.

The principal leaders of the Mountain were Robespierre and Danton.

Robespierre was cold and reserved in disposition, dogmatic in opinion, and domineering in character. He was clear and sententious as a speaker, but always passionless. A lawyer by profession, he was sent as a Deputy to the *Tiers-Etat*, or National Assembly, where he attracted no attention. His aim was to control the Revolution, and thus become Chief of the State. For this purpose he became the Head of the Club of the *Jacobins*, composed of all the desperadoes that thronged to Paris. He also obtained complete sway over the *Commune*, or Municipal government. With these auxiliaries, he proposed to exterminate every rival that might oppose his ambition. He hoped to manage the Convention by sending to the block the Girondists, who would be sure to resist his schemes of slaughter.

Danton was also a lawyer, but a striking contrast to Robespierre. Singularly endowed for a popular leader, his intelligence was prompt, his energy prodigious, and his courage reckless. He threw himself into the Revolution from love of action, more than from conviction or ambition. He founded the Club of the *Cordeliers*, of which Marat, Hébert, &c., were members, and this Club even surpassed its rival, the *Jacobins*, in ferocity. He stimulated the massacres of September, 1792, and hesitated at no atrocity that promoted the Revolution. Robespierre calmly plotted wholesale carnage to arrive at the Dictatorship; Danton passionately shared in universal butchery to promote the Cause he had espoused.

The leaders of the Girondists were men of higher culture and nobler sentiments than these chiefs of the Mountain, and therefore less influential with the populace of Paris. They sustained the Revolution to renovate France, and not to tyrannize over it anew. None of them, therefore, acquired the same prominence as the two unscrupulous chiefs of the Mountain.

The day the Convention assembled, September 21st, 1792, the Monarchy was abolished, and the Republic proclaimed. Absolute power was assumed by the Convention; political and social Equality decreed; by which law no superiority in talent, position, or fortune was in future to be acknowledged. In November an appeal was addressed to the people of all nations to rise against Monarchy. In January 17th, 1793, the Convention by a majority of 11 out of 721 votes condemned Louis XVI. to death. He was executed on 21st of same month.* In February, war was proclaimed against England, Holland, and Spain, and a levy of 300,000 men was ordered. In October, the Convention annulled the Gregorian calendar, and decreed that the French era should compute from the date of the Republic, September 22nd, 1792.†

Robespierre and Danton had concocted a scheme for getting the Executive power into the hands of their party; and they manœuvred the Convention into

* The King died with unruffled composure. Addressing the crowd he said, "I die innocent of all the crimes laid to my charge. I pardon those who have decreed my death, and I pray to God that the blood you are now going to shed may never be visited on France."

† This absurd arrangement was repealed in 1806 by Napoleon I.

creating, April, 1793, a "Committee of Public Safety," which was to wield Supreme power over France, reporting at intervals to the Convention. They now found themselves strong enough to assail their antagonists, the Girondists, whom they accused of seeking to check the Revolution and betray France. They were supported by the two clubs under their administration, the *Jacobins* and *Cordeliers*, as well as by the *Commune*, which they entirely controlled. By these means they roused the Parisian populace to insurrection, and on May 31st, the leading Girondist Deputies were imprisoned.

The Convention was now the tool of Robespierre and Danton. It was promptly decided to paralyze all France by fear. The "Reign of Terror" was inaugurated. A "Revolutionary Tribunal," without appeal, was decreed to try all "suspected" persons. A law detailing who were suspected persons embraced every one whom the Terrorists chose to destroy. A "Revolutionary Army" was organized to march about France, to shoot down the opponents of the Revolution. Committees were instituted in every village to receive denunciations, and the guillotine soon disposed of the accused. Absolute power, far greater than the Monarchy ever possessed, was lodged in the hands of the "Committee of Public Safety," which represented the majority of the Convention. Its control over the lives and property of every individual in France was undisputed. A tyranny so complete never existed, not even in the days of Nero. It was wielded in the name of Liberty, but it was soon evident that this cry was a pretext.

The extent of slaughter committed during the "Reign of Terror" is unparalleled in the annals of crime.

No class was spared; high and low, rich and poor, suffered alike. More than a million of persons* were sacrificed, merely to spread terror over the land, so that no one might venture to contest the authority of the "Committee of Public Safety."

The details of these terrible scenes would fill volumes and horrify every reader. On October 16th, 1793, Marie Antoinette, the wife of Louis XVI., was executed.† On the 31st., the leaders of the Girondist

* Prudhomme has given the following appalling account of the victims of the Revolution:—

Nobles,	1,278	
Noble women,	750	
Wives of labourers and artizans,	1,467	
Religieuses,	350	
Priests,	1,135	
Common persons, not noble,	13,623	
Guillotined by sentence of the Revolutionary Tribunal,—		18,603
Women died of premature child-birth,		3,400
In child-birth from grief,		348
Women killed in La Vendée,		15,000
Children killed in La Vendée,		22,000
Men slain in La Vendée,		900,000
Victims under Carrier at Nantes,		32,000*
Of whom were,—		
Children shot,	500	
Children drowned,	1,500	
Women shot,	264	
Women drowned,	500	
Priests shot,	300	
Priests drowned,	460	
Nobles drowned,	1,400	
Artizans drowned,	5,300	
Victims at Lyons,		31,000
Total,		1,022,351

In this enumeration are not comprehended the massacres at Versailles, at the Abbaye, the Carmelites or other prisons on September 2, the victims of the Glaciere of Avignon, those shot at Toulon and Marseilles, or the persons slain in the little town of Bedoin, the whole population of which perished.

† "At four o'clock in the morning of the day of her execution, the Queen wrote a letter to the Princess Elizabeth. 'To you, my sister,' said she, 'I address myself for the last time. I have been condemned,

* Carrier, finding that the guillotine did not despatch his victims quickly enough, caused ships full of them to be floated down the river and scuttled.

party, twenty-two in all, were also executed. On 6th of November, the Duke of Orleans, who took the name of Philip *Egalité*, and voted for the death of his cousin the King, went to the guillotine in his turn.*

Of the nine members of the "Committee of Public Safety," Robespierre was the most influential. He was far inferior to Danton in decision and courage, but made up for this by his superior activity. Whilst Danton gave himself up to luxurious indulgence, the plotting, austere Robespierre was cunningly paving his way to Supreme Power. He meant to play the *rôle* of Cromwell; but though he was the equal of the Protector in profound hypocrisy, he was wholly below him in capacity and daring.

The only rival who now stood in his path was Danton. The brutal, but popular Marat had been slain in July, 1793, by Charlotte Corday, whose motives were as patriotic as those of Jeanne d'Arc. The savage Hébert, who declared the Convention was too mode-

not to an ignominious death—that is only for the guilty—but to rejoin your brother. I weep only for my children; I hope that one day, when they have regained their rank, they may be reunited to you, and feel the blessing of your tender care. May my son never forget the last words of his father, which I now repeat from myself—Never attempt to revenge our death. I die true to the Catholic religion. Deprived of all spiritual consolation, I can only seek for pardon from Heaven. I ask forgiveness of all who know me. I pray for forgiveness to all my enemies."—ALISON.

"When led out to execution, she was dressed in white: she had cut off her hair with her own hands. Placed in a tumbrel, with her arms tied behind her, she was taken by a circuitous route to the Place de la Révolution. She ascended the scaffold with a firm and dignified step, as if she had been about to take her place on a throne by the side of her husband."—LACRETELLE.

* The Duke, not content with voting the death of his cousin, drove in an open carriage to witness his execution, and afterwards gave a *fête*. He spent great sums on the people, and hoped to reach the throne. As he went to execution, he was hooted by the mob. He shrugged his shoulders and said, "They used to applaud me."

rate, and proposed to transfer all its powers to the more sanguinary *Commune*, was by Robespierre's perfidy sent to the scaffold, March, 1794. Of all his brother-assassins, there was only one left between him and that Supremacy he steadily pursued. Thiers, in his "French Revolution," attributes to Robespierre these reflections:—"If Danton were sacrificed, there would be left not one prominent name out of the 'Committee of Public Safety;' and in the Committee, there would remain only men of secondary importance. By consenting to this sacrifice, he would at once destroy his rival, and above all heighten his own reputation for virtue, by striking down a man accused of having sought money and pleasure."

It was so resolved, and Robespierre set his satellites to work calumniating Danton as a Retrograde, though never uttering a word himself. Danton was warned, but his reply was, "They will not dare." When suspicion had been aroused, and Robespierre thought the mob ready for his purpose, the "Committee of Public Safety," of which he was the head, ordered Danton's arrest.* The Convention was thunderstruck, but dreaded, in the presence of Robespierre, to utter a protest. Danton now appeared before the "Revolutionary Tribunal" he had created, and which had hurried so many innocent victims into eternity. He clamored loudly and denounced his Colleagues with fury, but without being allowed a defence was sentenced and executed, April, 1794, along with Camille Desmoulins,† and three other of his friends—all members of the Convention.

* As he entered the prison, Danton exclaimed, "At length I perceive that in revolutions, the supreme power ultimately rests with the most abandoned."

† When Camille Desmoulins was asked his age by the judge on his

"After them," says Mignet, "no voice was heard for some time against the Dictatorship of Terror. It struck its silent reiterated blows from one end of France to the other. The Girondists had wished to prevent this violent reign, the Dantonists to stop it—all perished; and the more enemies the rulers counted, the more victims they had to despatch."

On the 10th of May, 1794, Madame Elizabeth, the devoted sister of Louis XVI., was sent to execution, and died with the same calm courage as the King and Queen.*

Robespierre was now at the head of France. He was the Chief of the "Committee of Public Safety," and was able to overawe the *Commune* and the Convention, neither of which were well disposed towards him. No one, not even his most devoted partisan, or humblest satellite, felt safe. His frown was a summons to the guillotine. History records no tyranny so bloody and so inexorable as the Dictatorship of Robespierre. For this, then, all that was noble, grand, and good in France had been sacrificed. For this, a million of men, women, and children, noble and common, rich and poor, had been ruthlessly slain.†

Robespierre began to feel that such a Regime must soon prove insupportable, and he showed a desire to

trial, he replied: "*Trente-trois ans, l'age du sans-culotte Jésus Christ lorsqu'il mourut*"—"The age of the democrat Jesus Christ when He died." The term "*sans-culotte*" was applied to the extreme Revolutionists at the time.

* In going to the guillotine, her handkerchief fell from her neck, and exposed her to the gaze of the multitude. She said to her executioners, "In the name of modesty, I entreat you to cover my bosom."

† Thiers says that at this epoch, "Death was rapidly descending from the upper to the lower classes of society." We find at this period on the list of the Revolutionary Tribunal, tailors, shoemakers, hairdressers, butchers, farmers, publicans, nay even labouring men, condemned for sentiments and language alleged as counter-revolutionary.

conciliate society. In May, 1794, he ordered the Convention to proclaim the Existence of a Supreme Being, in opposition to a previous Vote which had abrogated God. Up to this period, the savage fury of the Revolution had defied all authority human and divine. Not only were all the laws and institutions of France overthrown, but Christianity itself was ridiculed and abolished. France, stript of law, bereft of religion, paralyzed by terror, lay weltering in gore at the feet of a handful of brutal men who mocked at the havoc which surrounded them. There is no instance in history of a Nation reduced to such an extremity; and Robespierre, though insensible to human sympathies, had sense enough to perceive that such a state of things could only be transitory; and that to avert Anarchy among men, it is necessary to acknowledge the wonderful Order on which the Universe reposes—in other words, to recognize a First Cause or Supreme Being.

On the occasion of the Convention admitting the existence of a Supreme Being, May, 1794, Robespierre delivered a pompous harangue, wherein he stated that the Government, whilst proclaiming the worship of a Supreme Being, had no idea of restoring the Clergy. "What is there," he exclaimed, "in common between Priests and God? Priests are to morality what quacks are to medicine. How different is the God of Nature from the God of Priests! I know nothing so nearly resembles Atheism as the Religions which they have framed. By grossly misrepresenting the Supreme Being, they have annihilated belief in Him as far as lay in their power."

But though the Dictator was willing to give back religion and its consolations to desolated France, he refused from fear or ambition to relax his bloody terrorism. He hurried through the Convention a law dispensing with witnesses and official defenders for the unfortunate people dragged before the "Revolutionary Tribunal," which daily sent a hundred or more to the guillotine. He organized a legion of spies to denounce the most inoffensive. His only motive seemed to be to maintain his power by indiscriminate carnage.

At this time—May, 1794—the "Committee of Public Safety," of which he was the head, "exercised," as Thiers remarks, "an absolute dictatorship." They were all regarded as dictators; but it was Robespierre in particular, whose high influence began to dazzle all eyes. It was customary to say no longer that the *Committee wills it*, but that *Robespierre wills it.* Fouquier Tinville* said to a person whom he threatened with the guillotine, "If it please Robespierre, thou shalt go before it." The agents of the Government constantly named Robespierre in all their operations, and referred to him as the source from which everything emanated. Thus, after wading through seas of blood, after climbing over mountains of headless bodies, after consigning to destruction

* Fouquier Tinville was the government prosecutor before the Revolutionary Tribunal, and Dumas was the president. Fouquier seemed actually to revel in his daily butcheries. He had batches of sixty brought in and condemned at one time, but said this was waste of time, and ordered that space should be made for a hundred and fifty. One day a prisoner's name was not on the list, and he cried out, "I am not accused, my name is not on your list." "Give me your name," said Fouquier. "There it is on the list now, go to the scaffold with the rest." In June, 1794, Fouquier exclaimed with glee, that with the aid of Robespierre's new law to facilitate executions, he would be able to empty the prisons. "We shall be able to inscribe on their doors—'These Houses to let.'" "It goes well," he added, "heads fall like tiles, but it must go better next decade. I must have 450 at least." This monster was arrested three days after Robespierre, and beheaded in his turn.

nearly all his allies, Robespierre at last reached the pinnacle of Sovereign Power, June, 1794; but ere he could seat himself, Providence, as if in derision, hurled him precipitately into the same hideous gulf with his innumerable victims. For almost immediately, in the very "Committee of Public Safety" itself, jealousies began to break out among his colleagues at his assumption of exclusive power.

The leaders of his party—the Mountain—in the Convention, aware that even the populace of Paris were murmuring against the daily useless slaughter of the guillotine, began also to protest against the prolongation of this horrible terrorism. Robespierre, to silence these symptoms of reaction, deliberately resolved to execute at once several Members of the Committee and some fifty Deputies of the Convention. The Club of the *Jacobins*, composed of desperate men, was devoted to him. The *Commune*, which had the government of Paris in its hands and controlled all its military force, was wholly under his sway. He little dreamt that the Convention, always so submissive, would dare to confront such formidable odds. All was ready for the new murders he had planned, when Robespierre appeared on the 26th July, 1794, in the Convention to demand the arrest of the Members he had doomed. To his amazement he found himself bearded and denounced on all sides. His crimes were enumerated, and his downfall demanded. He made great efforts to speak, but his voice was drowned in shouts of fury. Livid with rage, and foaming at the mouth, he attempted to speak during a momentary lull, but his voice failed. "It is the blood of Danton chokes thee," said a member. The Convention decreed his arrest, and that of his two allies, St.

Just and Couthon. The brutal Commandant of Paris, Henriot, and the Mayor of the *Commune*, were also taken into custody. Robespierre and his companions, however, were rescued by a force of the *Commune* which had called on the forty-eight Sections of Paris to send their military contingent to the *Hôtel de Ville.* It was a critical moment, but the Convention displayed great energy and courage. They appointed a member, Barras, to command the troops that would support the Convention, and then sent deputations to the various Sections to rally them for the law and the Convention. It was soon evident that the sanguinary despotism of Robespierre had lost its hold on the popular mind; for the citizen troops of the Sections refused to obey the *Commune*, and declared for the Convention. Robespierre and his satellites were ensconced in the *Hôtel de Ville*, and when the officers of the Convention entered, some jumped from the windows, whilst Robespierre attempted suicide. He was seized and executed the following day, together with twenty of his accomplices.*

* "When Robespierre ascended the fatal car, his head was enveloped in a bloody cloth, his color was livid, and his eyes sunk. When the procession came opposite his house it stopped, and a group of women danced round the bier of him whose chariot-wheels they would have dragged the day before over a thousand victims. Robespierre mounted the scaffold last, and the moment his head fell the applause was tremendous. In some cases the event was announced to the prisoners by the waving of pocket handkerchiefs from the tops of houses."—HAZLITT.

"Robespierre was executed on the spot where Louis XVI. and Marie Antoinette had suffered. He shut his eyes, but could not close his ears against the imprecations of the multitude. A woman, breaking from the crowd, exclaimed, 'Murderer of all my kindred! your agony fills me with joy. Descend to hell, covered with the curses of every mother in France!' When he ascended the scaffold, the executioner tore the bandage from his face; the lower jaw fell on his breast, and he uttered a yell which froze every heart with horror. For some minutes the frightful figure was held up to the multitude; he was then placed under the axe. 'Yes, Robespierre, there is a God,'

With the death of Robespierre, the blood-stained march of the Revolution was arrested.

In reviewing its career, it may be said that from July, 1789, when insurrection broke out in Paris, down to 1792, the Revolution achieved immense benefits for France. All the Reforms that her writers and statesmen had invoked were accomplished. The Feudal fabric was finally overthrown, and the monstrous oppression of centuries was suppressed and avenged. But then appeared a band of reckless Demagogues, who, for the sake of power, played on the passions of the populace, and stimulated them to horrible deeds. By these means, Marat became an idol, Danton a minister, and Robespierre a dictator. The punishment which overtook them all was the just penalty of their criminal ambition.

After the fall of Robespierre Supreme Power re-

said a poor man, as he approached the lifeless body of one so lately the object of dread."—ALISON.

"On the very day of Robespierre's arrest, his adherent, Dumas, who was executed with him, had signed the warrant for putting sixty persons to death. In the confusion, no person thought of arresting the guillotine. They all suffered."—SCOTT's "Life of Napoleon."

"To the profound hypocrisy of Cromwell, he joined the cruelty of Sylla, without possessing any of the great military and political qualities of either of these ambitious adventurers. To observe the emphasis with which he boasted of having proclaimed the existence of the Supreme Being, one might have said that, according to his opinion, God would not have existed without him."—*Annual Register*, 1794.

"In the year 1785 he wrote an essay against the punishment of death, which gained the prize awarded by the Royal Society of Metz." —*Quarterly Review.*

"When Robespierre first appeared in the world he prefixed the aristocratical particle *de* to his name. He was entered at college as de Robespierre; he was elected to the States General as de Robespierre; but after the abolition of all feudal distinctions, he rejected the *de*, and called himself Robespierre."—*Quarterly Review.*

"In the space of eight or ten days after the fall of Robespierre, out of ten thousand suspected persons, not one remained in the prisons of Paris."—LACRETELLE.

verted to the Convention. Under the impulse of outraged humanity, vigorous measures to repress the desperadoes who had converted France into a slaughter-house were adopted. The Revolutionary Tribunal was suppressed, and Fouquier Tinville executed. The wretch Carrier, who destroyed 32,000 people at Nantes, was also sent to the scaffold. The club of the *Jacobins* was closed; the surviving Members of Robespierre's "Committee of Public Safety" were tried, March, 1795, and transported; the Sections of Paris were disarmed; the churches restored to public worship.

Later in the year the young daughter of Louis XVI., afterwards Duchess of Angoulême, was given to the Austrians in exchange for certain prisoners they had made. Her brother the Dauphin had died in prison.*

THE DIRECTORY.

Having thus calmed the perturbed mind of Paris and of France, the Convention set to work constructing a Constitution. After discussing it for three

* "Simon who was entrusted with the bringing up of the Dauphin, had had the cruelty to leave the poor child absolutely alone: unexampled barbarity, to leave an unhappy and sickly infant eight years old in a great room, locked and bolted in, with no other resource than a broken bell which he never rang, so greatly did he dread the people whom its sound would have brought to him! He preferred wanting everything to the sight of his persecutors. His bed had not been touched for six months, and he had not strength to make it himself; it was alive with bugs and vermin still more disgusting. His linen and his person were covered with them. For more than a year he had no change of shirt or stockings; every kind of filth was allowed to accumulate in his room. His window was never opened, and the infectious smell of this horrid apartment was so dreadful that no one could bear it. He passed his days wholly without occupation. They did not even allow him light in the evening. This situation affected his mind as well as his body, and he fell into a frightful atrophy."—DUCHESS D'ANGOULÊME.

months, they decreed the adoption of the "Constitution of the Year III.," as it was called, August, 1795. By this instrument the Executive power was given to five persons called the "Directors." The Legislative power was divided between Two Chambers, —the one, called the "Council of the Ancients," composed of two hundred and fifty members; the other, the "Council of Five Hundred," consisting of that number. The Directory was entrusted merely with the execution of the laws passed by the two Councils; with the direction, not the declaration of war; with the negotiation, not the ratification of treaties; and the five persons of whom it was composed decided by a majority. The Councils were elected by Universal Suffrage in the second degree, and the Directory was nominated by the two Councils. The judicial authority was committed to Elective Judges. The Press was declared free, as well as all Religions, which were not to receive support from the State. The Constitution, however, totally ignored the claims of the towns of France to Municipal independence; they were all retained under the control of the Central Authority.

The Convention decreed that the new Legislative body should be composed of two-thirds of their own body, and that one new third only should be elected. They seemed to dread that an entirely new legislature would turn round, under the influence of reaction, and punish many of those Members who had taken so active a part in the excesses of the Revolution. The Decree ordering the re-election of two-thirds of the Convention gave great umbrage to its numerous enemies, and an agitation was set on foot with the cry, "We accept the Constitution and reject the Decree." All the Departments of France voted the Constitution unanimously, and sustained the Decree by an immense majority. In Paris, however, the opposition was kept up and stimulated by the agents of the Royalists, by the journalists, and the literary men who were anxious to enter the new legislature. They propagated the belief that the Convention, if re-elected, would restore the Reign of Terror.

Finally, an Insurrection was organized, and the citizens of Paris, to the number of 40,000 men, enrolled themselves. The Convention could muster in its defence only some 8000 men, but 5000 of these were composed of troops of the line. Barras, the Member who had defeated the *Commune*, and Robespierre in July, was named the Commander of the troops of the Convention. He appointed as his second in command a young soldier of the name of Napoleon Bonaparte.* As Commandant of the artillery at the siege of Toulon he devised the plan which recaptured it. He afterwards obtained distinction in other operations, and was made General of Brigade. He was at this time in Paris unemployed and in great indigence.†

* Napoleon was the second son of Charles Bonaparte, and was born at Ajaccio, Corsica, then belonging to France, in 1769. The family was noble, and of Italian origin, dating from the twelfth century. Napoleon entered the Military School of Brienne at ten years old, and was made a Sub-Lieutenant in 1785, then sixteen. Napoleon had four brothers and three sisters.

† "At this period Napoleon passed most of his time in meditation and retirement. He went out but seldom, and had few acquaintances. He endeavoured to forget the sense of mortification and neglect by a more intense application to his professional studies. He sometimes went to the theatre, and frequented the Corazza coffee house in the Palais Royal, where the celebrated Talma is said once to have paid his reckoning for him, for which he had left his sword in pledge."—HAZLITT.

Barras believed in his capacity, and selected him at this critical moment as far more competent to deal with the situation than himself. Bonaparte was no sooner in command, than he seized all the artillery, which was parked at Sablons near Paris. He thus secured himself an immense advantage, and at just the right moment, for the cannon had scarcely been removed before a detachment of the Sections came in quest of it. Napoleon then made all his dispositions, and awaited the attack, which began at four P.M. on the 13th Vendémiaire (October 5th), and by six P.M. the assailants were routed, and the victory of the Convention complete.

The rough handling of the Parisians by the resolute Bonaparte was a lesson they long remembered. Rebellion in the streets disappeared, and the new Government went to work with great vigor. In the place of the *Commune*, which fell with Robespierre, Paris was divided, February, 1796, into twelve separate Municipalities, so as to render future insurrections less dangerous.*

The Directory resolved upon two important objects: first, to put down the civil war in *la Vendée*, west of France; and this they accomplished in six months; next, to carry on with energy the war against the foreign nations in conflict with France. Moreau was

* The reader may remember that the old city government of Paris was abolished in 1789, and a new organization called the *Commune* substituted, which concentrated all the municipal power in the hands of a Mayor. The object of this was simply to give the Revolutionists, through their instrument, the Mayor, the entire control of Paris. To get rid of this dangerous centralization of power, Paris was divided by the Convention, as stated above, into twelve municipalities, with as many Mayors; and this arrangement has been maintained to the present day. It was temporarily superseded by the *Commune* of 1871, but was immediately restored on the collapse of that sanguinary insurrection.

made Commander of the army destined for Germany; and Bonaparte, then twenty-six, obtained to his joy the army of Italy, at the time contending with Piedmont and Austria. The prodigies achieved by the young Corsican are briefly recounted in a foot-note.*

Whilst victory abroad rendered revolutionary France alarming to Europe, the political caldron at Paris was boiling fiercely. Three political Factions were struggling to obtain power. The Royalists aspired to restore the Monarchy; the "Patriots," as they styled themselves, desired to restore the reign of terror; and the Constitutionalists were anxious to preserve what existed. By degrees, and regardless of the results, cliques were formed in both the Upper and Lower Chambers of the Legislature to upset the Directory. The Royalists and Patriots hoped if they succeeded to seize on the Government. Besides the hostile combinations in the two Chambers, the Directory was divided against itself. Its two prominent members were Barras† and Carnot,‡ who detested

* General Bonaparte took command of the "Army of Italy," April, 1795, consisting of 30,000 men, beaten, disorganized, without food, clothes, or money. In a year he overthrew five armies, each more than double his own, and led by the first generals of Austria. He conquered Lombardy, and extinguished the ancient governments of Venice and Genoa. The King of Sardinia, the Pope, the Dukes of Florence, Parma, and Modena, begged for peace, and finally the Emperor of Austria signed the Treaty of Campo Formio, October, 1797, ceding to France Lombardy, the left bank of the Rhine, and the Austrian Netherlands. In Germany the French army under Moreau was also victorious, but the results were less important.

† Barras was of noble family, and began life as a soldier. He joined the revolution, and was active in the capture of the Bastille. He figured throughout the revolution; he owed his escape in the Reign of Terror to being on duty with the armies. He was the real head of the Directory till its fall. He was able, adroit, unscrupulous, and dissolute. He died in 1829, aged 74, at Paris, quite forgotten.

‡ Carnot was in the army when the revolution broke out, and immediately espoused the side of the opponents of the monarchy. He was a member of all the legislative bodies, as well as of the Committee of Safety. He abhorred Robespierre and his bloody acts, and had no

each other. A crisis was inevitable. Whilst the politicians in both Chambers were preparing for the explosion, and the Directors were intriguing against each other, the mob of Paris to the surprise of all were passive, if not indifferent. They seemed to have lost the ferocity which had transformed them from men into demons. Whether they had discovered that in all the changes they got nothing but the blows, whilst the Politicians pocketed all the profits; or whether the existence in Paris of a military force the Directory could depend on cowed them, the populace of Paris it was evident were no longer disposed to fight for another revolution, and left the demagogues to settle the matter to their liking.

On the 18th Fructidor—September 4th, 1797—the catastrophe came. Of the five Directors two joined Barras, making a majority. They ordered the military under General Augereau to surround the Chambers and seize the Members opposed to the Government. Two hundred were arrested and promptly transported. Forty-two journals of the Royalists were suppressed. All were doomed who attacked the Directory which now assumed Dictatorial power. The two Directors in minority, Carnot and Barthelemy, resigned, and were replaced. This Revolution was bloodless, a proof that revolutionary passions had cooled, and that the Opinion of the country kept the Politicians in check.

This *coup d'état* was effected by means of regular troops, and not by the mob as hitherto, showing that

share in them, being always absent with the armies. In military administration he was unrivalled. It was said of him that he "organized victory." After leaving the Directory he was frequently employed by Napoleon. He possessed great capacity and high principles, and died in 1823, aged 70, leaving a stainless reputation.

the military men who had been created by the wars the Revolution provoked, were destined to supersede the demagogues who had made it. From this time it will be seen that Soldiers, and not Politicians, were to govern France for a long period.

In December, 1797, General Bonaparte received a splendid ovation in Paris from the Directory. His renown filled Europe, and France regarded him as destined to restore her long-lost divinities, Law and Order. The Directory and the Politicians were already so jealous of his popularity that he was left without employment. Bonaparte knew the necessity of keeping the public eye upon him; and after incessant efforts he induced the Directory to give him an army to invade Egypt. He embarked with some 30,000 men in May, 1798, and in a brief period conquered the whole country, where he remained a little over a year. His constant victories, bold acts, and striking proclamations added daily to his glory, and electrified France.

During 1798, the Directory maintained order at home, and added to its credit by victories abroad. Yet the state of things was unsatisfactory. Everybody felt the Government was only provisional: the factions were always conspiring: some powerful hand, some master intellect, was necessary to crush them.

In July, 1799, another outbreak occurred. All the parties in the two Chambers, Royalists, Terrorists, and Constitutionalists united against the Directory, which was always divided against itself. This time there was no majority to call in the military. Only two of the Directors pulled together, Barras and Sieyès: the other three were unable to unite. The consequence was, that these three resigned, and were replaced. The Government now was weaker than ever, and the political bands were intent on a desperate struggle for power. Thus after ten years of terrible convulsions, France seemed no nearer to the promised land of Liberty and Order than at the beginning.

Speaking of this epoch, October, 1799, Thiers remarks—"It was not so much a defender that was needed at this moment as a chief to seize the reins of government. The mass of the population desired at any cost quiet, order, the end of dissensions, and unity of government. It was afraid of the Terrorists, of the Royalists, of the Chouans, of all the parties. It was the moment of marvellous fortune for him who should allay all their fears."* And it was at this propitious moment that the arrival of General Bonaparte from Egypt was announced, and the nation rose to greet him. Bonaparte was then just thirty, and the greatest Captain and profoundest Politician of his time. He accomplished a double object by his trip to the East. He added to his renown, and avoided contact with a disorganized Government and unscrupulous Factions. But his hour had come. He saw it with his eagle-glance; he seized it with his lion-courage.† Without

* Another author gives the following graphic sketch of France at the same time.—"Merit was generally persecuted; all men of honour chased from public situations; robbers everywhere assembled in their infernal caverns; the wicked were in power; the apologists of the system of terror were thundering in the tribune; spoliation was re-established under the name of false loans; thousands of victims were already designed, under the name of hostages; the signal for pillage, murder, and conflagration, anxiously looked for, couched in the words 'the Country is in Danger!' the citizens had no security for their lives; the State for its finances. All Europe was in arms against us. Our armies were routed; our conquests were lost; the territory of the republic menaced with invasion. Such was the situation of France previous to the revolution of the 18th of Brumaire and the establishment of the Consulate."

† A packet of French papers reached Bonaparte in Egypt. Devouring their contents, he exclaimed, "Heavens, my prediction is verified; the fools have lost Italy. All the fruits of our victories are gone. I must leave Egypt."

orders he crossed the Mediterranean amid the enemy's cruisers, and landing in France sped on to Paris. As he hurried onwards, bells rang, bonfires blazed, and shouts echoed from hill to hill. He comprehended this outburst: France hailed him as her Deliverer from new scenes of blood and anarchy.

He entered the Capital, October 18th, and every General came to offer his sword.* This was the main point. He sounded the Politicians. All the discontented and ambitious gave their adhesion. Two of the Directors, Sieyès and Ducos, agreed to resign: another, Barras, was ready to imitate them. On the 18th Brumaire, November 9th, 1799, the signal was given. Three of the five Directors resigned; and so the Executive power was dissolved. The Two Chambers were left: the Upper Chamber took the side of Bonaparte, and appointed him by decree Commander of all the troops in Paris. The Capital was quiet the whole day: Bonaparte forbade any interference with business.†

On the succeeding day, November 10th, the Two Chambers were to meet at St. Cloud. The General entered the hall of the Upper Chamber, and harangued the Members, who replied with hearty applause. He then went among the "Five Hundred," but had scarcely entered when he was surrounded and furiously denounced. The leaders of the Royalists and Terrorists who saw that the Government, at which they aimed, was falling into the hands of a great Soldier, were

* Three only held back, Bernadotte, Jourdan, and Augereau.

† The chief of the police had ordered the barriers to be closed, &c. Bonaparte indignant said to him, "Wherefore all these precautions? We go with the nation, and by its strength alone. Let no citizen be disturbed, and let the triumph of opinion have nothing in common with the transactions of days in which a faction prevailed."

frantic with rage. Probably the General, like Cæsar, would have been assassinated, were it not that his enemies dreaded the fury of the people. After a stormy scene, Bonaparte retired. The President of the "Five Hundred," Lucien Bonaparte, then declared the Lower Chamber dissolved, and called on the troops to disperse it. A battalion of Grenadiers appeared at the doors, and unlike their courageous predecessors of the Convention, the Members fled in all directions. They knew too well that the country was weary of anarchy.

The next day the Upper Chamber met, and created a Consulate of three members, Bonaparte, Ducos, and Sieyès. A portion of the Lower Chamber confirmed these decrees. Bonaparte was now at the head of the Government. The Executive power that had passed from the King into the hands of the "Committee of Public Safety"—all Politicians—and then into the hands of the Directory—again Politicians—now was deposited in the firm grasp of a Soldier. Military power became dominant, and the reign of the Demagogues was over.

THE CONSULATE.

NINETEENTH CENTURY.

ABSOLUTE Power was restored in France when Bonaparte became First Consul. This was the inevitable result of the fearful vicissitudes through which the country had passed since the Insurrection of July, 1789. So complete was the disorganization into which everything had fallen that it required nothing less than the wonderful genius and resolute will of Bonaparte to revive the civil and moral life of the Nation. With matchless sagacity and vigor he began the work of reconstruction.

The three Consuls named by the late Chamber of the "Ancients"—Bonaparte, Sieyès, and Ducos—set to work immediately to draw up a definite Constitution. Sieyès, who believed himself specially endowed for such a task, proposed an elaborate Scheme of Government which the practical genius of Bonaparte rejected as impracticable, if not absurd. A plan was drawn up under his direction concentrating the Executive power entirely in his own hands, with the title of First Consul, and for a period of ten years. Two other Consuls were created as "Advisers." A Senate of sixty-six Members, and a Legislative Body of three hundred were added more for ornament than utility; for no power was confided to them—not even the privilege of debate. The Senate was nominated by the First Consul; the Legislative Body was elected by the Senate: therefore both were composed solely of the adherents of Bonaparte.

This Constitution, which made him absolute master of France, was submitted to the sanction of the Nation 3rd December, 1799, and was approved by a Vote of three millions and upwards.

He next turned his attention to military matters, reorganizing every arm of the Service with wonderful celerity. In May, 1800, he crossed the Alps with an army, fell unawares on the Austrians at Marengo in June, and regained possession of Italy. He forced Austria to make Peace by the Treaty of Luneville in February, 1801. In March, 1802, he concluded a Peace with England, Spain, and Holland by the Treaty of Amiens.

This general pacification enabled him to enter on that vast scheme of internal Reform which constitutes his strongest claim to the gratitude of France. He ordered the entire legal system to be reorganized; and the most eminent Jurisconsults—Tronchet, Portalis, Merlin—were appointed to draw up new Codes, Civil, Commercial, and Penal.*

The Civil Code, known as the Code Napoléon, went finally into effect in March, 1804. Up to that period, France had been under the control of a variety of laws which were often contradictory—the written or Roman laws; the laws of custom, or Common Law; also those known as the Royal Ordinances: and Bonaparte rendered

* The Civil Code was divided into three books. The first treated of persons; the second of property; the third of the modes of acquiring property.

an immense service to his country by converting this legal chaos into order and unity.

In 1801, he made a Concordat with Pius VII. which restored the Catholic religion and the Papal authority in France, taking care to reserve for the Government complete control over the Church by the nomination of all its officials. In 1802, he instituted the Legion of Honor—an Order of Chivalry for the reward of merit civil or military.

His popularity had by this time become so universal that the Senate, at his instigation, proposed him for election as First Consul for life; and the new title was conferred on him in August, 1802, by a popular Vote of over three millions and a half.*

On 14th April of the following year he established the Bank of France, which from that day to this has been administered with incredible skill. It has surmounted the immense disasters which have befallen France for the last seventy years - three Invasions from abroad, and three Revolutions at home.

During the whole period of the Consulate the activity of the First Consul knew no bounds. In every direction, and by every means, he sought to develop the resources and promote the welfare of France. Canals were dug by his orders; harbors were built; roads and bridges constructed; taxation was reformed; and education enlarged. All this tended to make him more and more the idol of France; and in May, 1804, the Senate, again at his

* The National Convention of 1793 introduced Universal Suffrage into France. The Constitution of 1795 maintained it, but with some small modifications. Napoleon continued it, and it was not abolished till the Restoration in 1815.

own suggestion, offered him the Crown as the Emperor of the French. The Nation was consulted as before; and by a Vote of over three millions and a half against two thousand, he was raised to the purple. His Coronation took place 2nd December, 1804, amid great pomp at the Cathedral of Notre Dame. Pius VII. came from Rome to consecrate it by his presence.

EMPIRE.

NINETEENTH CENTURY.

Before giving a short *résumé* of the events of the Empire, it may be well to remark that the System of Centralization, which attained its full development under Napoleon, owed its origin to events many ages before him. The concentration of power in the hands of the Central Government began with the struggles between the feudal Nobility and the Monarchy. Under the Feudal System, as shown, France was broken up into endless jurisdictions independent of each other; but as the Monarchy gained ground these local governments gradually diminished. Louis XI. gave a great impetus to Centralization, and Cardinal Richelieu extended it still more. The Politicians who directed the Revolution of 1789 carried Centralization far beyond their Monarchical predecessors; for their object was to hold France in complete subjection to Paris as the centre of all political direction.

When Napoleon assumed the Government, he found the administrative machinery of the Revolution well adapted to his purpose. At that moment whoever held Paris controlled France. Every village as well as every Department was governed by a *Maire* and a *Préfet* sent from the Capital. Napoleon really had little to do to make the Centralization of Power more absolute than he found it. Certes, it lost nothing of its vigor in his iron grasp.

The rise of the Empire witnessed a formidable Coalition meant to destroy it. In August, 1805, Russia, Austria, and Naples joined England, already at war with France, for its overthrow. The battle of Austerlitz, in December, crushed this combination; and the Treaty of Presburg followed, which deprived Austria of all her Italian provinces, and raised Wurtemberg and Bavaria from Duchies to Kingdoms, for the benefit of Napoleon's German allies. Soon after, 1806, the King of Naples was dispossessed of his throne, which was given to Joseph, the elder brother of Napoleon. Another brother, Louis, was made King of Holland, and Murat, a brother-in-law, became Grand-Duke of Berg.

With a view to consolidate his position in Germany, Napoleon proposed to the feudal Princes under the tutelage of Austria and Prussia to form a Confederation, of which he offered to become the head and protector. His scheme was adopted by fourteen Princes; and thus was founded the 'Confederation of the Rhine,' which closed the career of the German Empire.

This event, coupled with the seductions of England and Russia, induced Prussia to enter into a new Coalition against France. The defeat of Prussia, in October, 1806, at Jena, and the double rout of Russia at Eylau, in February, and at Friedland in June, 1807, again left Napoleon master of the situation. The Treaty of Tilsit between Napoleon and Alexander, February, 1807, closed the war. It contained sundry secret Articles, which amounted to the partition of Europe, exclusive of England and Turkey, between them. Prussia was despoiled of large territories; a portion of which was annexed to Westphalia, of which Jerome, the youngest brother of Napoleon, was made King.

At this time, Napoleon planned his "Continental Blockade," to which Russia assented, by which he hoped to ruin the commerce of England, in closing all the European ports against her. To this effect were issued the Berlin and Milan Decrees in November, 1806, and in December, 1807.

The triumph of Napoleon over all the combinations of continental Europe seemed to convince him of the permanence of his dynasty. In March, 1808, he decreed the creation of an Hereditary Nobility. At this period, too, he set to work improving and embellishing Paris, and ordered an Exhibition of the Products of French Industry.

The condition of Spain next attracted the Emperor's attention. Charles IV. of Spain was wholly under the domination of his wife and her favorite, Manuel de Godoy, which induced the Prince of the Asturias, the King's eldest son, to put himself at the head of a popular movement and force his father to abdicate. The French Emperor offered himself as an Arbitrator between the two; and the tractable Charles abdicated finally in favor of Napoleon, who immediately transferred his brother Joseph from Naples to the throne at Madrid.

This transaction led to a general rising in Spain, in which all classes united, and which was powerfully aided by an English army. It was the origin of that famous Peninsular War, which from 1808 to 1813 witnessed the successive defeats of the best French Generals, and founded the military fame of the Duke of Wellington. During these five years, the French loss has been estimated at over 400,000 men.

In April, 1809, England succeeded in drawing Austria into another Alliance against France, which led, by the French victory at Wagram in July, to the complete subjugation of Austria. Instead of breaking up the Austrian Monarchy, as it was in his power to do, Napoleon proposed as the price of peace a marriage with Maria Louisa, daughter of the Emperor Francis. In December of this year, he divorced his first wife Josephine; in April, 1810, he married the Archduchess of Austria. Napoleon's chief motive in this marriage was doubtless to secure the permanent alliance of Austria; and he inferred, besides, it would add to the prestige of his dynasty.

In July of this year Holland was annexed to France, and Louis Bonaparte, who opposed the project, fell into disfavor. This may be considered the culminating point of Napoleon's career. From this period may be dated errors which showed that his judgment was disturbed by his marvellous success. Some of his best auxiliaries, as Fouché and Bernadotte, fell away from him; he quarrelled with the Pope, who excommunicated him; and, worse than all, his "Continental Blockade," levelled at England, greatly damaged the commerce of France and caused general dissatisfaction. In March, 1811, Maria Louisa gave birth to a son who was created "King of Rome"; and this was the last boon conferred on him by a bounteous Providence.

Unable to restrain his martial spirit, he declared war on Russia in June, 1812, without caring to secure the co-operation of Sweden or Turkey. He set out with an army of 450,000 men, and marched through Poland in pursuit of the Russians, who constantly retreated. It was only at Borodino near Moscow that a battle occurred, where the Russians were beaten. On the 14th September, Napoleon entered Moscow, and the day following a conflagration broke out which destroyed it. The Fabian tactics of Russia were then revealed. They had retreated before Napoleon only to lure him on to Moscow, which was burnt over his head. His situation was alarming. He waited for a month in the hope of peace; and on October 19th, began a retreat the most disastrous which history records. Only a fragment survived of the half million of men that left France. Quitting his army, he reached Paris in December.

In the following March, 1813, Russia was joined by Prussia in the war against him, and in August, Austria entered the Coalition. Meanwhile England was steadily forcing back the French forces in Spain. In April, Napoleon again took the field with a new army of 350,000 men, and in August defeated at Dresden the combined armies of Russia, Prussia, and Austria. In October, however, he was defeated at Leipsic through the defection of his Saxon auxiliaries, and was forced to fall back on France. In January, 1814, the Allies crossed the Rhine. The campaign which ensued is considered the most brilliant in Napoleon's career. He gained repeated victories, and the Allies offered terms of peace, which the Emperor rejected. He was manœuvring to enclose the enemy between himself and Paris ; but his plan was defeated by the sudden surrender of the Capital in March—an event attributed by some to treachery. In April he signed his Abdication, and retired to Elba, of which the Allies, as if in derision, made him the Sovereign.

RESTORATION OF THE MONARCHY.

NINETEENTH CENTURY.

Napoleon's downfall brought the old French Monarchy back, but under circumstances that rendered it only a phantom of its former self. Napoleon wielded the absolute power of Louis XIV., and could also boast—*L'état, c'est moi.* His successor, Louis XVIII., brother of Louis XVI., on the contrary, was transformed into that modern invention, yclept a Constitutional King—the first which appeared on the continent of Europe. On the death of his nephew, the Dauphin, in 1795, he took the title of King, and was recognized as such by Europe; and on the Abdication of Napoleon in April, 1814, the Senate, at the instigation of the European Coalition, called him to the throne. Louis XVIII. began his reign in the same month.

In spite of the moderation of the King, the conduct of the Royalists and the Clergy was so arrogant and reactionary, that the country soon became shocked and alienated. Napoleon, perceiving the tide was again setting in his favor, forsook his retreat, and boldly landed in France, March, 1815.

THE HUNDRED DAYS.

AMID the most enthusiastic demonstrations, Napoleon made his way from Cannes to Paris, and reascended the throne; his rival, Louis XVIII., retiring on his approach to Holland. The Allies, convinced that peace was impossible whilst the Emperor held power, resolved to renew the war, and in three months they advanced on France. Napoleon met them finally at Waterloo, and his defeat there closed his career. He was exiled by the Allies to St. Helena, where he arrived in October, 1815, and died in May, 1821.

As a warrior and an administrator, Napoleon is ranked with Alexander and Cæsar of the ancient, and Charlemagne of the modern world—considered the four greatest men that Europe has produced. He rendered eminent service to France by extinguishing the factions of the Revolution in 1799, and setting up a framework of society which has endured in great part to the present day. In repressing anarchy, reconstituting society, restoring religion, reorganizing education, creating the Code, and in placing France at the head of Europe, he established solid claims on the admiration of his countrymen.* This, however, comprises the useful part of his career. His insatiable thirst for war rendered his political existence incompatible with the safety of Europe, whilst his despotic

* The Empire founded by Napoleon is regarded as equal to that of Charlemagne; for it consisted in 1812 of 130 French departments—which included various German and Dutch provinces; 24 departments of Italy annexed to France, and 7 provinces of Illyria.

character was inconsistent with the permanent welfare of France, and his overthrow became an imperative necessity. His military exploits achieved immortality for his name, but yielded to the world nothing save wonder and regret.

SECOND RESTORATION.

Louis XVIII. reascended the throne in July, 1815. For sixteen years had Napoleon held France in his stern grip. His intellect, his will, and his glory, had confounded opposition; but with his disappearance, the Nation relapsed once more into the hands of Politicians.

The Allied Sovereigns and their Statesmen, who entered Paris a second time in 1815, must have pondered deeply over the situation. For twenty-six years France had been in their eyes little else than a common nuisance: first with her Revolution, its anarchy, bloodshed, and subversive principles; next with her Napoleonic Wars, assailing and subjugating all nations in turn. Twice had Europe risen in self-defence, and twice had France been stricken down. How to extinguish such a volcano must have been a perplexity to the conquerors. Various projects were discussed. Should the Feudal System be restored? Should the Absolute Monarchy be set up again? But Feudality without the Middle Ages, and Absolute Monarchy without the Seventeenth century, would be anachronisms and short-lived. Europe, irritated and bewildered, returned home, and left France to the solution of her own destiny.

Napoleon suppressed, and his conquerors gone, France, I repeat, fell once more into the possession of her Politicians; and her history since then is simply the record of their conflicts for supremacy—each set struggling in turn to outwit the others. A new Constitution, called the "Charter of 1814," inaugurated the return of Louis XVIII. This Constitution gave the Executive power to the King, and divided the Legislative power between two Chambers: an Upper Chamber composed of Peers, some hereditary and others for life; and a Lower one consisting of Deputies, elected by qualified suffrage.

Two parties immediately sprung up, which were the natural product of the circumstances. One consisted of the Aristocracy and Clergy, who had been persecuted and decimated by the Revolution. These naturally desired that France should return to the condition in which they were the dominant classes. They proposed that Agriculture should be the chief interest; that cultivation on a large scale should be restored; that great properties should be reconstituted with Entail and Primogeniture; that the Clergy should be supported by the State; and that the Administrative Centralization reorganized by Napoleon, which enabled the Government to control the country, should be abolished. In short, they hoped to revive the Feudal System, the system of the Middle Ages, the government of the Aristocracy, which Richelieu had suppressed. They were as much opposed to an Absolute Monarchy as to an Absolute Democracy. They always believed that France was their heritage, quite forgetting that they had been superseded by the Absolute Monarchy, and that both had been supplanted by the Revolution. This was the

Feudal party, which dreamt that ancient France could be galvanized and set up again.

Opposed to it was the party that was born in the seventeenth century, and survived the vicissitudes and horrors of the eighteenth century. They denied that the Supreme power belonged either to the Aristocracy or the Monarchy; it was, they contended, the property of the Nation, to be used by its agents or delegates for the benefit of all. This was the party of Modern France. It represented all the new interests that had grown up, and consisted of the new men that aspired to govern the country. It was composed of the parliamentarians, the bankers, manufacturers, merchants, physicians, and lawyers; in fact, the descendants of that Middle Class which once stood between the Aristocracy and the masses.

The struggles between these parties, between ancient France and modern France, filled up the reign of Louis XVIII. The King was a sensible man, with a love for *belles-lettres*, and no taste for politics and its noisy jargon. The lessons of his eventful life were not forgotten. The ancient Monarchy of France in the person of his brother had sunk in a sea of blood. An exile and wanderer for twenty-three years, he returned to France, not to sit on the throne of his ancestors—it had vanished—but to play the novel *rôle* of Constitutional King. Either from indifference or prudence, he held aloof from the contests that raged around him. He could feel no sympathy for a party that sought to resuscitate an Aristocracy meant to curb alike the Monarchy and the masses. He comprehended, on the other hand, the folly of resisting a party that impersonated the France of his day. For nearly ten years he held the balance evenly between them, choosing as his Minister, at one time the Duke Decazes, the leader of modern France, and at the other, M. de Villèle, the chief of the "Impracticables," as the party of ancient France was christened. When dying, he laid his hand on the head of his young grand-nephew, the Duke de Bordeaux,* and said, "Let my brother husband tenderly the Crown of this child."

* The Duke de Bordeaux, better known as the Count de Chambord, was born in September, 1820, and was grandson of Charles X. His father, the Duke de Berry, was assassinated, in February, 1820, as he was leaving the Opera-house, by the fanatic Louvel, a saddler, who declared his object was to extinguish the elder branch of the Bourbons.

DOWNFALL OF THE MONARCHY.

NINETEENTH CENTURY.

Charles X., brother of Louis XVI., and of the last King, succeeded to the throne in 1824. Up to this time he bore the title of Count d'Artois. He emigrated in 1789, and was active in urging the Foreign Powers to invade France and put down the Revolution. He returned in 1814, untaught by the fearful events that had occurred, and unconscious of the vast moral and material change that had ensued. This was exemplified by his reply when asked, on his arrival in Paris, if he found any alteration. "Only a Frenchman the more," he answered, alluding to himself. He was a man of small capacity, and great irresolution—just the combination to lead to a catastrophe. During his brother's reign, he identified himself with the reactionary party, and readily yielded to the perilous influence of the Clergy.

He was no sooner in power, than under the counsel of his Minister, M. de Villèle, he authorized the adoption of several indiscreet measures, which soon aroused public indignation. Alarmed at the outcry, he called M. de Martignac to his side, 1827, and calmed the universal dissatisfaction by a wiser policy. Unable, however, to resist the pressure of insidious advisers, and still profoundly ignorant of public sentiment in France, he made, in 1829, M. de Polignac his Minister, and resolved on a course of policy utterly opposed to the views and interests of the great majority of the Nation. The protests of the Opposition in the Chamber of Deputies were loud and threatening. They voted an Address to the King by a majority of 221, declaring that the "political views of the Government did not concur with the wishes of the people." In spite of this warning, and the many symptoms of an impending storm, the King persisted in extreme measures; and in July, 1830, he issued the famous Ordinances dissolving the Chamber of Deputies, suspending the Liberty of the Press, and changing the Electoral System. In a word, the Constitution of 1814 was glaringly violated.

Two days after, July 27, an Insurrection broke out in the streets of Paris, which in three days ended in the Abdication of Charles X., in favor of his grandson, the Duke de Bordeaux. The infatuated King again resumed the road to exile. He died at Goritz, in 1836, in his 80th year.*

Thus fell to the ground, where it is destined to lie, the Monarchy of the Middle Ages, impersonated in the elder branch of the Bourbons. It was put on its legs a second time by the Allied Armies in 1814, not so much perhaps out of respect for the "Divine Right" it represented, but that there was no other material out of which a Government could be manufactured. The Revolution had left neither a man nor a principle. The Empire naturally disappeared with Napoleon, its founder. There was nothing, therefore, but the old Monarchy to resuscitate, and an effort was made to adapt

* At the very close of the reign of Charles X., July, 1830, Algiers was annexed to France.

it to the altered circumstances by yoking it to a Constitution. Its fate is recorded.

The Government which succeeded that of Charles X. had for its chief exponent his cousin Louis-Philippe, of the house of Orleans—the younger branch of the Bourbon family. He was familiarly dubbed at the time "The Citizen King," to show that he was the representative of modern France.

I shall reserve my comments on this reign, of which I was an eye-witness, until I discuss it in the "History of my Times."

ENGLAND.

ENGLAND.

SAXON EPOCH.

A GLANCE, however rapid, at English history before the Middle Ages will be interesting. The islands of Britain and Ireland were first occupied by emigrants from Gaul —afterwards France—of the Celtic race.* Aristotle alluded to these islands some 350 years before Christ; yet little is known of them until the invasion of Britain by Julius Cæsar in the first century. Ireland never fell under the Roman, or Saxon yoke, and remained purely Celtic for several centuries: a fact which explains, in some degree, the dissimilarity of character between the Irish and the English. The Romans remained masters of Britain for four centuries, and did not retire until the fifth century, when the invasion of Italy by the Goths imperatively recalled them home. The Britons then became the prey of various German tribes, who conquered different parts of the island, and dispossessed the native Chiefs or Kings.

With the success of these tribes the period known as the Saxon Heptarchy begins. Under Egbert, King of Wessex—827—the Seven Kingdoms of the Heptarchy were united under one Government, and the country then took the name of England. The institutions,

* Gaul, Italy, and Spain were first occupied by roving tribes of Celts, supposed to have come from India.

laws, and language of the Saxons superseded those of the ancient Britons, who became the slaves of the new conquerors. The Kingdom was divided by degrees into shires or counties, each shire having its law courts. There were numerous cities and burghs. The Church had its hierarchy of Archbishops, Bishops, and inferior Clergy; cathedrals and monasteries were built and endowed; and poetry and literature were cultivated. The language spoken and written was Saxon. The Saxons held England for over four centuries, with the exception of an interval of twenty-seven years, when the Danes obtained possession of the country, and established a dynasty. In 1041, the Crown was restored to the Saxons.

It is curious to observe in some of the institutions of the Saxons the germs of what is now existing. For instance, the Government, though Monarchical, was limited by an Assembly—The Witan—composed of Priests and Nobles. "The pervading principle," says Rowland, "of the Saxon government was aristocracy." But what is more striking is, that the Saxons were divided into three ranks—the Nobles, the Freemen, and the Slaves. The Nobles and Freemen were Saxon, whilst the slaves were the descendants of the conquered Britons. This free, or Middle Class was engaged in agriculture, or when living in towns, in various handicrafts. The slaves were employed either on the land or in the houses of their masters. The freeman of the Middle Class could by successful industry raise himself to the position of a Thane,* just as at the present day

* The Thanes were divided into King's Thanes, or Nobility; and the middle and inferior Thanes, or Gentry. If a freeman became owner of a certain quantity of land, or made three voyages in a ship, and with a cargo of his own, he was made a Thane.

the prominent men of the Middle Class are advanced to titles and dignities.

The conspicuous feature of this social organization was the free Middle Class; and it is to this class, as we shall see, the masses of the world owe their enfranchisement. No such class existed elsewhere in Europe, or had ever existed before. The Franks, like the Saxons, were of German origin; like the Saxons, they enslaved the inhabitants of the conquered country, but then they established the Feudal System; under which two classes of society only existed, the Nobility and the slaves. The Saxons, on the contrary, who conquered Britain and enslaved the inhabitants about the same period, broke up into the three classes mentioned, because the Feudal System was unknown there. We shall see its effect when introduced by the French. It is true the Saxon Middle Class possessed no political or municipal privileges till the thirteenth century; whereas the French *communes* or Middle Class which had sprung up, as already described, from the abuses of the Feudal System, were endowed with Municipal liberty in the twelfth century. There was this immense distinction, however, in the two cases. The Saxon Middle Class, which existed since the conquest of Britain, say in the sixth century, had always been Freemen, and were consequently inspired by a spirit of independence which could never be broken, and which was the parent, finally, of the Independence of the United States and of the French Revolution in 1789. The French Middle Class, on the other hand, emerged from bands of fugitive serfs accustomed to obedience and submission; and therefore, though enfranchised by one King, was easily deprived of self-government by another at a later period, as we have already seen.

The last Saxon King was Harold II., who usurped the throne on the death of Edward the Confessor, his brother-in-law, in 1066.

THE NORMAN CONQUEST

MIDDLE AGES.

THE cursory review of England during the Saxon Régime will convey some general idea of the civilization of the country prior to the Norman Conquest. In October of 1066, William, Duke of Normandy, landed at Hastings with 60,000 men, claiming the English throne. A battle ensued in which Harold was slain, and the Saxon dynasty overthrown. Many of the Saxon Nobility were killed, many emigrated, and others accepted the new King.

This event was the grandest in its results that history records, for it led ultimately to the birth of civil and religious liberty. The Norman Conquest introduced a new people and a new language, but more important still, a new political organization into England. The Duke of Normandy imported his *Coutume de Normandie*, as it was then called—the Custom of Normandy—which was nothing else than the Feudal System as then established in France: and thus the Feudal System was transplanted to English soil, with its Military service, its Primogeniture, Knighthood, Armorial bearings, and all its "pomp, pride, and circumstance."

William divided the lands of England among his captains, as the King of the Franks had done with Gaul. The conquered country was split up into

Baronies, with a Norman Chief as the Lord of each. The share given was proportioned to the rank of the Lord, the number of his vassals, and the supplies furnished to the expedition. For himself the Conqueror appropriated fourteen hundred and twenty-two large estates in different shires, besides other lands and farms recently the property of the Saxon Kings and the great Thanes.

The foundations of the Feudal System were thus laid, but William insisted that it should be acknowledged and consecrated by a solemn ceremony. Accordingly, all the great landowners met the King at Sarum, 1085, went on their knees one after the other before him, and declared that they had received their lands from him as their Lord Paramount. In Norman-French they thus spoke:—"I become your man from this day forward, of life and limb, and of earthly worship; and unto you shall be true and faithful, and bear to you faith for the tenements I claim to hold of you." The King then kissed each liegeman on the cheek, and the Oath of Fealty was taken:—"Hear this, my lord; I will be faithful and loyal to you, and will bear to you faith for the tenements I hold of you, and will loyally perform the customs and services which I owe to you, at the times assigned. So help me God and his Saints."

This was not all an idle form, for every landowner was bound under it to furnish the King a soldier fully accoutred for war for every twenty pounds a year he received from his land. In this way the King raised troops, before those standing armies appeared which in other countries ultimately broke up the Feudal System. The Conqueror took care, like Charlemagne and Hugh

Capet, to conciliate the Clergy by bestowing large quantities of land on the Church; but under the Feudal System no immunity was granted to ecclesiastical property. Every Bishop and Abbot was called on to provide soldiers for every twenty pounds of revenue. We shall see how little the Saxon Clergy liked this feudal usage, and how gladly they always united with the Barons to diminish the Royal Power. It will also be seen how much English history differed from French, although the Feudal System prevailed in both countries during the Middle Ages. In England the Priests and Nobles worked cordially against the King, which in France was not the case. In England the Middle Class saw their interest was to sustain the Barons; but in France they allowed themselves to be utilized by the King against the Aristocracy until the rise of a standing army destroyed their importance as allies. In England the Barons and the citizens shrewdly opposed any standing army. King John, it will be remarked, was obliged to employ foreign troops during the struggle for *Magna Charta.*

The Conqueror, as King of England, took a different view of Feudalism from that he took as Duke of Normandy. In France, as a feudal Lord, he sought to increase his power and to weaken the Monarchy; but in England, as King, he curtailed the influence of the Barons and augmented his own authority. This was not Feudalism as the French Lords understood it, and they would have at once taken up arms against the King, as had been the practice for so many centuries in France, but that serious obstacles compelled them for a time to submit.

One of these obstacles was William himself. His

great capacity and resolute character awed them. It may be seen from the following sketch he was a dangerous opponent. "We see him bold and ambitious, stern without anger, and merciful without kindness, choosing sternness or mercy as best served his purpose; thinking only of what would retard or promote his success, and careless whether he used sword or poison to remove an enemy, provided that the enemy was removed. At the same time he was influenced by the improving spirit of the time, and had an honest and generous purpose in favour of right and order, which must not be overlooked."

To this graphic portrait I will add, as a further illustration of the Conqueror's character, a story told in the words of an old chronicle of the time, and lately repeated in a book of M. Guizot. It was related that "Baldwin, Count of Flanders, had a daughter named Matilda, who was beautiful, learned, pious, a model of virtue and modesty. William demanded her in marriage, but Matilda answered, 'I would rather be a veiled nun than given in marriage to a bastard.' Duke William heard what answer the damsel had made, and not long after he took certain of his followers and went privily to Lille, where the Count of Flanders abode with his wife and the damsel. He entered the hall and passed on as if he had business, and so reached the chamber of the Countess; and there he found the damsel, Count Baldwin's daughter. Her he seized by the hair and dragged round the room, and spurned her with his foot, and did beat her. Then he went forth from the chamber, leapt upon his horse, which one held for him at the hall, set spurs to it, and went on his way. At this deed was Count Baldwin wroth ; and matters remained thus for a time, and after that Duke William sent once again to speak with Count Baldwin concerning the marriage. So the Count told the damsel his daughter, and she replied that it pleased her well. And then with much joy they twain were wedded. After all these matters were ended, Count Baldwin did laugh, and he asked his daughter why she had at last lightly consented to a marriage which at first she had so cruelly refused; and she made answer that she did not then know the Duke as she did afterwards, 'For,' said she, 'if he had not great heart and high courage, he would never have been so bold as dare to beat me in my father's chamber.'"

Evidently, William was not a man to be tampered with, and his Barons carefully avoided a collision. There was another obstacle, however, to quarrelling with the Crown in England. The French Lords found their new vassals, the Saxons, a very different race from their impetuous countrymen.* They were a sober, patient people, who had already acquired a taste for liberty from the early Charters of their Kings, and from the "good old laws" of Edward the Confessor, 1041 to 1066.† They were, besides, sullen and hostile to their new masters. The Barons found themselves helpless between an adverse population and an Arbitrary Monarchy, and at once saw that the Feudal System as established in France was

* Under the Saxon Government, "the people," says Rowland, "had no direct political power; but they were not rigidly excluded from it. A large proportion of them were freemen, and there were various methods by which even the serfs could obtain their freedom."

† These laws were favorable to the people, and originated with King Canute, 1017, and were confirmed by Edward the Confessor.

not possible in England. In France, the people were born the vassals of one feudal Lord or another, and they had had no idea of any other existence. This was Feudalism, not only in France, but in Italy and Germany; for no Middle Class of freemen had grown up in these countries before Feudality arose, as in England.

The Norman Lords, under these circumstances, perceived that they had little chance of dictating to the Monarchy in England, and exercising the license which they enjoyed at home, unless they could find vassals to carry out their plans. They saw the only way to enlist support was to divide the spoils of victory. With these views, they agreed to share with their Saxon adherents the power that was wrested from the Monarchy. The conquered people, on their part, accepted readily an alliance with their Norman Lords, but they were more intent on gaining liberty for themselves than in building up the supremacy of the Aristocracy, as the sequel will show.

In 1087, the Conqueror died,* and his second son, William Rufus, succeeded. We hear little of the Barons during his reign.

In 1100, Henry I., third son of the Conqueror, ascended the throne. He was at once involved in a war with his brother Robert, and afterwards with the King of France. To secure the support of the Barons, who were rapidly becoming formidable, he was obliged to grant them concessions at the expense of his own power.

* One of the last acts of his reign was to order a Survey of all the landed property in England, which was made and recorded in "Domesday Book," and is still preserved in a perfect state. No less than 25,000 serfs, or one-eleventh of the population of England in 1087, are registered in "Domesday Book."

This was the first advantage, the first triumph of the Aristocracy over the Monarchy.*

Stephen, Henry II., and Richard I. succeeded; but in their reigns there was no trouble with the Barons, who were quietly preparing for a decisive struggle. Henry II. had a violent contest with the Church, in which he was completely subdued.† The rule of these three Kings covered 64 years.

When John ascended the throne in 1199, over a hundred years had elapsed since the Conquest; and by this time the Saxons and the Normans, or the Freemen and the Barons, were in complete accord, and ready for action. Their motives were identical.‡ Each aimed at reducing the arbitrary power of the Monarchy, and both were resolved to appropriate a share of the political booty they meant to extort from the King.

* A grand event distinguished this reign. Trial by jury, never known before, was organized. For the first time also, nobles and commoners, clergy and laity, were taxed alike; and thus was established the principle of equal taxation.

† Henry II. attempted to reduce the power of the clergy in England, and issued decrees called the "Constitutions of Clarendon"—so named after his palace at Clarendon—which limited the jurisdiction of the ecclesiastical tribunals. This led to a revolt of the clergy against the king, in the course of which Thomas à Beckett, the Archbishop, was assassinated in the Cathedral of Canterbury. Henry was excommunicated by the Pope, and to conciliate the Church he revoked the "Constitutions of Clarendon," and did penance at the tomb of Thomas à Beckett. Abandoned and persecuted by all, he died in 1189.

‡ By this time, say various authorities, a new language began—Saxon blended with Norman. Also, all distinctive peculiarities of Saxon and Norman attire had disappeared. The process of the amalgamation of the two races was nearly complete.

FEUDALITY VANQUISHES THE MONARCHY.

MIDDLE AGES.

John began by usurping the throne, and plotting the murder of his nephew Arthur, the legal heir. He next engaged in a quarrel with the Pope, which led to his excommunication. To escape from this, he agreed to hold his Crown as the vassal of the Holy See, and to pay an annual subsidy. In a war with the French King, he lost Normandy, and all his fiefs in France. These and other acts made him odious.

The Barons saw that the opportunity for striking a blow at the Monarchy had arrived, and the Yeomen readily joined them. Their co-operation led to the birth of popular freedom in the shape of the *Magna Charta*. This is the first time in the world's history that the Supreme Power ever acknowledged "the rights and liberties of the people." This, too, is the first time that the Aristocracy and People ever united for such a purpose, and it could not have been accomplished without this co-operation.

It was in the Easter of 1215 that the Barons, followed by their vassals, appeared before Oxford, where John was then residing, resolved to wrest from him certain concessions or "liberties." Alarmed at their approach, the King sent to know what were the liberties they wanted. In reply, the confederates sent a list of their demands, which threw his Majesty into a rage, and provoked the exclamation, "And why do they not demand my crown also? By God's teeth, I will not grant them liberties that will make me a slave." The Barons declared war at once: but the King, startled at this decisive measure, proposed a Conference, which finally took place, in the "meadow called Runimede," on the 15th of June.

The Church united with the Barons and Freemen on this occasion, and Langton, the Archbishop of Canterbury, was one of the chief instigators of the movement. In consequence the Church obtained its share of the concessions that were made.

After the Church and the Barons came the turn of the Middle Class, or Freemen. Among the various clauses that were meant to protect them, there is one worth citing, as showing the iniquities then prevalent. Clause 38 says: "There shall be one measure of wine and one of ale through our whole realm, and one measure of corn, that is to say, the London quarter, and the weights shall be as the measures." This proves that it was common at that day to use false weights and measures, and that no law prevented it. There was another clause, however, worth all the rest, and that contained a pledge that had never before been uttered. This was the first time, as just stated, that a Government entered into a compact with the People, and bound itself to renounce tyranny and oppression. Clause 44 runs thus: "*We will sell to no man; we will not deny or delay to any man right or justice.*"

Strange that thousands of years had elapsed before such a bulwark against despotism was raised; strange that a combination of French Lords and Saxon Yeomen should have extorted from arbitrary power a confession of its wrongs; strange that but for these memorable words such a Government as that of the United States might never have existed.

English lawyers and historians are agreed in forming the highest estimate of this Charter. Sir Edward Coke spoke of it, in 1600, as "the foundation of all the fundamental laws of the realm." Hallam says, "It is the keystone of English liberty." Sir James Mackintosh remarks, "It contains maxims of just government applicable to all places and times, of which it is hardly possible to overrate the importance."

The liberties they obtained, however, were soon threatened. In spite of his solemn covenant, the King never intended to carry out the Charter; and no sooner had the Barons withdrawn, than he applied to the Pope for assistance. His Holiness issued a Bull forbidding the Barons to exact the observance of the Charter, and dispensing the King from paying any regard to it. John hired foreign troops and renewed the civil war. The Barons called on the son of the French King—afterwards Louis VIII.—to come and assume the English Crown; but in the midst of these commotions John died, 1216.

His son, Henry III., was no better disposed than his father to respect the Charter, and he violated it so often that the Barons had recourse to various expedients to enforce him to observe it. On one occasion they prepared an imposing ceremonial in the great Hall of Westminster, 1254, at which the King was present with his Barons and Prelates—the latter in full pontificals, and carrying burning tapers in their hands. The *Magna Charta* was then read before the Assembly, and the Ecclesiastics pronounced the sentence of excommunication against every one who should hereafter violate this fundamental Law. Then, throwing their torches on the ground, they exclaimed, "May the soul of every one who incurs this sentence so stink and corrupt in hell!" The King added —"So help me God, I will keep all these Articles inviolate, as I am a man, as I am a Christian, as I am a Knight, as I am a King, crowned and anointed!" The Pope, however, as in King John's time, stepped in with a dispensation, and relieved Henry of his oath.

Finally, the Barons resolved on a more decided course; and, under the lead of Simon de Montfort,* Earl of Leicester, induced the King to call a Great Council at Oxford, 1258, which consisted of Prelates and Nobles. These came to the Assembly attended by their vassals, and, taking the King prisoner, forced him to sign some new Laws known as the "Provisions of Oxford."

These Laws, which the King again swore to observe, put the Government under the direct control of 24 Barons, selected for the purpose. Henry once more applied to the Pope, who in a new Bull denounced the "Provisions of Oxford," and relieved the King of all obligation. A war then ensued between the Barons and the King, who was routed at the battle of Lewes, 1264, and taken prisoner. His son Edward was also detained in Dover Castle as a hostage.

This led to another great event, only second in im-

* Simon de Montfort was son of Count de Montfort, the Crusader, and was a Frenchman. He inherited, by his father's marriage with an Englishwoman, large possessions in England, and came to settle there in 1236. He was welcomed by Henry III., who gave him his sister's hand, and made him Governor of Gascony. He was afterwards, however, recalled in disgrace, and readily joined the conspiracy of the Barons against the King.

portance to *Magna Charta*, namely, the Representation of the People, by the creation of a *House of Commons*. Up to this period, both before and after the Christian era, there had been numerous Assemblies regulating and controlling the destiny of nations, but they had always consisted of the Upper Classes only. This was the first time the phenomenon occurred that any class below the Nobility and the Clergy was called on to send its Delegates to take part in the creation of laws for the common government of all.

At this epoch in England the King engrossed the whole power. The Executive control was entirely in his hands, and he was the author of all the laws, asking when he chose the mere formal assent of his Prelates and Barons. Furthermore, the King held possession of the Kingdom as he might of a private estate. Not only did he derive a large revenue from the Royal domains, but, by the feudal laws, the Barons held their lands as if from his bounty, and paid him a large income. The King also levied tolls on the Royal towns, or received in place of tolls a fee-farm rent. The merchandise imported and exported also paid tribute to him; and he had a right to the prisage of wine—two casks out of every ship. The money so derived he spent as he pleased: in the expenses of his Government; in his own household; in peace or in war. When this revenue was sufficient, the people were spared, and were content; but when the King required larger subsidies from his subjects, he assembled his great Council of Priests and Nobles, and called for their co-operation.

The vast importance of the great change I am speaking of may be estimated when it is seen that it swept away this irresponsible despotism, and wrested the right of taxation from the hands of the King and the Aristocracy, to deposit it in those of the Commonalty, where it has since remained.

The capture of Henry III. at Lewes, as related, vested the Sovereign power in the Barons, and they decided promptly to call on the freemen of the Middle Class to co-operate with them in curbing the tyranny of the Monarchy. Evidently this was the surest means to strengthen themselves and weaken the King. Accordingly they authorized their leader, Simon de Montfort, to summon, in the name of the captive King, a Great Council or Parliament to meet in London, January 20th, 1265.

The Prelates and Barons were summoned by writs in the King's name, as were also two Knights from each county. The records show that 23 lay Lords and 122 Ecclesiastics, including Abbots, Priors, and Deans, attended the Assembly.

It also appears by the record that writs were sent to all the cities and boroughs of England, commanding them to send "two of the more discrete, lawful, and honest of their citizens and burgesses" to the Parliament.

This beyond all question is the first appearance of the People on the political stage. Hallam remarks, "After long controversy, almost all judicious enquirers seem to have acquiesced in admitting that this is the origin of *popular representation*." In the writs addressed to the "citizens and burgesses" the purpose of their attendance was stated to be "to treat on the King's affairs, with the King, Prelates, and Magnates."

Not long after Prince Edward escaped from Dover Castle, and took up arms against the Barons, who were beaten at the battle of Evesham, August, 1265, and

Montfort was slain. The King was released from bondage, and no more was heard of popular representation during his reign.

Edward I. succeeded Henry III. in 1272. He was constantly engaged in war. He conquered Wales, and annexed it. He had also frequent conflicts with Scotland. To obtain the subsidies demanded, he found it necessary at last to adopt the example set by the Barons; and in the twenty-third year of his reign he, too, summoned the "citizens and burgesses" to Parliament. What the father of Edward regarded as an usurpation was now by the act of Edward himself established as the law of the land. Only two years later he consented to a Statute which restricted the power of the King over taxation. He bound himself to the Lords spiritual and temporal and to the Commonalty of the land that "for no business he would take any aids, tasks, nor prises, but by the *common assent of the realm*, and for the common profit thereof."

In this way and at this early date, nearly 600 years ago, was the foundation laid in England for the redemption of the masses, the world over, from the bondage and tyranny they had endured, utterly helpless, for thousands of years.*

In the reign of Edward II., who succeeded in 1307, the power of the Barons and the Freemen gradually increased.

In the second year of this Monarch's reign a Petition of the Commons appears on the Rolls of Parliament. It is couched in humble terms, but complaints at that

* Rowland remarks that it required 85 years to establish the *Magna Charta* as settled law, from its grant by King John down to the 28th year of the reign of Edward I.

day were bold innovations. It ran thus:—"The good people of the kingdom, who are come hither to Parliament, pray our Lord the King, that he will, if it please him, have regard to his poor subjects, who are much aggrieved, by reason that they are not governed as they should be, especially as to the articles of the Great Charter; and for this, if it please him, they pray remedy." The grievances are then enumerated: "that the King's purveyors seize great quantities of victuals without payment; that new customs (duties) are set on wines, clothing, and other imports; that the collectors of the King's dues in towns and fairs take more than is lawful; that men are delayed in civil suits by writs of protection; that felons escape from punishment by procuring charters of pardon." In reply to this petition, which was written in Norman-French, the King promised redress; and, in return for this promise, the Commons granted him a subsidy of a twenty-fifth of their movables. This grant was made by them alone, apart from the Barons, and to affect only the property of their own order, which was a novelty of considerable importance.

Edward II. was a debauchee, and completely under the control of his favorites. Great abuses were the result of the ill conduct of the King. The Barons again confederated, and forced him to sign new Ordinances curtailing his prerogatives. Among them was one by which the King bound himself "to hold a Parliament once in every year, or twice if there should be need." Another Ordinance was, that "money should not be altered without great occasion, and then by the common advice of the Baronage in Parliament." Ten years afterwards the King raised an army, and defeated the

Barons at Burton. The Ordinances were repealed, and the King reasserted his prerogatives—at the same time, however, acknowledging the joint authority of the Lords and Commons. Five years later Edward was again assailed by the Barons. The Earl of Mortimer landed at Harwich with some Flemish troops, and, being joined by numerous Lords with their vassals, raised the standard of rebellion. The King fled to Wales, but was captured. He was then formally deposed by Parliament for various gross abuses duly set forth, and his son Edward III. was proclaimed King.* In thus driving Edward II. from the throne, and giving to this action legal form, the Parliament added to its prestige.

In the reign of Edward III., the power of the Commons made gradual advances. They were now regularly appealed to when money was required, and they never failed to demand some new concessions before granting it. At a Parliament in the thirteenth year of this reign they said, "They would vouch to the King 2,500 sacks of wool whereon to borrow money immediately, but that if the conditions they had proposed were agreed to by the King they would raise the grant to 30,000 sacks."

In this reign the Commons began to sit separately from the Lords in the Chapter House of Westminster Abbey. It was also in this reign that the Commons

* The unfortunate King was imprisoned by the Earl of Mortimer, and cruelly murdered, a hot iron being thrust into his entrails. Three years later, 1330, his son Edward began to govern, and he immediately hanged Mortimer and imprisoned his mother, who was suspected of conniving at the assassination. During the reign of Edward II. the victory of Bannockburn was won by the Scots under Robert Bruce, which heightened the unpopularity of the King. Edward II. was the first to bear the title of Prince of Wales.

exercised for the first time the power of Impeachment. Articles were framed against Richard Lyon, a merchant of London, and the Lord Latimer, one of the King's Councillors, for certain abuses, one of which was bargaining with the King's creditors, for their claims, and procuring the King to pay them in full. Lyon and Latimer were imprisoned, and suffered forfeiture of their goods and chattels. In the fifty-first year of this reign we find the first mention by name of a Speaker of the House of Commons, Sir Thomas Hungerford, Knight.

It was Edward III. who founded the Order of the Garter—1349—and built Windsor Castle. He also ordered, with the assent of the Lords and Commons, that the statutes and law proceedings should be in English, instead of French, as hitherto.

Richard II. succeeded to the throne in 1377.

During his minority an Insurrection of the villeins or serfs occurred in the neighbourhood of London. Their leader was Wat, a tyler by trade, who killed a collector of taxes, and raised a formidable revolt. The insurgents marched on London, and before they could be checked great damage was done. The palace of the Archbishop of Canterbury was burnt, and the Archbishop murdered. Other palaces were destroyed, and besides the Archbishop, several persons of distinction were killed. To conciliate the rebels, the young King offered them freedom. A parley took place, at which the King was present. Wat, however, having been guilty of some act of insolence, was killed on the spot by the Lord Mayor. A band of armed men overawed the rioters, and compelled them quietly to disperse. So ended the Rebellion.

The Parliament unanimously demanded the recall of the manumissions granted by the King under the influence of the tumult, but the Commons blamed him as the chief cause of it.* They closed their remonstrance in these words :—"To speak the real truth, these injuries lately done to the poorer Commons, more than they ever suffered before, caused them to rise, and commit the mischief done in their late riot."

In the tenth year of this reign, the Commons impeached the Lord Chancellor. The King resented this act, but the Commons were not intimidated. They resolved, "they neither could, nor by any means would, proceed in any business of Parliament, or despatch so much as the least article of it, till the King could come and show himself in person amongst them, and remove Michael de la Pole from his office." This demand was finally complied with.

The King's conduct, however, continuing to grow worse, the Parliament determined to depose him, and his cousin the Duke of Lancaster was raised to the throne as Henry IV. The Commons impeached several other persons during this Parliament, a proof of their growing importance. Richard was adjudged to perpetual imprisonment, and it is supposed he was assassinated by order of his successor.

We find in the ninth year of Henry's reign a remarkable proof of the extent to which the Commons had consolidated their power. The King had demanded a

* A record of the time states that "from this time we find little more of the villeins. Their manumission required neither letters patent of the King nor Act of Parliament. The lords relaxed, and gradually abandoned, their right to their services; and when that was given up, the villeins were not distinguished in condition from their free fellow-subjects."

subsidy of the Lords in Parliament. The Lords having complied, the King desired the Commons to follow the example of the Upper House. The Commons declared this was "a derogation of their liberties;" and it was finally settled that "it should be lawful for the Lords to commune amongst themselves of the state of the realm, and that it should be lawful for the Commons on their part to commune together, and that no report should be made to the King of any subsidy by the Commons granted, and by the Lords assented to, before the Lords and Commons should be of one assent and accord in such matters, and then in manner and form as had been accustomed, that is by the mouth of the Speaker of the Commons." This was a great triumph for both Houses of Parliament, for it established the independent action of each, whilst it required the assent of both "to any report to the King," that is, to any law. "The two Houses of Parliament," observes Rowland, "thus acquired the constitutional action that now exists. In other words, the Regal or *Executive* functions ot the government were separated from the *Legislative*; placing the latter in two distinct Houses, representing the aristocratic and democratic classes, with definite although similar functions, with separate power of deliberation, and with separate wills; but requiring joint concurrence in any measure that should be presented to the King, and his assent to it before it became a law."

It is assuredly remarkable that Constitutional Government should have made such progress as this in England in 1407. What a contrast to the condition of France and the rest of Europe at this time, which were wholly under the sway of force, and where such phrases as "popular liberty," and "constitutional rights and usages," would have been unintelligible!

Henry V. succeeded his father in 1413, and suddenly forsook the dissolute ways to which he had abandoned himself while a Prince.

Seeing that France was a prey to a civil war between two Aristocratic factions contending for power, he declared war against her, won the battle of Agincourt, and finally became the Regent, after conquering nearly the whole of France.

Amid the din of war, little is heard of Parliament. In the second year of this reign, however, the House of Commons protested against statutes passed without their assent, "considering," as their Petition to the King declared, "that the Commons of your land, which is, and ever hath been, a member of your Parliament, are as well assenters as petitioners." The King, in his reply, promised that henceforth they should not be "bound without their assent."

Henry VI. was only eight months old when his father died, 1422. He was proclaimed King of England and France under the Regency of his uncles.

The war with France was carried on for some years; but peace was finally concluded, and cemented by the marriage of Henry with a French Princess, Margaret of Anjou.

The Government of England fell entirely into the hands of the Queen, as Henry was weak to imbecility.

A few years later, the Earl of Warwick, the "King-maker," who was connected with the York branch of the Royal Family, endeavored to raise the Duke of York to the throne occupied by Henry of the Lancaster branch. The leaders in this civil war, the "War of the Two Roses," * were Warwick and Margaret. The Barons sided with either faction, and after several battles, Margaret was forced to fly. Henry was imprisoned in the Tower, and Edward IV. of the York branch was made King, 1461. Warwick afterwards quarrelled with Edward, 1469, and espoused the side of Henry, who was restored to the throne, Edward being put to flight in his turn. In less than a year Edward returned with foreign troops, and, joined by his partisans, gave battle to Warwick at Barnet, 1471. Warwick was defeated and killed; Henry went back to the Tower; Margaret ultimately to France, and their son was assassinated. Edward IV. resumed the Crown, and for the rest of his reign gave himself up to the control of his favorite, Jane Shore.

Amid all the commotions of this tempestuous reign, the art of Printing, invented in Germany, crept into England. Caxton studied it whilst a merchant in Holland, and returning home in 1472, published the first printed book in 1474.

Edward V. was proclaimed King on his father's death, 1483, but being only 12 years old, his uncle, the Duke of Gloucester, assumed the Regency. Two months later he was assassinated with his younger brother, in the Tower, by order of Gloucester, who then usurped the throne as Richard III. Detested for his many atrocities, Richard was defeated and killed at the battle of Bosworth Field, 1485, by the Earl of Richmond, who claimed the throne as descended from the widow of

* The "War of the Two Roses" was so called from the rival parties wearing badges inscribed with a red or a white rose. The Lancaster party wore a red, and the York party a white rose.

Henry V., who married Owen Tudor, a Welsh gentleman.

With the death of Richard III. and the accession of the Earl of Richmond as Henry VII., the civil war between the factions of York and Lancaster, which lasted some thirty-three years, ended.

THE MONARCHY AGAIN IN THE ASCENDANT.

SIXTEENTH CENTURY.

THE growth of Parliament was utterly checked during this stormy period. From the date of *Magna Charta* down to Henry VI., the Barons and the Middle Class had co-operated to increase their power at the expense of the Monarchy. The civil war wholly changed the position: for the Barons and Middle Class were divided in their support to the rival pretensions of the two Royal claimants, and so wasted the energies hitherto concentrated on constitutional victories. The result was that when Henry Tudor, Earl of Richmond, mounted the throne, 1485, he found it easy to restore the Monarchy to the power it enjoyed before the birth of Parliament. "The destruction of the nobility in the civil wars," says Rowland, "by lowering the power of the aristocracy, placed Henry VII. in a condition to acquire and exercise absolute power." The number of Barons was reduced to 40: the Clergy were thus in a majority in the House of Lords, and the Clergy gave their support to the King. The Commons, having lost their old leaders, made no opposition to Royal authority. The spirit of independence formerly displayed by the "citizens and burgesses" in Parliament was never visible during the period when the Tudor family occupied the throne. Henry VII. set the example of keeping the Nobility down, and his son Henry VIII., and his grandchild Elizabeth, adopted his tactics. The consequence was that the Middle Class, deprived of their former chiefs in the House of Lords, were completely cowed, and remained so down to James I., when the Nobility raised their heads once more, and renewed their old opposition to Absolute Monarchy. Henry VII. was always on his guard against the Barons, "for he kept," says Lord Bacon, "a strait hand on his nobility, and chose rather to advance clergymen and lawyers which were more obsequious to him, but had less interest in the people; which made for his absoluteness, but not for his safety. For his nobles, though they were loyal and obedient, did not co-operate with him, but let every man go his own way." This passage from Lord Bacon, who wrote in the reign of Elizabeth, shows that the Nobles had been so exhausted by the civil wars, that they dared no longer stimulate the Middle Class to resist arbitrary power.

During this reign Canada and Nova Scotia were discovered by the Cabots, who were patronized by the King.

We now enter upon the sixteenth century, usually considered the close of the Middle Ages; but it is questionable if the epoch known as Modern Times can be said to commence before the institutions of the Middle Ages were overthrown; that is, until the year 1688 in England and the year 1789 in France.

Be that as it may, the sixteenth century is renowned for the successful effort in England to suppress the despotism of the primitive Church. For centuries the Papacy had controlled the Governments of Europe by its spiritual power over the masses. Kings and Princes struggled against the yoke, but were fain to submit. Superstition began to lose ground in the sixteenth century; and Luther dared to protest against the domination of the Pope, and to call on the people to read the Scriptures and work out their own salvation. The invention of Printing now made the Bible accessible to all.

This rebellion against the authority of the Church in the sixteenth century in England was the forerunner of the rebellion against the authority of the State in the seventeenth century.

To England belongs the glory of having pioneered the human race to its emancipation. She became, from the accidents of her history, the champion of humanity against the arbitrary power which the Minority had always, in the name of religion and government, exercised over the Majority of men. The alliance of her Aristocracy and Middle Class, a phenomenon impossible elsewhere, forced Absolute Monarchy, in the thirteenth century, to surrender "rights and liberties" never before conceded to mankind. The hope of freedom thus engendered led the nation, in the sixteenth century, to support a hot-brained King in his impassioned assault on the Papal power. Whilst the growth of political liberty in England is due to the union of her Aristocracy and Freemen, it is equally clear that her religious liberty could not have been secured if this partnership had not been maintained. In the reigns of Henry VIII. and Elizabeth, when the ecclesiastical monopoly was abolished, and free trade in religion initiated, it is true the hands of the Aristocracy and Middle Class were not so visible as in the political struggles of previous reigns, but neither Henry nor Elizabeth could have conquered the Pope if the Aristocracy and Middle Class had not supported them. The Aristocracy may have been divided by religious scruples, as was also the Middle Class; but the majority of both foresaw that the downfall of religious despotism would necessarily prepare the same fate for political tyranny.

The Tudor Kings, from Henry VII. to Elizabeth—1485 to 1603—were more absolute than either Norman or Plantagenet, and simply because the Aristocracy were crippled by the civil wars, and unable, as before, to lead the Middle Class against the common enemy. Thus it was that during the Tudor dynasty, Parliament seemed to abdicate its old *rôle* of extending its privileges and curtailing those of the Monarchy. No doubt the peremptory commands of Henry and Elizabeth were cheerfully obeyed when Papal domination was in question; but that no opposition was made to the efforts of Philip and Mary to restore it, is difficult to explain, save by the fear of an invasion from Spain, whose King was the father of Philip. This invasion was actually attempted in the reign of Elizabeth.

These preliminary remarks will awaken attention to the great event of the sixteenth century.

Henry VIII. succeeded to the throne in 1509. He married soon after at eighteen, Catherine, daughter of Ferdinand and Isabella of Spain. She had previously married his brother Arthur, who died at the end of five months. The legality of her second marriage was doubted at the time, and at a later period, Henry made this uncertainty a pretext for a divorce.

During the earlier years of his reign he left the Government in the hands of Cardinal Wolsey, his Minister and favorite. The Clergy sustained by Wolsey exercised unbounded power: and hesitated at no abuses or exactions. "It was common at this time for persons, after committing great crimes," says Rowland, "to go into the priesthood to avoid punishment."

Subsidies for the wars with France were constantly demanded of Parliament, who humbly remonstrated, but dared not refuse. The King frequently resorted to forced loans, if the grants were inadequate.*

England at this period was writhing under the double tyranny of the Church and the Crown. Parliament, that had formerly deposed two Kings, and forced Henry IV., a hundred years before, to retreat before their energetic resistance, was now dumb in the presence of the insolent Wolsey, who, as Cardinal and Minister, wielded the thunderbolts of both Church and State.

At this dreary moment occurred "one of the greatest events in history," as Hallam calls it. The language of Bacon is no less striking when he says, referring to Henry's first marriage, "The secret providence of God ordained that marriage to be the occasion of great events and changes." After living eighteen years with Catherine of Arragon, the sensual King conceived a violent passion for Anne Boleyn, a Maid of Honor to the Queen. Resolved to divorce Catherine, and marry Anne, he applied to Pope Clement, 1527, for a Bull to dissolve his first union. Henry had been a zealous son of the Church, and had, by writing a book against the

* The danger of refusing to subscribe to these loans may be seen in the fact that an Alderman of London, Richard Reed, who would not contribute, was sent down to serve as a common soldier on the Scottish border, and the General in command there was ordered to employ him on the hardest and most perilous duty.

heresy of Luther, secured for himself the title from the Pope of "Defender of the Faith." His Holiness was anxious to oblige the enamored King, and grant the divorce, but Charles V., Emperor of Germany and King of Spain, who was nephew to Catherine, forbade him to do so.

With the Pope's consent, however, a trial for divorce began in London at the Black Friars' Convent, 1529, before the Legates of the Pope, Cardinals Campeggio and Wolsey. Catherine appeared in person, denied the jurisdiction of the Court, and appealed to Rome. After sundry delays the Court broke up, by order of the Pope, without pronouncing a divorce. Wolsey was disgraced for this failure, and stript of his honors and wealth.

Thomas Cranmer, a Professor of Theology in Cambridge University, sustained the divorce, and suggested to the King to ask the opinion of the Universities of Europe, on the question whether a marriage with a brother's widow were lawful. This was done, and the Universities, including those of Oxford and Cambridge, supported the King. Cranmer was sent to Rome, where several of Henry's Ambassadors had already gone, to obtain if possible the coveted Bull for the divorce.

Irritated at the Pope's indecision, Henry summoned a Parliament, 1529, after an interval of seven years, to give legal expression to his anger. The House of Commons, eager to avenge itself on the Clergy, showed great readiness to carry out the King's purpose. They sent a Petition to the King, reflecting severely on the "vices and corruptions of the clergy," adding this singular phrase: "which were believed to flow from men who had Luther's doctrines in their hearts." This is a proof how little the Reformation was foreseen or meditated by Parliament or the King. To alarm the Pope, Henry had three Statutes passed in this Parliament, curtailing the privileges of the Clergy.

No attack was yet made on the authority of the Pope. In the Parliament of 1531, as a new menace, a Law was enacted depriving the Pope of his fees for the consecration of English Bishops; and it was stated in the preamble that "£160,000 had passed in this way out of the realm since the second year of Henry VII."

As His Holiness still procrastinated, the Parliament of 1532, at the desire of the King, aimed a serious blow at the Papacy, by a Statute "For the Restraint of Appeals to Rome." By this Law whoever carried his case "out of the jurisdiction of the realm" for decision at Rome, as was customary hitherto, incurred the severest penalties. Henry withheld for a time his signature to this decided act of hostility. At last, driven furious by the Pope's inaction, he made Cranmer Archbishop of Canterbury, and ordered him to assemble a Court of Inquiry, at which the Archbishop presided. This Court in May, 1533, pronounced the desired divorce; but the amorous King had already married Anne Boleyn in November, 1532, and she gave birth to a daughter, the Princess Elizabeth, in September, 1533.

The Pope declared the sentence of Cranmer null, as well as the second marriage. All hope of reconciliation with the Pope was now abandoned; and, expecting the thunders of excommunication to fall on him for this contempt of Papal authority, Henry resolved upon open war.

The first step of the King was to secure the allegiance of the English Clergy. They were summoned to choose between the spiritual authority of the King and that of the Pope. The Clergy, in equal dread of the Parliament and the Crown, promptly recognized the King as the Head of the Church in England. Statute now followed statute against "the Bishop of Rome, otherwise called the Pope." New modes of consecrating the Archbishops and Bishops were provided, and new processes devised for carrying on the spiritual affairs of the Kingdom. Everything was planned to put an end to the power of the Pope in England, and to prevent him extracting pecuniary benefit from the English people. The House of Commons sent a Petition to the King, saying "that his subjects were greatly decayed and impoverished by the intolerable exactions of the Bishop or the See of Rome, pretending and persuading them he had the power to dispense with human laws in causes which were called spiritual, whereas your Grace's realm, recognizing no superior under God, but only your Grace, hath been, and is free from subjection to any man's laws—but only such laws as have been made within this realm, and not the laws of any foreign prince, potentate, or prelate—which the King, the Lords temporal, and the Commons in Parliament have full power to abrogate and annul as to them shall seem meet for the good of the realm."

This was the old spirit of resistance to arbitrary rule which the Lords and Commons had displayed from *Magna Charta* down to the civil wars; and if the impetuous King had been more sagacious he would not have rekindled the flame of independence which was still smouldering in the breast of the Nation. With the keenest relish the Lords and Middle Class followed the headstrong Henry in his war on the despotism of the Pope, secretly meaning when the time came to put a similar check on the tyranny of the Crown.

Amid the booming of the Parliamentary guns, the King of France, Francis I., tried to reconcile Henry with the Pope. The attempt was foiled by a mere accident.

The Parliament of 1534 declared "the King's Grace to be the authorised Supreme Head of the English Church," which the Clergy had already felt themselves constrained to acknowledge. All persons were required to subscribe to this declaration by Oath. The Oath was generally taken throughout the Kingdom. Some persons refused, and were executed for High Treason. Amongst those who hesitated was the celebrated scholar, Sir Thomas More, formerly Speaker of the Commons, and who had succeeded Wolsey as Lord Chancellor. He resigned this post, disapproving of the King's quarrel with the Pope. Cranmer urged him vehemently to take the "Oath of Supremacy," but in vain. He was imprisoned in the Tower for some months, and, persisting in his obstinacy, was tried and executed. Some Charter House Monks also refused the Oath, and were beheaded in their ecclesiastical dress.

The heaviest blow at Papal influence, however, was given in the Parliament of 1535 when the Monasteries were attacked. The King was glad enough to enrich his coffers with the spoils of the Church, and the people generally thought that this confiscation of the Monasteries might diminish taxation. Still as there was great reverence for these ancient establishments, it was thought politic to undermine them adroitly before breaking them up.

Commissioners were consequently appointed for a general inspection of the "smaller Monasteries." The Report of these Commissioners was laid on the table of the House of Commons, and was made the basis of the Law dissolving the Monasteries. The preamble is full of animosity against these establishments, declaring that "manifest sin, vicious, carnal, and abominable luxury is daily used and committed in such little and small abbeys, priories, and other religious houses of monks, canons, and nuns. Amendment has been long tried, but their vicious living shamelessly increaseth and augmenteth." The remedy adopted was "to suppress such small houses, and that the religious persons therein be committed to great and honorable monasteries of religion in this realm wherein (thanks to God) religion is right well kept and observed." The Law then gave the King all the small Monasteries, "with their lands, tithes, and tenements, and all their ornaments, jewels, goods, moveables, and debts."

Four years later a Statute was levelled at the larger Monasteries. This Statute stated that the abbots, priors, abbesses, and prioresses had "of their own free and voluntary minds, goodwill, and assents," renounced their monasteries, abbeys, and priories, which with all their lands and other property were given to the King.

His Majesty apparently cared little for the lands, for he gave some away, and sold more at low prices to the nobility, gentry, merchants, and traders. "The liberation of so much property," says Rowland, "from the inertness of monastic rule and its distribution and diffusion amongst so many persons could not be but a benefit to the nation." Hallam thinks that a great many estates of the families of the day, both within and without the Peerage, obtained their titles at this time and in this way. Certes, most of the Nobility who had lost their property in the civil wars were glad to get these lands cheap, which enabled them to build up again their political and social importance. Thus it happened that the English Monarchy in driving the Pope out of England unwittingly put weapons in the hands of the Aristocracy and Middle Class which were afterwards destined to destroy its own power.

One effect of the abolition of the Monasteries was striking. Twenty-six Parliamentary abbots and two Parliamentary priors lost their seats in the House of Lords; and thus at the ensuing Parliament there were present only 20 spiritual Peers to 41 temporal Peers. Sooner or later this change was destined to have considerable influence on the position of the Crown.

It should not be inferred from the overthrow of the Papacy that the Catholic religion had been superseded in England. This was by no means the case, as will be seen from the six new Dogmas Henry desired Parliament to enforce by law:—

First, the Real Presence at the Sacrament; second, Communion in one Kind only; third, that Priests may not marry; fourth, that Vows of Chastity or Widowhood ought to be observed; fifth, that Private Masses be continued in the English Church; sixth, Auricular Confession. Any person teaching, preaching, or holding opinions contrary to these Articles was to suffer death, and to forfeit his lands and goods as a felon. It is plain from this that in Henry's time the Reformation had made very little progress, though he unquestionably prepared the ground for it very effectually.

It is singular that the frantic passion of the lustful King for Anne Boleyn led to the advent of Protestantism in England; and yet in three short years he beheaded her on the pretext of adultery. The day after, he married Jane Seymour, who had been a Maid of Honor to Anne, as the latter had been to Catherine. His third wife died in a year, after giving birth to a son. The fourth wife, Anne of Cleves, he repudiated by Act of Parliament, and then married Catherine Howard, grand-child of the Duke of Norfolk. He beheaded her two years afterwards on the charge of infidelity, and married Catherine Parr, the widow of Lord Latimer, who survived him.

Henry wound up his turbulent career by restoring to the Crown some of its "ancient prerogatives" granted away by his progenitors. Parliament ventured on no resistance to his tyrannical instincts, satisfied with their emancipation from the gripe of the Church. The reckoning with Royalty was reserved for hereafter. During this reign the first Bankrupt law on record was passed.

Edward VI., son of Jane Seymour, succeeded in 1547. Being only nine years old, the Kingdom was administered by his uncle, the Duke of Somerset, as Lord Protector, with a Council of which Archbishop Cranmer was the head.

Parliament under the influence of these two distinguished men continued its legislation against Rome.

It was declared High Treason to say or write that the King was not Head of the Church, or that the Pope was. The Parliament also took away benefit of Clergy, or Sanctuary, from persons convicted of murder and sundry other offences, but declared that "a Lord of Parliament or Peer of the realm, should of common grace have benefit of clergy, *though he could not read*, for the first offence." It likewise repealed many of the late tyrannical statutes of Henry VIII.

The reign of Edward lasted only six years; but the Schism in the Church was actively promoted by Archbishop Cranmer and Bishops Latimer and Ridley. The Protestant sect made rapid progress. The Book of Common Prayer now used dates from this reign.

Mary, daughter of Catherine of Arragon, succeeded in 1553, being then thirty-seven years old. She was the first Queen Regnant since the Conquest. Mary inherited her father's barbarous disposition, and began her bloody reign by executing Lady Jane Grey—a descendant of Henry VII., and only seventeen years of age—for aspiring to the throne. This accomplished Princess was involved in this attempt against her will by the intrigues of the Duke of Northumberland, who was also beheaded.

Mary was a rigid Catholic, and married her relative, the bigot Philip, son of Charles V. of Spain, 1554. The Queen and her husband began a fierce crusade against the Protestant converts. Archbishop Cranmer was arrested as a heretic, and though he retracted, was executed. During Mary's brief reign of five years, one Archbishop, three Bishops, and many Clergymen, with three hundred of the laity, perished at the stake, whilst many others died in prison.

Parliament was forced to pass a Law repealing all the Acts of Henry and Edward against the See Apostolic of Rome; but it was found impossible to restore the Church property granted away, and Her Majesty was less anxious on this point, as a good deal of it still belonged to the Crown. The power of the Monarchy at this time may be measured from the fact that Parliament could thus be forced to abolish all its recent legislation against the Papacy.

Mary died, in 1558, of grief at the neglect of Philip,* who abandoned her two years after their marriage. The loss of Calais, which had been reconquered by the French, is said to have hastened her demise.

Elizabeth, daughter of Anne Boleyn, succeeded in 1558, being then twenty-five years old. Her father at first excluded her from the throne, calling her illegitimate, and consigned her to seclusion. This hardened her character, and stimulated her intellect. She acquired extensive knowledge, and was mistress of the French, Italian, Latin, and Greek languages.

No one contested her title in England, but the Pope forbade her to assume the Crown without his consent, and claimed England as a fief of the Papacy from the time of King John; at the same time assuring the Queen of his friendly disposition, if she would acknowledge his Supremacy. Elizabeth recalled her Ambassador from Rome, and set the Pope at defiance. She gave liberty to all imprisoned for their religion, and selected for her Ministers those favorable to the new Sect. A Parliament was called, which readily restored to the Crown the ecclesiastical supremacy vested by Mary in the Pope; re-enacted the laws of Henry and Edward, and then went heartily to work to build up the new worship. The new church, or Church of England, was organized on the basis of the "Thirty-nine Articles"

* It would seem that Philip was much fonder of pork than his wife, for he used to dine on it daily, and eat so much as to be frequently ill. Even up to this time pork was in general consumption, and some centuries earlier it constituted almost the only article of food, as beef, veal and mutton were comparatively unknown. In France, Charlemagne kept in his forests immense droves of swine.

agreed on by the Convocation of Bishops, where it reposes to this day.

Elizabeth inherited the domineering spirit of her father, and she was resolved that no one should govern in England but herself—neither Pope, Nobility, nor Middle Class. She displayed great vigor in extinguishing the old religion, and such was the jealousy of foreign influence that popular feeling sustained her. The legislation against the Catholics became more and more severe. An Insurrection at last broke out in the north of England to supersede Elizabeth by raising Mary Queen of Scots to the throne. The Pope encouraged the effort, and issued a Bull, excommunicating Elizabeth, and depriving her of the Crown for "her heinous crimes against the Church." The rising was unsuccessful, and new laws of greater rigor followed. Every kind of penalty up to death was distributed against those who read or listened to Bulls, or who brought into the realm "things called *Agnus Dei*, or any pictures, crosses, beads, or such like superstitious things, consecrated, as it is termed, by the Bishop of Rome."

In nearly every Parliament of her long reign, Popery in all its phases was passionately denounced. In that of 1581, penalties were decreed against "every one who should say or sing Mass." In that of 1585, an Act was passed, expelling "Jesuits, seminary priests, and other such like disobedient persons." In that of 1593, a Law was made, "restraining Popish recusants to some certain places of abode."

All these statutes were meant to establish the supremacy of the Crown, as against all foreign Potentates, as well as to settle the national religion. This extreme legislation was acceptable to the Nation, not so much out of love for the new doctrines, as the desire to be independent of all foreign domination. Great misery must have ensued from these cruel edicts, but no complete record exists of the thousands who suffered from fines, imprisonment, and banishment. Historians compute that some two hundred Catholics were put to death in this reign of forty-five years.

During most of her sway, "Queen Bess" had been so engrossed in her struggle with the Catholics, that she failed to perceive a New Sect had developed itself until it was actually standing upright before her. Well might the Queen be puzzled by the appearance, and more still by the novel ideas of this Sect. This mysterious band of devotees entirely approved the persecution of the Catholics; did not dispute, like the Papists, the temporal authority of the Queen; did not even desire to separate from the new national Church, but only to reform it. Here had Elizabeth spent nearly all her life enforcing on the poor Catholics her Reformed religion, and now a new-born organization had sprung up which proposed to reform that! Luther, too, who had so recently picked holes in the time-worn garments of Catholicism, now had his new drapery of German manufacture disparaged even before its gloss had gone. One form of scepticism had already created another. Heresy was on its march. Elizabeth and her advisers must have been perplexed by these new-comers, who were not only anxious to carry out the Reformation, then all the vogue, but wished to carry it further than the Protestant Elizabeth or her Protestant Ministers of State had ever meditated. They proposed dropping all forms and ceremonies which the express word of Scripture did not support. They did not approve of the symbol of the Cross, of the surplice, of the ring in marriage, or of kneeling at the altar during the Sacrament. But that was not all. They fully agreed that the ecclesiastical authority should not be vested in the Pope; but, then, they did not see why it should be invested in anybody, either in King, Queen, or Hierarchy.

This was reforming the Reformation in a way Queen Bess neither understood nor liked. It occurred to her, doubtless, that if this new batch of reformers—known by the odd name of Puritans—were allowed to topple over all ecclesiastical authority, they might, before long, aspire to pull down all political authority also, especially in the shape of Absolute Monarchy. It is clear she suspected their intentions towards Monarchy were not strictly honorable, for she ordered Parliament to enact forthwith that "Any persons above the age of sixteen years, refusing to come to the church established by law, and who should willingly join in, or be present at, any unlawful assemblies, conventicles, or meetings, under color or pretence of the exercise of religion, should be committed to prison; there to remain until they should conform and come to church." Again, "Any person who should not within three months after conviction, conform himself when required to do so, should abjure and depart from the realm, and if he returned without license, should be adjudged, and suffer as a felon."

These point-blank Laws compelled the proscribed Sect either to abandon its convictions, or to conceal its dislike of the Romish ceremonies still retained in the Church of England, or to seek a land where they could carry out the Scripture in all its "purity." Choosing the last course, many of the so-called Puritans embarked for Holland; whence in 1620 they sailed across the sea, and landed on Plymouth Rock, North America. Thus, unwittingly, the Virgin Queen became the mother of the American Democracy, and Henry VIII. must be regarded as its grandfather, from having introduced the Reformation into England.

A goodly number of the Puritans, however, remained in England, and caused Elizabeth no small vexation. A certain Peter Wentworth, Member of the Commons, was a great stickler for the privileges of Parliament, and was frequently sent to the Tower. In 1571, he got up "a Petition to the Lords to be Suppliants with the Lower House to the Queen." This was the old combination of the Aristocracy and Middle Class which had given so much trouble to Elizabeth's predecessors. The project was nipped in the bud by locking up Wentworth in the Tower. Nothing daunted, we find the plucky Puritan, four years later, declaiming in Parliament for the right of "free speech." "Two things," he said, "do great hurt here. One, a rumor which runneth about the House—'Take heed what you do; the Queen's Majesty liketh not such a matter.' The other is a message sometimes brought into the House, either commanding or inhibiting, very injurious to the freedom of speech and consultation. Would to God, Mr. Speaker, that these two things were buried in hell. The King hath no peer or equal in the kingdom, but he ought to be under God and the law, because the law maketh him a King." Of course Wentworth was again assigned to the Tower. Three years afterwards, still refractory, he put a series of Questions to the Speaker in Parliament, to wit: "Whether this House be not a place for any Member freely to utter any of the griefs of the commonwealth? Whether honor may be done to God, and benefit and service to the Prince and State, without free speech? Whether there be any councils besides Parliament which can make, add to, or diminish from, the laws of this realm?" Wentworth's curiosity cost him a third trip to the Tower. No wonder Elizabeth lost her temper with these inquisitive Puritans. The genius of the future Yankee might be discerned in their prying propensities.

There can be no doubt that England prospered under the intelligent despotism of Queen Bess. In agriculture, commerce, and navigation, the Nation made progress; letters flourished; the finances were economized; Sir Francis Drake sailed round the world; Bacon's philosophy and Shakspeare's poetry immortalized the epoch: yet Monarchy was never so despotic since the date of *Magna Charta*. "The administration of the law," says Rowland, "in civil as in religious matters, was directed by the Queen's personal wishes. In the Court of Star Chamber she was the sole judge, and might fine, imprison, and punish corporally by whipping, branding, slitting nostrils and ears." The High Commission Court, instituted by Archbishop Whitgift by her orders, carried into effect the terrible penalties against the Catholics and Puritans. "No man," wrote Elizabeth to the Archbishop, "should be suffered to decline, either to the right or left hand, from the drawn line marked by authority." This was the quintessence of tyranny. Martial law constantly superseded the ordinary courts and juries, and was often used against religious offenders. The rack, though not acknowledged by the laws of England, was freely employed in her reign, and not only by the authority of the Queen, but by that also of her Secretaries and Privy Councillors, each of whom might imprison anyone he suspected, and at his own discretion order him to the rack. Hallam declared that the Courts of Justice, in cases of Treason, were little better than "caverns of murderers." The laws were frequently superseded by Royal proclamations.

Elizabeth's sway over Parliament was absolute. It was not allowed to legislate on religious or state affairs. In the Session of 1571 she told them—"They should do well to meddle with no matters of State, but such as should be propounded unto them." In the Parliament of 1592, the Speaker, by command of the Queen, said, "Her Majesty's present charge and command is, that no bills touching matters of State, or reformation in causes ecclesiastical, be exhibited. And upon my allegiance I am commanded, if such bill be exhibited, not to read it." She wondered "that any would be of so high commandment to attempt a thing contrary to that she hath so expressly forbidden." Any obstinate Members who infringed the Royal commands were summoned to the Privy Council, where they were so startled by the punishments held over them, that "when they returned to their seats, their terror was visible in their faces, and communicated itself to all around." Elizabeth had an ingenious mode of increasing her pocket-money by granting monopolies for the exclusive sale of commodities, some of them the common necessaries of life. A list of those granted to her courtiers was read in the House of Commons in 1601, when an indignant Member asked, "Is not bread amongst them?"

The imprisonment for eighteen years of Mary, Queen

of Scots, who had thrown herself on the protection of the English Queen, and her final execution on a mere pretext, in 1587, is one of the foulest crimes of Elizabeth's reign.

Though stern and relentless, she seemed to have a sentimental vein, for her love of the Earl of Leicester, whom she covered with honors, never abated whilst he lived. Her passion, too, for the Earl of Essex was so profound that remorse is said to have shortened her life from having, in a moment of fury, signed his death-warrant. She died not long after Essex's death, in 1603.

The "Act for the Relief of the Poor," 1601, known as the Poor Law, is the only one that reflects any credit on the legislation of this reign.

The story of the sixteenth century in England is now told, though briefly. How little the two chief actors comprehended their *rôles!*

Henry VIII., enraged at the Pope's opposition to his divorce, declared himself the Head of the Church in England; and then to obtain money seized on the property of the Catholic Priesthood. These acts of the King encouraged a small band of religious Reformers, fervent disciples of Luther, to propagate their new doctrines. They translated the Bible into English, calling on all to form their own opinions on religious matters, and to be governed no longer by the authority of the Pope and Priesthood, as in past centuries. The King little understood what this meant. It was sheer rebellion against the control of the Church that had so long governed the minds of men. Many such rebellions against the Papacy had been attempted before in various countries, but were crushed because the people were superstitious and clung to the Pope. Other Kings before Henry VIII. were anxious to concentrate the spiritual and temporal power in their hands, but dared not. Those who attempted it were excommunicated, and to save their crowns were forced to make peace with the Pope. In England, as has been shown, the long struggle of the Barons and the Middle Class against the absolute authority of the Monarchy had ripened the popular mind for independence. They were ready when the sixteenth century came for rebellion. The King's personal quarrel with the Pope opened the door, and the Nation rushed into the arms of the Reformation.

The Church of England, however, did not satisfy such sceptics as Peter Wentworth and his class. The Bishops of the new Church insisted on *passive obedience* just as the Bishops of the old. The Puritans of England, and the Presbyterians of Scotland, were bent on saying their prayers in their own way—standing up, or sitting down, or in any other fashion that suited them. This was setting all ecclesiastical authority at defiance.

Elizabeth foresaw, as was said, what such diabolical heresy might lead to. If people were allowed to snap their fingers at the authority of the Church of England, they might some day venture to dispute the authority of the Crown of England. So she locked up the Puritans, or bade them "abjure and depart from the realm." The Puritans remembered, however, that she and her father rebelled against the Pope simply because they wished to be independent, and they resolved sooner or later to profit by their example. The most impatient among them embarked for the wilds of America, and the rest remained to carry out their plans at home.

The reader can hardly fail to recognize that these resolute opponents of arbitrary power in Church and State were no other than the descendants of those Saxons of the Middle Class, "the freemen," whom the Norman Barons were obliged to take into partnership in order to clip the wings of the Monarchy. The two fought their way successfully together, constantly curtailing the Royal power and adding to Parliamentary control down to Henry V., 1413, when the wars with France stopped the constitutional struggle.

Then, as stated, came the civil wars of "the Roses," which led to the advent of the Tudor dynasty.

It was shown, also, that the policy of Henry VII., the first of the Tudor line, was, as Bacon expressed it, "to keep a strait hand on his nobility, and chose rather to advance clergymen and lawyers, which were more obsequious to him, but had less interest in the people." This conduct of the King was sagacious beyond doubt, for he knew the Aristocracy had always been the leaders of the Middle Class in their joint crusade against the Monarchy.

His son, Henry VIII., adopted similar tactics, and kept the Nobles in check, preferring to advance obsequious Clergymen, such as Archbishops Wolsey and Cranmer.

Elizabeth, the last of the Tudors, did not forget the example of her grandsire. "She seemed to delight," says Buckle, "in humbling the nobles. On them her hand fell heavily." He also remarks: "Whatever explanation we may choose to give of the fact, it cannot be denied that during the reign of Elizabeth, there was an open and constant opposition between the nobles and the executive government." No doubt there was, for the Aristocracy had now recovered from the exhaustion of the foreign and civil wars, and were ready to unite with their old allies of the Middle Class to reduce Monarchy to constitutional limits. Elizabeth, too, employed "clergymen and lawyers," dreading to put power in the hands of the Nobles. Cecil, Walsingham, and Whitgift were able men, but they were the obsequious tools of the most despotic Sovereign England ever knew.

It is singular that the learned Buckle, whose democratic bias is decided, should glorify Elizabeth for oppressing the Aristocracy when he must have known that the conjunction of the Aristocracy with the Middle Class had been the sole means of promoting popular freedom. He also applauds the "Great Queen" for pushing on the Reformation—which she did whilst it enhanced her power—yet he strangely refrains from censure when she turned like a tigress on the Puritans who logically sought to make the Reformation a reality. Her two favorite aversions were the Aristocracy and the Puritans, and who were these but the descendants of those very Barons and Freemen whose "singular alliance," as Buckle elsewhere calls it, "was the condition of the popular privileges" obtained centuries before? His strong admiration for the tyrannical Elizabeth led the historian into grave contradictions, as well as incorrect interpretations of facts. No sooner had his "Great Queen" passed away than the Aristocracy and Puritans raised their heads once more, and the consequences to Monarchy were serious indeed.

DECLINE OF THE MONARCHY.

SEVENTEENTH CENTURY.

WE now enter the seventeenth century, memorable for the birth of Civil Liberty, and the downfall of Absolute Government in England.

James I. of England was son of Mary Queen of Scots, and therefore King of Scotland. He ascended the English throne in 1603, as the great-grandson of Henry VII., whose daughter Margaret married James IV. of Scotland. He was the first of the Stuart family* to reign in England, and the Crowns of the two countries were united thenceforth. He took the title of King of Great Britain.

His welcome in England was most cordial, and above all by Parliament, for it not only rejoiced at escaping from the clutches of the despotic Elizabeth, but saw in the advent of a foreign King, whose influence would naturally be less, an opportunity for extending Parliamentary authority, and diminishing Monarchical power. Parliament had been so trodden upon by the Tudors, that it yearned to avenge itself upon Arbitrary Monarchy. It had yielded grimly to this oppression, not only for the causes cited, but also because Henry

* The Stuarts were descendants of Banquo, Thane of Lochaber, assassinated in the eleventh century by Macbeth.

9*

VIII. and Elizabeth had, though for their own special purposes, promoted the Reformation, which Parliament and the Nation desired. But now the course was clear. An Arbitrary Church had been overthrown, and *religious freedom* had been secured. An Arbitrary Monarchy was next to be assailed, and *civil liberty* was the trophy to be won. It was such ideas as these that inspired the Parliament which met in 1604..

King James, on the other hand, who was an amiable and learned man, entertained no doubt of the Divine Right of Kings, and the passive obedience of the people. "A perfect kingdom," he declared, "is that where the King rules all things according to his own will," and he even wrote a book to prove this thesis. With such dispositions as these on both sides a collision was inevitable. "It was with the Stuart kings," says Rowland, "that the battle between prerogative and freedom was fought."

It is somewhat strange that for the first two years, the King and the Parliament, who were destined to become such bitter antagonists, never met without using the gentlest language towards each other—for all the world like two duellists shaking hands before drawing swords.

An attempt to blow up with gunpowder both the King and Parliament, 1605, was discovered only the day before the King was to open the Session in person. Guy Fawkes, a Catholic officer, was arrested as he was about to fire several barrels of powder concealed in the cellars under the House of Lords.

This was a suitable moment for panegyric. "No nation of the earth," says the Act of Parliament, passed on this occasion, "hath been blessed with greater benefits than this kingdom now enjoyeth; having the true and free profession of the Gospel, under our most gracious sovereign lord King James, the most great, learned, and religious king that ever reigned therein."

This billing and cooing was, however, short-lived, for after passing sundry cruel laws against the Papists, the House of Commons began to display a sense of its importance that must have astounded the King. It declared on one occasion that it alone was the judge of the election-returns of its Members. On another, it decided that Members were free from arrest, and sent to the Tower the Warder of the Fleet Prison for contempt in not giving up Sir Thomas Shirley, arrested for debt. Then followed a document, drawn up by a Committee of the House, and addressed to the King, which summed up their opinion of their rights and privileges in these words:—"Our privileges are our right and due inheritance, no less than our lands and goods."

Such volcanic language as this, brought a trumpet-blast from the indignant King. "The state of Monarchy," he said to the Parliament of 1610, "is the supremest thing upon earth, for Kings are not only God's Lieutenants upon earth, and sit upon God's throne, but even by God himself they are called Gods. Kings have like power with God; they make and unmake their subjects, have power of life and death; are judges over all their subjects and in all causes, and are accountable to God alone." Elizabeth never uttered such thunderbolts as these. Her custom was simply to send for the mischief-makers in the House, and threaten them with the rack. Conduct so energetic had the desired effect; but the pedantic speech-making of the milder James had no terrors for Parliament. On the contrary, they persisted in their audacious course, and even went so far as to adopt the strategy of the old Parliaments, which often adjourned chuckling at having voted no subsidies. This period—1614-1620—is described as "halcyon days in England; no taxes being paid, trade open to all parts of the world, profound peace."

The struggle between James and Parliament grew more and more obstinate. When he dissolved the Parliament of 1620, the Commons entered a vigorous protest on their journals. The King sent for them, "and rent out the protestation with his own hand," denouncing "the ill-tempered spirits" who had contrived it. This time, however, his anger took a more practical turn, for he sent Sir Edward Coke, the great lawyer, and Sir R. Philips to the Tower, and Messrs. Selden, Pym, and Mallory to other "prisons and confinements."

The Parliament of 1623 was eager to support Protestant Germany in a war against Catholic Germany, and agreed to vote large subsidies, but on condition that "eight citizens of London were appointed treasurers" of the fund, and "two other selected persons to be His Majesty's Privy Council for the war," and, further, "that all these should be accountable to the Commons in Parliament." This was considered "an extraordinary innovation," as indeed it was; but it arose from the conviction of Parliament that the King's Ministers were all corrupt men. The chief of them, the Duke of Buckingham, it cordially detested.

We find a glaring proof of the prevalent dishonesty in high places in the conduct of the Lord Chancellor, the learned Bacon. This celebrated man began life as a lawyer. He entered the House of Commons in Elizabeth's reign, but made no further progress at that period. James, appreciating his great abilities, advanced him rapidly, until he reached the woolsack* in 1618. Not long afterwards, he was impeached by the Commons, and tried by the Lords for selling places and privileges within his gift. He was condemned to imprisonment in the Tower; £40,000 fine, and future disqualification —1621. The accusation and sentence were principally inspired by the bitter hostility of Parliament to Buckingham, whose creature it considered Bacon to be. The King remitted the imprisonment and fine, but the disgraced Lord Chancellor, fortunately for posterity, retired from public life, and gave himself up to philosophy. His intellect was the greatest of his age. Since Aristotle, no such master-mind had appeared.†

One of the last acts of Parliament in this reign was to abolish those grants of monopolies by the Crown in which Elizabeth had so freely indulged. One case only was excepted, that of a new invention, to which a monopoly for fourteen years was allowed. This was the origin of the familiar Patent Law. The first lottery drawn in England was instituted in this reign.

It is perhaps worthy of notice that in the struggles between Parliament and James, the House of Commons was always in the van. This may be attributed to the

* The woolsack was first introduced in the House of Lords as the Chancellor's seat in the time of Elizabeth as a memento of an Act which was passed against the exportation of wool, that commodity being then the main source of the national wealth of England. It is composed of a large square bag of wool without either back or arms, and covered with red cloth.

† Bacon is called the Father of Experimental Philosophy, since he proposed that facts, instead of hypothesis, should be the basis of all reasoning. He wrote copiously on History, Politics, Morals, and Philosophy. In his "Novum Organum" he attacked the deductive method of Aristotle's Logic and advocated his own—the inductive.

strategy of the Lords who, though just as eager for the reduction of the Royal prerogative, did not desire to figure too prominently. The perfect accord between them is seen in the fact that the Commons constantly abandoned what the Lords refused to sanction. Their joint action was, of course, necessary to any successful attack on the Crown. In this way the old alliance of the Nobles and Middle Class was gradually working miracles in the cause of Constitutional Government.

The next reign begot events that nullified for a time this ancient partnership, and the result of the breach was after years of turmoil the advent of a subtle despot who "ruled all things according to his own will."

The contest which had arisen in the previous reign between Parliament and the King was based on the determination of the Nation, through its representatives, not to be governed by Absolute Monarchy. The struggle of the Nobles and Middle Class against despotic power, which had begun in the days of the *Magna Charta*, 1215, had been continued for over four centuries, and, except in the interval occupied by the Tudor dynasty, the Nation, through Parliament, had constantly acquired increased control over its destinies. In spite of King James's lofty notions of his prerogative, Parliamentary Government steadily advanced ; but the reign of Charles I. was destined to witness the eclipse of both Parliament and King.

The temporary overthrow of the ancient Government must be ascribed more to glaring defects in the nature of Charles I., than to want of intelligence. His alternate waywardness, indecision, and levity, to say nothing of his childish duplicity, exposed him to the pernicious counsels of incompetent and unprincipled men. Such a character as his coming in contact with the passions of that time necessarily entailed the catastrophe which ensued. The unfortunate Charles is well described in a phrase of the Latin poet, *Nil fuit unquam sic impar sibi*—no man ever exhibited such a mass of inconsistencies and contradictions. This much said, let us follow the events.

Charles I., son of James, ascended the throne in 1625. He was twenty-five when his reign began, and three months afterwards married Henrietta Maria, daughter of Henry IV., one of the wisest and best of French Kings.

Soon after his accession he engaged in war with Spain on religious grounds, and summoned his first Parliament to obtain supplies. Their antipathy to the Duke of Buckingham, the Minister of Charles, as he had been of his father, was so great that they procrastinated until the King in anger dissolved Parliament. As no money had been voted, Charles resorted to the old expedient of forced loans. This measure led to grievous exactions, and yet was inadequate.

The King resolved then to call a second Parliament—1626. The new House of Commons was in scarcely a better mood than its predecessor. Still it showed a disposition at times to vote supplies, but some impetuous act of Charles led to new difficulties. He imprisoned two Members of the Commons for language offensive to him, and likewise a Member of the Lords, the Earl of Arundel. The Lords, by conciliation, effected the release of the Members of the Commons, and obtained the discharge of their own Member by an unanimous demand. Finding the Commons still lingering over the supply so frequently called for, Charles dissolved Parliament a second time within a year. New schemes were adopted to raise money, which Charles considered his prerogative fully authorized; but Parliament held a different theory. The Nobility were called on for contributions; and a loan of £100,000 was demanded from the City of London. The subsidies which the Commons had discussed without voting were exacted in the shape of loans. Many distinguished men refused to pay the loans, and were imprisoned.

An expedition to relieve French Protestants at Rochelle was fitted out with the money so obtained, but failed. Furthermore, the war with Spain and France, coupled with the onerous taxation, caused much agitation, and Charles was compelled to reassemble Parliament for the third time in 1628.

The King's opening Speech to Parliament was unconciliatory. He said money was the sole object of calling Parliament, and he would "use but few persuasions; for if these be not sufficient, then no eloquence of men or angels would prevail." After sundry other expressions of the same tenor, he concluded, "Take not this as a threatening, but as an admonition, for I scorn to threaten any but my equals."

The unsatisfactory condition of things led to long debates in both Houses. At the end of two months, a "Petition of Right" was passed by Lords and Commons, which, after reciting *Magna Charta* and ancient statutes, required that henceforth no man should be taxed in any manner without consent of Parliament, and that no Freeman be imprisoned without cause shown. The King came to Parliament House, and in the presence of the Lords and Commons assented to the Petition. Not long after, a subsidy was granted, and the Parliament was then prorogued.

Several of the Clergy offended Parliament by sustaining the King's abuse of power, and one of them, Dr. Mainwaring, was impeached by the Commons, tried by the Lords, and condemned to prison during the pleasure of the House. He was also fined £1,000, and disabled from holding any ecclesiastical dignity. Mainwaring, however, was promptly pardoned by the King.

Parliament met after a prorogation of six months. New complaints of the illegal acts of the Crown resounded on all sides. Mr. Rolles, a Member of the Commons, said his goods had been unlawfully seized for duties. Mr. Selden said the "Petition of Right" had been violated. He referred to the case of a Mr. Prynne, who had been deprived of his ears by sentence of the Star Chamber. Oliver Cromwell made his first appearance at this time, and stated that some of the Clergy of the Church of England were preaching "flat Popery." The antagonism of the Commons daily increased, and at last the exasperated King ordered the Speaker to adjourn the House for a fortnight. The majority of the House, however, compelled the Speaker to disobey the order of the King and drew up an indignant protest. The King, hearing that the House would not receive a message from him, and that the doors were locked, fell into a rage, and sent a guard to force an entrance. Before the guard had arrived, however, the House had adjourned.

The open defiance of Parliament inflamed the King. He published a proclamation against the seditious conduct of certain Members of the Commons, and announced the dissolution of Parliament, which soon followed. Nine of the prominent Members of the Commons were imprisoned. The Judges refused bail, and they were committed to the Tower during the King's pleasure, and Sir John Elliot, as the ringleader, was fined £2,000.

At this period the Commons were divided into two sections bitterly hostile to each other—the Court party and the Puritan party. The Lords frequently acted as peace-makers between the Lower House and the King, but always co-operated with the former in all attempts to limit the power of the Crown. Thus far the old alliance of Nobles and Middle Class was maintained. The power of the King now appeared so irresistible that several of the Puritan party went over to him and accepted office, for, says Rowland, sarcastically, "their patriotism seemed to promise no reward." Amongst others, Sir Thomas Wentworth left the popular party, and was made Earl of Strafford.

The King now determined to govern without a Parliament, and to strengthen himself, made peace with France and Spain. An interval of eleven years elapsed without a Parliament, during which, says Lord Clarendon, "there was peace, plenty, and universal tranquillity;" but the principles of the Constitution, as well as the laws on taxation, continued to be violated. Amongst other imposts created by the Crown was that of "Ship Money," or a tax to provide ships. John Hampden, a cousin of Oliver Cromwell, declared the demand illegal, and refused to pay his assessment of twenty shillings. "Thousands for defence," he exclaimed, "but not a penny for tribute."

To complete his difficulties, the King at this moment became involved in a deadly quarrel with Scotland. Archbishop Laud, one of his chief advisers, undertook to force the liturgy of the Church of England on

Scotland, which had adopted Presbyterianism, introduced by John Knox in 1558. The Scots rose *en masse*, made a "Solemn League and Covenant" to abide by their Kirk; organized an army, and met the forces of Charles at Berwick. A parley ensued, and Charles agreed to withdraw the project of Laud.

Want of funds compelled the King to call his fourth Parliament in April, 1640; but as it began discussing grievances, Charles abruptly dissolved it in three weeks.*

The English Clergy, under the lead of Archbishop Laud, and with the approval of the King, continued their aggressions on Presbyterianism. Exasperated by this, the Scotch sent an army into England. An engagement took place, and the King's forces were defeated. The Nation was aroused to fury by these events, and petitions came from every quarter for a new Parliament, London being specially clamorous.

* American readers may not be generally aware that a Dissolution of Parliament involves new elections, which a Prorogation does not.

THE REVOLUTION.

SEVENTEENTH CENTURY.

The above heading is usually applied in England to the bloodless change of Government that took place in 1688, whilst that of "Commonwealth" is affixed to the epoch following the reign of Charles I. Both titles are clearly misnomers as applied to these different periods. The tempest which swept away the throne, and left an *interregnum* which was filled by an Absolute Government, can only be designated as a Revolution; and therefore I attach this word to the present chapter, which will describe those events. On the other hand, I will head the chapter which narrates the pacific substitution of William III. for James II. as simply the Limitation of the Monarchy, for that was the true meaning of what occurred.

The Revolution, in my opinion, originates from that juncture when it was evident that both King and Parliament were engaged in a deadly struggle for the supremacy. From this point dates the rise of those waters of discord which were destined to flow and swell in volume till, finally, they overspread and deluged the land.

The King then called his fifth Parliament in November, 1640—better known as the "Long Parliament." The Government of the King had brought him into such discredit that Parliament was resolved to give him no quarter. The Commons were eager for the fray; "the

Lords," says Rowland, "were animated by the same feeling;" and both went to work in earnest. The Commons impeached the Earl of Strafford, the King's chief adviser, and the Lords tried him for High Treason. He was condemned and executed. Sir F. Windebank, Secretary of State, was next impeached, but he escaped to France. The new canons of the Clergy were all denounced, as not having the consent of Parliament; the tax called "Ship Money" was declared illegal; and the Commons expelled four of their Members for being monopolist patentees. The impeachments of Archbishop Laud and the Lord-Keeper Finch followed. The Lords condemned the Archbishop, who was afterwards executed. Finch fled to France.

The King was alarmed, and resorted to strategy. He summoned both Houses, and made a conciliatory speech. More politic still, he offered office to the Puritan party. Oliver St. John, one of his bitterest enemies, became Solicitor-General. The Earl of Bedford, one of the Puritan leaders of the Lords, and Mr. Pym, of the Commons, were tempted with high appointments; but they waived their claims until their fellow-leaders were provided for.

Parliament, however, pressed on. They passed an Act that neither House should be dissolved or prorogued without their consent. The High Commission Court and the odious Star Chamber were abolished—both effective instruments of tyranny in previous reigns. The King was completely cowed. He assented to all those Acts stripping him of the prerogatives his predecessors had enjoyed. He remonstrated sometimes. "You have taken the Government almost in pieces," he said once: "it is almost off the hinges."

The surrender of the Royal power was so complete

that a popular reaction in the King's favor took place. Demonstrations of loyalty and affection burst forth whenever he appeared. This alarmed Oliver Cromwell, who had now become the real leader of the Puritan party, and bent on the downfall of the unfortunate Charles. So adroitly had he played his *rôle* that few suspected it was his hand skilfully guiding the various movements which were fast precipitating the country into civil war. Cromwell counted on the fatuity of his intended victim, and was not disappointed. The Puritan party in the Commons suddenly proposed a "Grand Remonstrance" against any control over legislation by the Crown. It was debated twelve hours, and passed—159 to 148. Cromwell said to Lord Falkland, as they left the House, "If the Remonstrance had been rejected, I would have sold all that I had the next morning, and never have seen England more." Hume refers to this Remonstrance as aiming at "an abolition almost total of the Monarchical Government of England." Hallam considers that "it was put forward to stem the returning tide of loyalty, which threatened to obstruct the further progress of the popular leader." Other attacks on the Crown followed. The Commons accused twelve Bishops of High Treason, and the Lords ordered their arrest.

The unanimity of the Lords and Commons—the Nobles and Middle Class—during this epoch is striking. The Lords aimed at the establishment of Parliamentary Government, and the abolition of absolute power. So did a portion of the Commons, to the number of 148. Another portion, counting 159, with Oliver Cromwell at their head, had a very different project in view, which neither the Nation, the Lords, nor a half of the Commons suspected at the time.

The King, after he had accepted the "Grand Remonstrance" and several other measures strongly obnoxious to him, at last determined to yield no more. Accordingly, he ordered four Members of the Commons, Pym, Hampden, Haselrigge, and Strode, with one Member of the Lords, Kimbolton, to be accused of High Treason—January, 1642. He even went in person to the House of Commons with a guard to arrest the objects of his resentment; but they escaped as he entered. The King then asked the Speaker if the accused were present. Falling on his knees, the Speaker replied, "I have neither eyes to see nor tongue to speak in this place but as the House is pleased to direct me, whose servant I am here, and humbly beg your Majesty's pardon that I cannot give any other answer than this." The House then adjourned in great excitement. Next day they passed a declaration that the King's proceedings were a breach of the rights and privileges of Parliament, and adjourned for a week. The House of Lords made a similar adjournment.

On reassembling, the accused Members took their places. The King admitted his impetuosity, offered a free pardon, and appealed to the Lords to mediate once more between him and the Commons. The appeal, however, came too late. The Commons grew more defiant. They demanded, with the concurrence of the Lords, that the town of Hull, with its magazine and arms, should not be given up without their authority. Both Houses next passed a Bill removing the Bishops from Parliament; and to this Bill the King, contrary to expectation, assented. They then insisted on taking the command of the Militia; but with this demand the King resolutely refused to comply, and thus the final breach was made.

From this brief *résumé* it will be plainly seen that Parliament was triumphant in every contest with the vacillating Charles. It stripped him of all his prerogatives, and extinguished irresponsible power in England. When the King signed the law which made Parliament indissoluble but by its own vote, his surrender was complete. If Parliament, therefore, merely sought for a preponderance over the Sovereign, the struggle was ended. In all the previous conflicts between King and Parliament, the concessions of the King terminated the contest. In this way for centuries Parliamentary power grew up, and Royal authority was cut down. It is often asserted that Charles was faithless, and would have reclaimed the power he had yielded; but if Parliament was strong enough to take it from him, how could he recover it? The truth is, as subsequent facts proved, there was a wing of the Puritan party in the Long Parliament of 1640, called the "Root and Branch Men," and afterwards known as the "Independents," who aimed at something more than the union of Legislative and Executive power in the hands of Parliament—a faction whose real object was to suppress the Monarchy itself. The opportunity was favorable, for the King though able, was irresolute, and controlled by the influences about him,* so that Par-

* The wife of Charles exercised a fatal ascendency over him. She was intrepid, but ignorant of England and the situation. It was she who forced the hesitating King to attempt the seizure of the five members of the Commons, his bitterest antagonists. "Go, coward," she exclaimed, "and pull out these rogues by the ears, or never see my face again." When the conflict became inevitable, she escaped to Holland, and sold her own and other jewels to buy arms. Eluding the cruisers, she landed soon afterwards on the Yorkshire coast. A few hours later, four Parliamentary ships came up, and opened fire on the village she occupied. Fleeing with her attendants to a ditch in the outskirts, she crouched there for a time in concealment, until the Queen remembered she had

liament was constantly able to overcome him. Cromwell, who had put himself at the head of the Independents, saw that victory over such an antagonist in the field was certain, and would place the Government in his grasp.

There was one other man in England who foresaw this. "Who is that sloven?" said Lord Digby, one day, to Hampden, pointing to a Member of the Commons. "That sloven," he replied, "will be the greatest man in England, if we ever come to a breach with the King, which God forbid." The sloven, Oliver Cromwell, and his cousin, John Hampden, had resolved on a breach with the doomed King, and they accomplished it.

The attempt to obtain the command of the Militia proved that the Puritan leaders had resolved on civil war. This was so evident that the King decided to leave London, March, 1642, and prepare for the conflict. There was no standing army in England, and both sides were compelled to enroll troops. In June, Parliament obtained money from the Corporation of London and other sources. In the same month, they voted "nine proposals" of reconciliation with the King, which required that all civil, military, and reli-

left her pet lapdog behind. Heedless of the danger, she flew back, and brought off her favorite in her arms. A soldier was killed near her in the ditch, and her party were covered with earth by a ball striking the ground near them. On another occasion, when a Parliamentary ship was in chase of her, she commanded her captain not to strike, and, to the terror of all, bade him at the last extremity to blow up his vessel. During the campaign of 1644 she gave birth to her last child; and a few days later she was forced to escape in disguise, and wandered to Falmouth, whence she embarked for France, where her nephew, Louis XIV., then reigned. She had many noble traits; but, being a Catholic, she was hated by the Puritans and Presbyterians. She said once, "Though they hate me now, perhaps they will not always hate me; and if they have any sentiments of honor, they will be ashamed of tormenting a poor woman who takes so little precaution to defend herself."

gious affairs should be placed in their hands. The King, then at York, rejected these indignantly, and an appeal to arms was the result. In July, Parliament voted an army. In August, the King raised his standard at Nottingham. The forces of Parliament amounted to 20,000 men, of which the Earl of Essex was made Commander-in-chief, and the Earl of Bedford second in command. The King's army numbered some 12,000 men, which he commanded in person. The first battle occurred in October, 1642, at Edgehill, and the issue was doubtful.

OLIVER CROMWELL.

Not long after this conflict the energy and prowess of Cromwell in the field became so conspicuous that his future distinction was a foregone conclusion. The prophecy of Hampden was daily becoming more probable. As Cromwell was destined to become from this period the prominent figure in English history for some years, it will be interesting to give a short sketch of his antecedents.

This extraordinary man was born at Huntingdon, in 1599. His family was an old one, and claimed descent from the founder of the House of Stuart, which would have made him a relative of Charles I. Cromwell once remarked of himself, "I was by birth a gentleman, neither living in any considerable height nor yet in obscurity."

His early life was boisterous. At seventeen he was sent to Cambridge University, but was more addicted to frolic than study. At twenty-one he married the daughter of Sir James Bourchier. Soon after this he became a zealous Puritan, and prayed and preached with great fervor. Cromwell already comprehended that Puritanism was little else than Democracy in a religious disguise; but to the last he concealed his ambition under copious quotations from Scripture.

At twenty-nine he entered Parliament. He was again elected eleven years later, for the Short Parliament of 1640, and was returned for the Long Parliament in the same year. At once he joined the Ultras, then known as "Root and Branch Men," and soon perceived that a storm was brewing, which he determined to guide to his own advantage. He spoke passionately when he rose in Parliament, but was not given to debate. He was an active party man, and during the first year of the Long Parliament figured on eighteen Committees, ardently promoting the most hostile measures to the King, and calmly awaiting the hour when Charles should stand at bay. The Lords and Commons, wholly intent on securing the supremacy of Parliament, were vastly elated at their repeated victories over the Crown, little foreseeing the day when both Parliament and Crown would vanish before the wand of the necromancer from Huntingdon. Cromwell may not have yet clearly seen that such a feat was possible, but the amazing skill of every step he took shows that his purpose was as fixed as his ambition was boundless.

Before the Royal standard was unfurled, he despatched arms to Cambridgeshire, and, leaving London, began forming a troop. He gave the keenest attention to discipline, but, with the instinct of genius, he felt that something more was necessary. In the Royal army, the "King's name was a tower of strength," and the principle of allegiance stimulated thousands to rise. Cromwell appealed to the religious passions then so strong, and by this means, as much as by his masterly generalship, achieved wonders.

In the campaigns of 1643, '44, '45, Cromwell acquired great military renown. His daring strategy fascinated the army, and startled the Nation.

Cromwell now felt strong enough to throw aside the Nobles and Middle Class who were still fighting as in centuries past against Absolute Monarchy. They merely aspired to Parliamentary Government, and were wholly unconscious that they had been simply playing into Cromwell's hands. But these were not his only dupes. There was, besides, a small band of political enthusiasts—Ludlow, Vane, Sidney, and Harrington—who threw themselves into the Parliamentary contest against Charles, hoping to found a Republic on the ruins of the Monarchy. It was the destiny of both these factions to hold the ladder by which Cromwell ascended, and to discover at last that they had been his tools.

In 1645, Cromwell's prestige was so great that he began to display more boldness and less craft than hitherto. He declared one day in Parliament that the war would never end so long as Members of either House held commands in the civil or military service; and a law was passed, the "Self-denying Ordinance," which disqualified Lords Essex, Manchester, and others, though Cromwell retained both his command and seat in the Commons by special permission. He next insisted that the army should be new-modelled; and Parliament ordered the three armies to be concentrated into one, and gave the command to Sir Thomas Fairfax, an instrument of Cromwell. By these adroit measures Cromwell removed the Presbyterians or Moderates from his path, and secured the control of the army.

The success of his military operations was as great as that of his Parliamentary intrigues. By a series of brilliant victories he crushed the Royalists everywhere; and at last the defeat of Lord Astley, 1646, ended the English civil war. "You have done your work, my masters," exclaimed Astley to his victors, "and may go to play, unless you choose to fall out amongst yourselves."

Cromwell was now the leading man in England. Parliament voted him a revenue of £2,500, and made him a Baron.

The unfortunate King, in desperation, gave himself up to the Scotch army, who handed him over to Parliament.

The majority of Parliament was Presbyterian, and adhered to Monarchy. To get rid of them, Cromwell began a series of intrigues * as skilful as his tactics

* The Presbyterian leaders, fully convinced that Cromwell entertained designs against Parliament, meant to order his arrest if proofs could be obtained. One day two officers informed them that Cromwell had declared that it would soon be necessary to purge the House of Commons. The two officers were brought before the House, who repeated the very language of Cromwell, who was then present. Perceiving his danger, and that a desperate effort alone could save him, Cromwell immediately fell on his knees, "wept bitterly, and with a vehemence of words, sobs, and gestures that moved the whole assembly, he poured forth invocations and fervent prayers, calling every curse of the Lord on his head if any man in the kingdom was more faithful than he to the House. Then, rising, he spoke for more than two hours of the Parliament, the King, the army, of his enemies, of his friends, and of himself; touching upon and mixing up all things; humble and bold, prolix and impassioned; particularly repeating that he was unjustly accused, compromised without reason." Cromwell so completely blinded the House by his wonderful dissimulation and matchless acting that the conclusion was general that he had been slandered. Too wise to risk another display of his powers of deception, he secretly abandoned

in the field; cunningly stirred up quarrels between the army and Parliament; and in the end marched into London, and reduced Parliament to obedience. Most of the Presbyterian leaders fled at his approach. A short time previously, by a secret order of Cromwell, a band of troopers had abducted the King from the residence assigned by Parliament. Cromwell was now master of Parliament and the King's person.

Fearing a bargain between Charles and his political enemies, he induced the King to go first to Hampton Court, and then to Carisbrook Castle, of which his nephew was Governor. The intended victim was now under lock and key. Cromwell at this time, 1647, must have seen his way to the Sovereign authority. The "Independents," his own party, controlled the House of Commons, and the army, which was quite devoted to him, was the only real power in the country. The King, though a prisoner, was a stumbling-block, and it was resolved to dispose of him. To compromise him as an obstacle to order, Parliament was instigated to involve him in disputes, which were abruptly terminated by a Vote declaring it High Treason to hold further communication with him. Insurrections in his behalf broke out in Wales, but were promptly suppressed; and some Scotch Royalists who took up arms were quickly overpowered by Cromwell.

Determined to remove the King, who barred his way, he expelled by force 160 Members of the Commons whom he feared to trust. This act is known in

London on the very day this scene occurred, June 10th, 1647. He put himself at once at the head of the army and threw off all disguise towards the Presbyterians and the House, "for," as Guizot remarks, "it had now become impossible, even with his consummate hypocrisy, to preserve it any longer."

history as "Pride's Purge," from its being carried out by a body of soldiers under Colonel Pride. The fifty Members who remained were his passive tools, and readily voted to bring the King to trial. A High Court of Justice was improvised, and Charles was brought before it. He denied its jurisdiction, but was summarily sentenced to death.

Charles had for months suffered contumely and ill-treatment, but his equanimity never forsook him. On his trial, his conduct was intrepid and dignified, but resigned.* Insults were heaped on him, to provoke some intemperate word or act. The soldiers were ordered to spit on him as he proceeded to the Court. He bore all without a murmur. He slept soundly the night before his execution, and died with sublime composure—January, 1649—forgiving his enemies with his last breath. "I go from a corruptible to an incorruptible crown," exclaimed the unfortunate Monarch, as he laid his head on the block. Cromwell is said to have witnessed the scene from a window, and made merry over it; but soon discovering the Nation was shocked at the decapitation of the King, he affected to consider it a sad necessity.†

* When the names of the Court were read by the crier, that of Fairfax was called, when a voice among the spectators said, "He has more wit than to be here." When the indictment was read, "In the name of the people of England," the same voice exclaimed, "Not a tenth part of them." The disturber was ordered to be seized, and it turned out to be Lady Fairfax, wife of the Parliamentary General. She was, of course, released. A soldier was struck down by his officer for praying for the King. "The punishment exceeds the offence," exclaimed the compassionate Charles.

† The following anecdote from Guizot's "History of the English Revolution" is strikingly characteristic of Cromwell's grim insensibility under the most tragical circumstances: "The body of the King was already enclosed in the coffin when Cromwell wished to see it; he considered it attentively, and, taking up the head in his hands, as if to make sure that it was severed from the body; "This," he said, "was a well-constituted frame and promised a long life."

The House of Lords had now dwindled to a shadow. The Vote of the Commons for the King's trial had been rejected unanimously by the Lords, then only sixteen in number. This enraged Cromwell, and a week after the execution, the Commons, at his command, voted that the House of Lords was "useless, dangerous, and therefore abolished."

The old Firm, as it may be called, of the Nobles and Middle Class, whose co-operation had given birth to liberty, and who had striven for five hundred years to preserve it, was now dissolved by force. A Military despotism succeeded, which destroyed the ancient organization of England, and ignored the rights and privileges of all alike. The upper, middle, and lower classes lost the protection of the old laws, and were at the mercy of an armed force in the hands of a man of genius, bent on his own aggrandisement. Of course the suspension of the Nation's vitality could only be temporary. The struggle of centuries against tyranny, whether of King or Usurper, was sure to be renewed, and Cromwell if not blinded by ambition must have foreseen this.

After the King's death, a Council of State of thirty-eight members, with John Milton as Secretary, was organized as the Executive Government. This body was composed of Cromwell's partisans, and obeyed his wishes.

Ireland was in arms for the Monarchy. The Council of State and the mock Parliament desired Cromwell, at his own suggestion, to take measures to reduce it to submission. He embarked at once for that country, where his disciplined troops and fearless strategy overcame all resistance. He gave no quarter, and the wholesale massacres at Drogheda and Wexford struck all with terror.

He returned from Ireland—May, 1650—to find that Scotland had proclaimed Charles II. King. He set out forthwith for the North. The contest in Scotland lasted over a year, and ended with the battle of Worcester, 1651, where the Scots, under Charles II., were completely routed. The young King, after numberless perils, escaped from England. "The numerous prisoners were driven," says a contemporary, "like cattle to London, where many perished for want of food in the prisons, and the rest were sold as slaves to the Plantations." Cromwell was so elated by this victory that he proposed to knight some of his officers on the field, but abandoned this idea on being reminded that Knighting was a Royal usage.

The three Kingdoms now lay at his feet, and Cromwell, conscious that he was the sole depositary of Absolute Power, became more imperious in manner, and dealt less in that extraordinary dissimulation and religious cant which all the writers of the time have described. Though the Executive and Legislative power was in his hands, for the Council of State and the Commons were composed of his dependents, still he was embarrassed. It would have been better if he had carried out his darling project at once, and assumed the Crown; but he dreaded the opposition of his officers, who professed Republicanism, and, above all, the ridicule of the Nation. For eighteen months he coquetted and intrigued with his political and military allies as to the form of the Government and his own position.

At last his hesitation led to insubordination amongst his creatures in the Commons, the Independents; but he put a sudden end to the growing discontent, in April, 1653, by going down to the House one day with a regiment of soldiers; and after vilifying the members in violent language, he turned them all into the street and locked the doors.* It was rough treatment for the men who pretended to represent "the people of England," and who had voted the King's death and the abolition of the House of Lords at his bidding. This decided act of despotism, however, was applauded, for this paltry remnant of the Long Parliament was so steeped in crime that its overthrow by the man who had prostituted it was considered just retribution.

Thus the war begun in 1642 by Parliament seeking to become absolute over the King, ended in the disappearance of both Parliament and King. King, Lords, and Commons—all were gone. Nothing was now left but Oliver Cromwell at the head of his army. Since William the Conqueror, no King had wielded a power so unmasked, so absolute. With extraordinary genius he had played one faction against the other till all were overthrown.

Yet Cromwell knew that the Nation would not tamely submit to such unmitigated despotism. He desired to retain his omnipotence, but felt it necessary to conceal

* Hearing that the Commons were not disposed to dissolve, as he desired, Cromwell went down to the House with a body of soldiers, whom he placed at the door. Then entering, he sat down for a time, when, suddenly starting up, he loaded the members with the vilest reproaches for their tyranny, oppression, and robberies. Then, stamping his foot, a signal for the soldiers to enter, "For shame," he cried, "get you gone; you are no longer a Parliament. The Lord has done with you; he has chosen other instruments for carrying on his work." Taking hold of Martin by the cloak, he exclaimed, "Thou art a whoremaster." Then to another, "Thou art an adulterer." To another, "And thou an extortioner." To a fourth, "Thou art a drunkard and a glutton." He commanded a soldier to seize the mace. "What shall we do with this bauble?" he said. "Take it away." Ordering the soldiers to clear the House, he went out the last, directing the doors to be locked. Sir Harry Vane protested. "O Sir Harry Vane!" cried Cromwell; "the Lord deliver me from Sir Harry Vane!"

it under the forms and usages so long established. Accordingly, he determined to call another House of Commons, but took care to fill it with his retainers. It consisted of 156 Members, and met in July, 1653. It was composed of men of the lowest condition, the "very dregs of the fanatics," remarks Hume, and was nicknamed the "Barebones Parliament," after one of its conspicuous Members, Barebone, a leather-dresser. It was the policy of Cromwell to employ as his military and political agents individuals of low condition, for they readily carried out his illegal acts, whilst men of capacity would have refused.* The Barebones Parliament soon fell into ridicule as Cromwell intended; and upon his hint a majority of its Members, with the Speaker, came to him one day with their resignations. Hearing that some of the minority were not willing to depart, he sent one of his Colonels with a party of soldiers to disperse them. "What are you doing here?" asked Colonel White. "We are seeking the Lord," responded the recalcitrants. "Then you may go elsewhere," returned the Colonel, "for to my certain knowledge he has not been here these many years."

Having brought Parliamentary Government into contempt, which was his object, Cromwell thought the time had come to throw aside disguise, and make him-

* Buckle gives the following account of the original vocations of Cromwell's officers. Colonel Pride, who expelled a part of the Commons, known as "Pride's Purge," was a drayman; Admiral Deane, a servant; General Whalley, an apprentice to a draper; Colonel Goffe, ditto; Skippon, commander-in-chief in Ireland, a private soldier. Berkstead, a pedlar, and Selway, apprentice to a grocer, were Councillors of State; as also Berners, a servant, and Holland, a link-boy, Bond, a draper, Colonel Okey, a stoker, Colonel Horton, a servant, Colonel Hooper, a haberdasher, Major Rolfe, a cobbler, Colonel Fox, a tinker, Colonel Hewson, a cobbler, Colonel Jones, brother-in-law of Cromwell, a servant, &c. &c.

self the avowed Head of the State. A Council of his officers drew up what was called "The Instrument of Government," a sort of charter by which Cromwell was to be the supreme magistrate under the title of Protector. He was to nominate to all places, and to have the right to make peace or war, and alliances. A Council of State of not less than thirteen persons was created to cooperate with him. A Parliament was to be summoned by him every three years, to sit for five months. *A standing army was to be maintained under the sole control of the Protector.* This new political contrivance concentrated all authority in Cromwell, and was of course designed by himself. It was sworn to by his officers, and the Protector was installed in office, December, 1653. He appointed fifteen of his adherents to the Council. The Parliament was to meet in September, 1654.

If the Lords and Commons of 1640—the Nobles and Middle Class—had foreseen the revival of such perfect Absolutism as this, far beyond that which roused their ancestors against King John, they would have rested on the vast concessions of the pliant Charles, and avoided the civil war, with its crimes and miseries. Cromwell taught the Politicians of his time a lesson not likely to be ever forgotten.

His Highness the Lord Protector, as he was now called, promptly restored Monarchical usages. He received the foreign Ambassadors seated in a gorgeous chair of State. All the Royal palaces were fitted up with magnificence for his residence. He gave sumptuous banquets, and attired himself in robes of State.* The

* Seven tables were daily set at Whitehall, as follows:—A table for His Highness, a table for Her Highness the Protectoress, a table for

country, exhausted by eleven years of war and turmoil, accepted Cromwell's despotism with resignation. The bulk of the people, however, remained Royalist. The Presbyterians as well as his former allies the Independents equally hated Cromwell, but were powerless.

The Parliament proposed by the Protector was to consist of 400 Members for England, 30 for Scotland, and 30 for Ireland. All the lower class was excluded from the franchise, as an estate of £200 a year was necessary to a vote. All Royalists were also excluded. The elections were conducted with freedom, as Cromwell was anxious to know the sentiments of the country. This Parliament met in September, 1654, and lost no time in denouncing the new Government. Bradshaw, who sentenced the King, was now chief of the Opposition. Cromwell, losing his patience, locked the Members out of the House, and allowed none to return without signing a document declaring that his Government was legal. Two-thirds gave their signatures, but continued their opposition, till Cromwell in a rage dissolved the Parliament.

This experiment proved that the Protector could only maintain himself by force. He divided England into twelve military districts, appointing a General to the command of each with unlimited authority. "Never, before nor since," says an historian, "has England known so iron a rule."

Cromwell's foreign policy was bold, successful, but impolitic. He carried on a victorious war against Holland; cultivated the French alliance; and made war on Spain, seizing the Island of Jamaica. He was

chaplains and strangers, a table for stewards and gentlemen, a table for the gentlemen, two other tables for upper and lower servants.

ably assisted in his wars by Admiral Blake, though that officer had no love for the Protector. "It is our duty," Blake said, "to fight for our country."

His administration at home was skilful and vigilant. He promoted good men to the bench, and showed a cautious lenity to the various religious denominations. Scotland and Ireland he treated as conquered provinces.

Hoping that success abroad and tranquillity at home had popularized his Government, he summoned another Parliament in September, 1656. He used every influence to secure the return of his partisans, but found, to his chagrin, the majority against him. Without hesitation he set a guard at the doors of the House, and excluded all who would not sustain his acts. Finding that the Generals he had set up as *Pachas* over the military districts were growing dangerous, he adroitly got the Parliament to censure them, and they were removed.

And now he attempted to scale the last round of the ladder he had so skilfully mounted, and to clutch the prize he had so ardently pursued. His heart was set upon the Crown, and he fondly hoped that by obtaining it he would consolidate his power. The Assembly he had packed with his adherents gladly complied with his secret yearnings, and voted him the title of King in April, 1657. To his dismay, a furious opposition broke out. His Generals, one and all, denounced the project. Lambert; Fleetwood, his son-in-law; Desborough, his brother-in-law, threatened to resign their commissions. Colonel Pride, the "Purger," got up a Protest against Cromwell's attempt to restore the throne, which was signed by all the officers in London; and mutiny began to spread rapidly through the army, which was the Protector's chief support. Cromwell, after "the agony and perplexity of long doubt," says Hume, was compelled to refuse the darling object of his ambition. For the first time he suffered a galling defeat In his wrath he dismissed Lambert and all the officers who had opposed his ambitious design ; and consoled himself by getting his obedient Legislature to vote a new charter, called " A Humble Advice and Petition," by which he had the right to nominate his successor, and, furthermore, to create a House of Lords for life.

After this remodelling of the Government, Cromwell was again inaugurated as Lord Protector with great pomp, and the Parliament was adjourned. He then called many of the old Nobility to the new House of Peers, but they refused to attend, and he was forced to compose it of such materials as he could find. In 1658, he summoned his new Parliament of two Houses. The Upper consisted of some 60 persons. To his chagrin he found the majority in the Lower House, lately so submissive, now decidedly refractory. Greatly incensed, he dismissed them in fifteen days.

In spite of his marvellous success, in spite of the prodigies his genius had accomplished, Cromwell could no longer blind himself to the fact that the Nation he had enslaved would submit only whilst force compelled it. The upper, middle, and lower classes longed for the hour of emancipation. Ambition had blinded him, else he might have known that a people who were the first in the world to organize a Representative Government would never again endure the tyranny of any man, however gifted, however successful.

The last year of his life was a bitter expiation for all his greatness. The army, his only prop, was filled with disaffection. He knew not at what moment it might hurl him from his high estate. Surrounded by treacherous friends or secret enemies, he found not even in the bosom of his family sympathy or support. His favorite child, Mrs. Claypole, on her death-bed reproached him so keenly for his many sanguinary crimes as to fill him with melancholy, if not remorse. The dread of assassination haunted him day and night. He wore armor under his clothes, and was always provided with sword and pistols. He never moved without guards; never returned by the road he went, and travelled at a furious gallop; never slept twice in the same room, nor without sentinels at every door. He employed a legion of spies, and fifteen conspiracies were detected. All his arts and policy exhausted—treacherous to every party and false to every friend—corroded by care and preyed on by disease — he still recoiled from death with singular timidity. He fainted when his physicians announced his malady mortal, and, recovering, declared their statement false. "I tell you," he exclaimed, "I tell you I shall not die of this distemper; I am well assured of my recovery." His illness lasted but a week. The night before his death he frequently uttered exclamations that showed the torment of his mind. "Truly, God is good. Indeed he is, he will not"—here his voice failed him. At times he would denounce himself, and then again would express dread of the obloquy the world might cast on him. What a contrast to the placid end of his victim, Charles! After violent paroxysms, Cromwell expired, September 3d, 1658, in his fifty-ninth year.

In this concise sketch of his life many singular traits of this remarkable man have been omitted. His love of buffoonery has often been noticed, but this was only an artifice to hide some politic purpose. For instance, he held a consultation with a band of his trusted adherents after the King's execution as to the future form of Government. After all had spoken, to avoid giving his own views, he suddenly threw a cushion at the head of General Ludlow, and ran away. Again, when he signed the death-warrant of Charles, he smeared the face of Martin who sat next to him with ink, and the latter, when he signed, practised the same joke on Cromwell. His object in this was to make light of a tragical event. With all his grimness, he was not deficient in humor. One day, at Hampton Court, a corkscrew dropped from his hand as he was opening a bottle of wine. His Courtiers and Generals at dinner threw themselves on the floor to recover it, when Cromwell burst into laughter. "If any fool," he said, "were now to look in upon your posture, he would say you were seeking the Lord, whilst you are only seeking a corkscrew." Austere as he was reputed to be, he was not above temptation. His intrigues with the beautiful Lady Dysart are incontestable; and she is said to have saved her husband's head, after the battle of Worcester, by submitting to Cromwell's familiarities. No public man ever excelled Cromwell in dissimulation; and the religious cant so universal in his epoch enabled him to veil his meaning in such exquisite jargon as to defy comprehension. In a note will be found a sample.*

* The following is Cromwell's speech to the Committee of the Commons, when they waited on him with a tender of the Crown. He dared not openly accept it, yet shrank from refusing it. To avoid either, and gain time, was the secret of the rigmarole he spoke, and which, in its way, is a masterpiece. "I confess, for it behoves me to deal plainly with you, I must confess, I would say, I hope, I may be understood in this; for

It is useless to dwell on the numberless private executions and wholesale slaughters that disfigured his rise to power. Literally he waded through rivers of blood to satisfy his ambition. Take him all in all, he is the most extraordinary man that has figured in English history. Guizot, who has analyzed the career of Cromwell with equal felicity and impartiality, remarks that "Providence rarely bestows on the same man the double power to destroy and create; but it seems to have bestowed on Cromwell these two opposite gifts, for no sooner was the Revolution completed than the Dictatorship was organized."

Richard, eldest son of the late Protector, was proclaimed by the Council of War as his successor the day after his father's death. He accepted reluctantly a position for which he was unfitted from his mild character and ignorance of public affairs.

indeed I must be tender what I say to such an audience as this; I say I would be understood, that in this argument I do not make parallel betwixt men of a different mind and a Parliament which shall have their desires. I know there is no comparison, nor can it be urged upon me that my words have the least color that way, because the Parliament seems to give liberty to me to say anything to you, as that, that is a tender of my humble reasons and judgment and opinion to them: and if I think they are such, and will be such to them, and are faithful servants, and will be so to the supreme authority, and the legislative, wheresoever it is: if, I say, I should not tell you; knowing their minds to be so, I should not be faithful, if I should not tell you so, to the end you may report it to the Parliament. I shall say something for myself, for my own mind, I do profess it, I am not a man scrupulous about words or names of such things I have not: but as I have the Word of God, and I hope I shall ever have it, for the rule of my conscience, for my informations; so truly men that have been led in dark paths, through the providence and dispensation of God; why, surely it is not to be objected to a man; for who can love to walk in the dark? But Providence does so dispose. And though a man may impute his own folly and blindness to Providence sinfully, yet it must be at my peril; the case may be that it is the Providence of God that doth lead men in darkness; I must needs say, that I have had a great deal of experience of Providence, and though it is no rule without or against the Word, yet it is a very good expositor of the Word in many cases."

Cromwell's death left his authority in the hands of the army. The influential Generals whom the late Protector had dismissed—Lambert, Ludlow, &c.—promptly reappeared, in the hope of supplanting the incompetent Richard. To escape this danger, he called a new Parliament in January, 1659; but perplexed by the situation, it wasted time in idle debates. Dreading the cabals of the conspiring Generals, they voted that there should be no Councils of Officers without the consent of the Protector. This act of hostility enraged the Generals, and they insisted with threats, that Richard should dissolve the Parliament. He did so, but immediately resigned the Protectorship in April, 1659—only seven months after he had assumed it.

England was now without a Government. Divided amongst themselves, the Generals agreed to call together the remains of the Long Parliament formerly dispersed by Cromwell. This Assembly, known as the "Rump Parliament," met in December, 1659, and was composed of the party called "Independents," of which Cromwell was formerly the chief. When he expelled the Presbyterians—166 Members—from the House, it was the Independents who, at his instigation, voted the King's trial. The country regarded the return of these violent fanatics to power with alarm and disgust. Undismayed they set vigorously to work; appointed a Council of State of their own adherents, and undertook to bring the Generals under control. Partial insurrections broke out in different parts of the country, and the "Rump" were compelled to call on the army for protection. Lambert marched into Wales, and suppressed the rising there; and, on his return, organized a Military Council, to be independent of the

"Rump." Greatly startled by this measure, they promptly cashiered Lambert and his nominees. Lambert, adopting the tactics of his old master, marched into London, and turned the "Rump" into the street. A "Committee of Safety" was then organized, consisting of twenty-three persons. England thus fell into the hands of a military faction, and was on the verge of dissolution. Payment of taxes was generally refused. All classes were filled with apprehension. The Nobility and Middle Class dreaded loss of life and property; the People trembled at the perils in store for them.

At this juncture the eyes of the Nation were suddenly concentrated on General Monk, whom Cromwell had left in command of Scotland. This sagacious man comprehended the situation. He saw when Richard Cromwell retired that anarchy was inevitable unless the ancient Government were restored. This was impossible whilst an army of mercenaries, commanded by unscrupulous men, held the country in subjection. His force consisted of 6,000 men, whilst the army in England exceeded 30,000. It was, therefore, his interest to avoid a collision which would expose the country to unknown disasters. Silent and impenetrable, he waited the moment for action. When Lambert expelled the "Rump" Parliament, he protested, and began his march to London. This induced other Generals, jealous of Lambert, to side with the Parliament. As Monk advanced all classes hailed him as a deliverer, but to none would he disclose his purpose. Many suspected that he aspired like Cromwell to the supreme authority. Lambert alarmed left London to confront him. "The Rump" taking advantage of this reassembled, and sent a deputation to Monk, who gave them no explanation. They next sent orders to the troops with Lambert to return to the quarters assigned. The troops obeyed, abandoning Lambert to a man, and Monk entered London without conflict.

After coquetting awhile with the "Rump," he demanded that the 160 Members who had been driven out by Cromwell should take their seats, and they did so without opposition. This left the Independents in a minority, and was the end of that violent faction which under the lead of Cromwell had overthrown the old Constitution of King and Parliament, and which was in its turn suppressed by that crafty Politician for his own aggrandizement. The majority of Parliament again consisted of the Presbyterian party which had begun the collision with the unhappy Charles, and whose object was simply, as previously stated, the ascendency of Parliamentary Government. They discovered too late that they had provoked a Revolution they could not arrest, and expiated their folly when trampled under the feet of Cromwell and the Independents. Conscious that England owed to them the loss of her ancient liberties, and the miseries of the civil war, they readily obeyed the desire of Monk and the demand of the Nation to dissolve themselves, after summoning a free Parliament to decide on the destinies of England. This was the last act of the Long Parliament of 1640, which, as described, was alike the parent of the civil war and Cromwell's Protectorate. A Council of State composed of "men of character and moderation" administered the Government in the interval.

An explosion of pent-up enthusiasm for the old institutions now shook the land like a volcano from one end to the other. The elections filled the House of Commons with men pledged to the restoration of the throne, and the ancient Nobility forthwith returned to their seats in Parliament. The Nobles and the Middle Class resumed once more their co-partnership of centuries, temporarily broken up by a successful soldier whose advent their own indiscretion had provoked. They were still resolved on a due limitation of the power of the Crown; but, enlightened by misfortune, they were equally resolved to avoid the errors that had entailed such dire calamities.

The Commons had no sooner assembled than Monk announced that an Ambassador from the King was at their door with a letter from His Majesty. The Ambassador was admitted to the House, and the letter of the King read, which offered a general amnesty and liberty of conscience. The wildest acclamations resounded on all sides, and were re-echoed by the whole country as the news spread abroad The King was solemnly proclaimed at different points of London in presence of both Houses; and Committees from the Lords and Commons were sent to Holland to invite Charles to return to his vacant throne. The King entered London, May 29th, 1660, amid universal enthusiasm. From Dover where he landed, his way to the metropolis was lined with thousands of people who rent the air with cries of joy. Charles expressed his wonder and delight, whilst all marvelled at the utter disappearance of the faction which had so recently tyrannized over the land.

THE RESTORATION.

SEVENTEENTH CENTURY.

CHARLES II. was just thirty when his reign began. Guizot remarks that "Charles II. recovered his throne without foreign aid or domestic struggle, and even without the assistance of the Royalists, by the spontaneous impulse of the nation, who were thus delivered from oppression, anarchy, and revolutionary fluctuations, and only expected at the hands of the King order and stability." This is perfectly true, for all classes had suffered so much materially and morally from twenty years of political and religious agitation, and civil war, that all yearned for repose, and all believed it was to be found only in the restoration of their old institutions of King, Lords, and Commons.

If Charles II. had been an ambitious man, it would have been easy to restore the Royal power to something like the vigor it possessed under Elizabeth; but he was of a tolerant nature, a sound understanding, and an amiable disposition. Besides, the sad fate of his father and his own misfortunes indisposed him for conflicts which might have ended in another civil war and his own dethronement. As he showed no desire to strain his authority, the Nobles and Middle Class gave their attention to practical reforms of the most salutary character. Buckle remarks that "during the reign of Charles II. more steps were taken in the right direction than had been taken in any period of equal length during the twelve centuries we had occupied the soil of Britain." It was called by Fox "the era of good laws and bad government."

The prudent conduct of the King gave no cause for political dissensions, but the Church of England, which was restored with the Monarchy, exhibited less moderation. Having suffered so much persecution under the régime of the Presbyterians and the Independents, the Church was eager to take revenge on both these bodies of Dissenters. But neither the Nation nor the King sympathized with their zeal for Protestantism. So ridiculous and criminal had been the excesses of fanaticism during the reign of the Independents, so disgusted were all classes with the cant and sanctified hypocrisy that prevailed under Cromwell's Government, that a reaction bordering on scepticism had ensued, and most persons, high and low, felt an utter indifference to the quarrels amongst the Clergy of whatever denomination. As for Charles himself, he was a Freethinker much more than a Protestant or Catholic, and openly professed an admiration of Hobbes, the Materialist, who was cordially hated by the Clergy. All the great intellects of this epoch were likewise impregnated with disbelief. Locke was an Unitarian, Newton a Socinian, Milton an Arian.

To this sceptical condition of the public mind must be ascribed the various schemes resorted to by the Ecclesiastics and Politicians to dissipate the political and religious lethargy prevailing. In this way may be explained one of the strangest events of this reign. The "Popish plot to assassinate the King" can be regarded only as an invention to stir up the prejudices of the country against the Catholics, and so bring about a religious revival. The King, on his part, never for a moment believed in the conspiracy; but such was the number of false witnesses suborned—Titus Oates amongst the rest—that the smouldering hatred of Papacy was rekindled, and before it was extinguished a number of innocent lives both noble and plebeian were ruthlessly sacrificed.*

The Politicians worked zealously to utilize the Anti-Catholic fury, and to carry out their ambitious projects. Lord Russell, Algernon Sydney, and others united in bringing a Bill into the Commons to exclude James brother of the King from the throne, as he was a known Papist. The Bill being rejected by the Lords, these disappointed men entered into a conspiracy to incite an insurrection which would have entailed on England the horrors of another civil war. The Duke of Monmouth, a natural son of Charles, was at the head of this conspiracy, and aimed at the succession to his father. Lord Russell did not seek to overturn the Monarchy, but was ready to employ this odious means to redress what he considered grievances. Algernon Sydney, a son of the Earl of Leicester, aspired to found a Republic. Lord Shaftesbury, an unscrupulous Politician, fomented actively this wanton plot.

* The aged Viscount Stafford, a Catholic noble, was accused of conspiring to raise a Papal army to subdue England. This absurd accusation was sustained by false witnesses, whose statements were disproved, yet the House of Lords, under pressure of the mania prevailing, condemned him to death. The King commuted the sentence of "hanging and quartering" to that of decapitation, an exercise of prerogative which Lord Russell, in the House of Commons, called in question. The infirm old man on the scaffold protested his innocence in language so firm and pathetic that the populace forgot their insane delusions, and melted into tears. They shouted repeatedly, "We believe you, my lord; God bless you, my lord!" The executioner was so much affected that twice he lifted the axe, and it was only on the third attempt that the head was severed from the body.

In spite of the Anti-Popery frenzy that had been aroused by such detestable means, the Nation was not at all disposed to rush into another civil war. They knew the King was not tyrannical whatever might be his other faults, and they were not so easily duped by the Politicians as the last generation had been. Thus the conspirators were obliged to postpone the intended rising till all was discovered in June, 1683. Hume remarks that, "the whole gang of spies, witnesses, informers, and suborners who had so long been supported and encouraged by the leading patriots now turned short upon their old patrons, and offered their services to the Government." To escape arrest many fled. Monmouth absconded. Lord Russell was seized and sent to the Tower, as were also Lord Essex, Sydney, and others. Many of the conspirators confessed all; and it was made evident that a plan of insurrection had been fully settled, and that the assassination of the King was intended.

Lord Russell was tried by a jury "of men of fair and reputable characters." He did not deny his share in the projected insurrection, but declared that he harbored no design against the life of the King. He was found guilty, and condemned to death. The King commuted the legal sentence of "hanging and quartering," saying, "Lord Russell shall find that I am possessed of that prerogative which, in the case of Lord Stafford, he thought proper to deny me." Great exertions were made to save Russell's life. The Earl of Bedford, his father, offered £100,000 to the Duchess of Portsmouth, who had great influence with the King, but in vain. As several of the inferior agents of the conspiracy had been executed, the King was not disposed to interfere with the law to save those who had originated the plot, however lofty in rank or strong in connections. No one questioned the justice of Lord Russell's sentence, but many regretted that a man with so many noble traits had allowed his ambition to seduce him into a plot which, if carried out, would have involved a fearful sacrifice of life. Nothing could prove more clearly the wanton folly of resorting to violence to redress the grievances Lord Russell complained of than the events which ensued in the reign that shortly followed; for the infatuation of James II. was punished without resorting to a bloody revolution.

Algernon Sydney was another of the band of noble conspirators. He had fought against Charles I.; then denounced the usurpation of Cromwell; and, on the return of Charles II., had retired to the continent, refusing the Act of Amnesty. After some years he solicited the King's pardon, and obtained it though his name figured on the list of the Judges of Charles I. He was enthusiastic for a Republic on the ancient model, and was even willing, says Hume, "to seek a second time through all the horrors of civil war for his adored Utopia." Like Russell he was tried by a jury; like him he did not deny his guilt, and was condemned and executed.

Another prominent incident of this reign was the rise of the two great political parties which have so long conducted the public business of England. There can be no more positive proof of the great change in the condition of the country than the advent of these two parties. It was not until the power of the Church and the Monarchy had been overcome by the alliance of the Nobles and the Middle Class so often mentioned, that the existence of these parties became possible. They were composed of men whose position was wholly different from the Statesmen who had abounded at all epochs in modern Europe, and who were simply the agents of Royal authority commissioned to manage the business of the State. Nor did they at all resemble the public men of ancient Europe, who often aspired to the Sovereign power; for in Greece, as in Rome during the Consulship, they contended with each other for the supreme magistracy. It was reserved for England, in the seventeenth century, to develop a political sect hitherto unknown. The Church and Monarchy being stripped of that monopoly of power which they had jointly wielded in previous centuries, it fell into the hands of the Nation itself; and then arose a new category of public men who aspired, in the name of their views or principles, to act as Trustees of the National Will.

This new breed of Politicians arrayed themselves in opposite camps—those who considered further innovation dangerous, and those who persisted in new modifications. The first were content with the conquests achieved over Church and King; but the latter demanded more. These antagonistic opinions were professed in the time of Charles II. by two contending parties, who were then christened Tory and Whig.

This was the real distinction between these two sets of rival Politicians, though at the time they seemed merely to differ on the expediency of excluding James, brother of the King, from succeeding to the throne on account of his religion. The Whigs, who professed to be the popular or patriotic party, denounced James as a Catholic, which was consistent, as they were the authors of the furious crusade against the Catholics that ended in so many executions. They likewise excluded by the *Test Act*, of which they were the framers, all Protestants from Parliament and office who dissented from the Church of England. This Act of the Whig leaders remained unrepealed till the reign of George IV. Charles and the Tory party resisted this oppression of the Catholics and Dissenters; but the popular rage excited by the Whigs against Popery ran so high that the King as usual gave way and signed the *Test Act*.

It will thus be seen that the Whig, or so-called patriotic party, blundered fearfully at the start. They first robbed their Catholic and Protestant fellow-countrymen of their equal rights, because they dissented from the National Church. They next sought to throw the country into a Revolution, because they failed by legal means to obtain control of the Government. Such, beyond question, were the motives of Russell, Essex, and Sydney. The disrepute into which the party fell shows how hateful such designs were to the Nation at large; for the Whig party, after the discovery of the plot against the King, was completely overthrown. "This mighty faction," says Hume, "which has shaken the throne and menaced the royal family, was totally subdued, and by their precipitate indiscretion exposed themselves to the rigor of the law and to public hatred."

From that day to this political leaders whether Tory or Whig, Conservative or Liberal, have gone on amicably struggling for the Trusteeship of that power which no longer rests in the hands of a Church or a Monarch, but in those of the Nation. The mistakes of the Whig Politicians of the time of Charles II. have never been repeated: argument, and not force, is relied on as the only passport to political power.

After this summary of the principal incidents of this reign, it is unnecessary to enter into many details. The first Parliament of Charles II. met in April, 1660, and so overflowed with loyalty that the King would have been sustained in any abuse of his power. He made "the most eminent men of the nation, whether Royalists or Presbyterians, his Ministers," says Rowland. Sir Edward Hyde, afterwards Lord Clarendon, was selected as Prime Minister.* The second Parliament, quite as loyal, assembled in May, 1661, and was not dissolved for nearly seventeen years. The third Parliament assembled in March, 1678. Two other Houses of Commons, elected in 1680 and 1681, being under Whig influence, were refractory, but still in the main loyal.

A large number of highly beneficial laws were passed during this reign, diminishing the privileges of the Clergy and Nobility, and giving additional guarantees to the liberty of the subject. The right of the People to be taxed solely by their Representatives in the Commons was settled at this time, it being enacted that all money Bills should originate in the Lower House. The Feudal System imported by the Normans was wholly abolished; and thus was closed finally in England the régime of the Middle Ages. New laws regulating the liberty of Printing were also passed. It is to this reign also that England owes the *Habeas Corpus Act*. The writ of *Habeas Corpus*, which

* This able Minister and upright man became, from various causes, so unpopular that he was stripped of power in 1667, and banished by Act of Parliament. He wrote in his retirement, "The History of the English Rebellion."

requires that cause shall be promptly shown for depriving any subject of his liberty, and which was intended to prevent arbitrary imprisonment, originated with the "Writ of Inquisition" in *Magna Charta*, and was enlarged by statutes in the reign of Edward III. —1327–77. This law, so ancient in its origin and so necessary a safeguard of individual liberty, was not finally and indisputably settled until the twenty-eighth year, 1679, of Charles II.'s reign.*

Charles II. died in February, 1685. In spite of the events of the war with the Dutch, and the cry raised against him that he had sold himself to Louis XIV., Charles was immensely popular at his death. Hume in describing him says: "Far from being stately or reserved, he had not a grain of pride or vanity in his composition, but was the most affable, best-bred man alive. He treated his subjects like noblemen, like gentlemen, like freemen; not like vassals or boors. . . Upon the whole, it appeared to many cruel, and even iniquitous, to remark too rigorously the failings of a Prince who discovered so much facility in correcting his errors, and so much lenity in pardoning the offences committed against himself."

Charles II. was unfortunate in his marriage with a Portuguese Princess—May, 1662. She was unattractive in person, and proved to be sterile. This, doubtless, encouraged Charles in those habits of libertinism which became so prevalent after the rigid austerity of the

* The well-known statesman Charles James Fox spoke of the *Habeas Corpus Act* "as the most important barrier against tyranny, and best framed for the liberty of individuals, that has ever existed in any ancient or modern commonwealth." Sir James Mackintosh declared "the writ of *Habeas Corpus* and trial by jury to be the most effectual securities against oppression which the wisdom of man has hitherto been able to devise."

previous epoch. It was thought at one time that he would divorce his Catholic Queen; and at the height of the Anti-Popery mania no step would have been more popular. In spite of his interest, and even the safety of the throne, the King had the generosity to protect her. "They think," he said, "I have a mind to a new wife, but for all that I will not see an innocent woman abused."

Charles was noted for his quick wit. It was a current phrase that "the King never said a foolish thing, nor ever did a wise one." * When this saying reached his ears, he retorted, "That is easily explained, for my discourse is my own, but my actions are my Ministry's." He remarked once of the Duke of Ormond, "I have done everything to disoblige that man, but it is not in my power to make him my enemy." A proof of his sensibility may be seen in the observation of the Duke of Buckingham one day when the Duke of Ormond came to Court. "Sir," said Buckingham, "I wish to know whether it be the Duke of Ormond that is out of favor with your Majesty, or your Majesty with the Duke of Ormond, for, of the two, you seem the most out of countenance."

In all his public conduct Charles always displayed great tact, as well as a lively recollection of his father's ill-advised struggles with Parliament; always shunning any conflict which might possibly end in his fall and exile. One day when his brother James was urging some inexpedient act upon him he sagely replied, "Brother, I am too old to go again to my travels; you may if you choose it."

* Attributed to the Earl of Rochester.

THE MONARCHY LIMITED.

SEVENTEENTH CENTURY.

JAMES II., second son of Charles I., succeeded his brother, February, 1685, and was then fifty-two years old. This Prince had some good traits of character. He displayed great courage in the Dutch war; but was suspected and feared by the Nation for his bigoted devotion to the Catholic religion. He called Parliament together in May; and his professions to respect the laws, and religion as then established, were so plausible that the Commons promptly voted him the revenue of the late King for life, in spite of the remonstrances of some of the Tory Members. He thus became independent of Parliament.

The first year of his reign was marked by a foolish attempt of the Duke of Monmouth to stir up a Rebellion. The Duke was popular with the masses, and a staunch Protestant; but the Nation dreaded another civil war, and James had a disciplined army of 30,000 men. Monmouth was easily routed, and, being taken prisoner, was beheaded in July, 1685.*

* This favorite of the people, a natural son of Charles II., was attended to the scaffold by crowds in tears. He warned the executioner not to fail, as he had done with Russell, and be obliged to repeat the blow. This suggestion only unmanned the executioner. He struck a feeble blow, and Monmouth was able to raise his head, and look him in the face, as if to reproach him for his failure. He gently laid his head a second time

Parliament met for a second Session in November after the Rebellion. James, elated by his fancied strength, ventured now to reveal his plans, and showed that he was clearly resolved on restoring the Catholic religion, and on asserting his Absolute authority. Shallow and conceited, he seemed to forget altogether the past history of England and the tragic fate of his father. He began by calling on Parliament to vote supplies for a standing army, and to repeal the Test Acts, which excluded the Catholics from office. The House of Commons soon perceived the tendency of the King's proposals, and combining with the House of Lords, no less eager in defence of the Protestant religion and the rights of Parliament, set to work preparing resolutions condemning the conduct of James. Thus we see, as of old, the Nobles and the Middle Class again uniting to resist the encroachments of arbitrary power. James perceiving a storm in the horizon, prorogued this refractory Parliament, and never called another.

In the following year, 1686, James revived the Ecclesiastical Court created by Elizabeth, abolished by the Long Parliament, and again prohibited in Charles II.'s reign. He next boldly annulled the Test Acts by a Declaration of Indulgence, 1687, and followed this up by a Declaration for Liberty of Conscience —April, 1688. These acts of Toleration, since carried out by law in England, were then utterly repugnant to the Nation; for in the minds of the people Catholicism, which James openly avowed his purpose of reviving,

on the block, and the executioner struck him several times ineffectually. He threw down the axe, and declared he could not finish the bloody work. The Sheriff obliged him to renew the attempt, and with two blows more the head was severed from the body.

was identified with Absolute Monarchy. The Bishops were particularly zealous in opposing the policy of James. Seven were sent to the Tower, and being afterwards tried for misdemeanor were acquitted amid the shouts of the people. These insane proceedings of the King aroused the deepest disgust, and a determination to get rid of him was adopted by the leaders of both parties.

In the previous reign the Tories had refused to exclude James from the throne, while the Whigs had organized a conspiracy to carry out this object, but in the present emergency these differences were forgotten; the leaders of both parties dismissing all factious considerations, and thinking only of the interests of the country. This spectacle of party patriotism was remarkable, but it would be an exaggeration to suppose that the Politicians of that day were less ambitious or more disinterested than those who have succeeded. The unanimity of the Tory and Whig chiefs was probably in great part produced by the fact that behind them stood the combination of Nobles and Middle Class, who dictated, as of old, the course to adopt.

In June, 1688, an invitation was sent to William Prince of Orange, Stadtholder of Holland, to come to England and take the throne. The Prince of Orange was the grandson of Charles I., and had married his cousin Mary, the daughter of James II. He and his wife were both ardent Protestants. He was, besides, a man of distinguished ability, one of the first soldiers in Europe, and of unbending strength of character. All these qualities he had already shown, for he had contended successfully for years against all the power of Louis XIV. of France. William, though ambitious, was eminently prudent, and, were it not that he plainly perceived that the English Nation would be satisfied with nothing less than the expulsion of his infatuated father-in-law, would probably have refused the offer of the English Crown. He sailed for England with 14,000 men; and had barely landed when James, to his amazement, found himself standing actually alone. His army, officers, the Lords and the Commons, the people, even his own family, abandoned him, and welcomed William. Not a blow was struck. The King, terror-stricken, flung the Great Seal into the river, and fled to France.

Upon this, the Lords assembled in their House for deliberation, and William invited all persons who had been Members of the Commons in Charles's reign, together with the Lord Mayor and Corporation of London, to meet forthwith. One hundred and sixty Members met, and adopted unanimously an Address, already voted by the Lords, asking William to take charge of the Government temporarily, and to call by circular letters a new Parliament. The Prince consented to carry out these resolutions, and on January 23d, 1689, the Parliament—or, as it was then called, the Convention—met. The Whig party were in a majority, as their former opposition to James rendered them popular at this moment. The Convention first employed itself in debating whether William should be made Regent; or his wife, the daughter of James, be declared Queen Regnant; but the Prince declined both these suggestions. The Crown was then conferred by Vote of both Houses on William and Mary, but subject to the limitations contained in a Declaration of Rights which accompanied the gift. The King and Queen accepted the Crown on these conditions.

From that day the English Crown ceased to be held on the maxim of Hereditary or Divine Right. Its title has ever since reposed on a Contract with the Nation, according to which allegiance is given only on condition that the rights and liberties of all, as guaranteed by law, shall be respected. From that day the Monarchy of England was limited to such an extent that Supreme power virtually passed into the hands of the two Houses of Parliament. Thus triumphed Government by Parliament over Government by King; thus ended the conflict begun by John, in 1215, with his Nobles and Freemen of the Middle Class. From this moment commenced the era of Constitutional Government, a Government that is regulated by the laws and usages of the country. The overthrow of the despotism of the Church in England in the sixteenth century led to the birth of *religious freedom* in the world. The overthrow of the despotism of the Monarchy in the same country in the seventeenth century led to the advent of *political liberty*. Both these blessings were secured to England by the Compact entered into with the Nation by William and Mary for themselves and their successors; "and it may justly be affirmed," remarks Hume, "that we in this island have ever since enjoyed, if not the best system of Government, at least the most entire system of liberty that ever was known amongst mankind."

From William and Mary, through the reigns of Anne, the Georges, and William IV., down to the present day Limited Monarchy and Parliamentary Government have lived in perfect harmony. It is true that Government by Parliament has obtained such ascendency that the Monarchy has dwindled into a mere pageant, though it still has its uses, social and political. It is also true that the House of Commons has extended its sway so far as to diminish the salutary influence of its old ally the House of Lords. This is subversive of that balance of the three elementary principles of Government which has been considered the striking merit of the British Constitution, and to maintain which the King, the Lords, and the Commons should each exercise their legitimate influence.

We have now seen how, at the beginning of English history, the Kingly power preponderated ; how, as time went on, the Lords and Commons combined to limit it; and how, after long struggles, they succeeded in finally accomplishing it in 1688. Since then the House of Lords, as just remarked, has lost much of its ancient authority ; whilst the House of Commons has steadily increased its control until it has well nigh absorbed both the Executive and Legislative power. In spite of this defect in the political balance, the English Government is admirably administered, and the reasons for this I will undertake to show when I shall speak of England from personal observation. The theory of "checks and balances" in political machinery, however, is not wholly impracticable, as will be seen when commenting on the Constitution of the United States.

Before closing this sketch, it may be interesting to add a few items of curious information, selected from Hume and others, by way of showing the material progress that was made after the Restoration. Hume says that the commerce and riches of England did never during any period increase so fast as from the Restoration to the Revolution—1660 to 1688. The recovery or conquest of New York and the Jerseys was a considerable accession to the strength of the English Colonies, and, together with the settlement of Pennsylvania and Carolina, effected during the reign of Charles II., extended the English empire in America. Dr. Davenant affirms the shipping of England to have more than doubled in these twenty-eight years. Several new manufactures were established, as iron, brass, silk, hats, glass, paper, &c. One Brewer left the Low Countries, and brought the art of dyeing woollen cloth into England; and this improvement saved the Nation great sums of money. Charles II. gave a Charter to the Hudson's Bay Company, and revived the Charter of the East India Company. Sir Joshua Child states that in 1688 there were on 'Change more men worth £10,000 than there were in 1650 worth £1,000; that £500 with a daughter was in the latter period deemed a larger dowry than £2,000 in the former; that gentlewomen in 1650 thought themselves well clothed in a serge gown which a chambermaid in 1688 would be ashamed to wear; and that, besides the great increase of rich clothes, plate, jewels, and furniture, carriages had increased a hundred-fold. The Duke of Buckingham introduced from Venice the manufacture of glass and crystal into England. The first Law for erecting turnpikes was passed in 1662. In 1670, a second Treaty between England and Spain was made, by which both States renounced the right of trading with each other's Colonies. The French King, in Charles II.'s reign, laid some imposition on English commodities. England retaliated by making the commerce with that kingdom almost prohibitory.

In 1641, when the Star Chamber was abolished, the Long Parliament maintained the old restrictions as to printing of books. The same rigor was maintained by

Cromwell. It was not till 1694 that these restraints were taken off, to the great alarm of William III. and his Ministers. In 1677, the old Law for burning heretics was repealed. The philosophical body known as the "Royal Society" was created by Charles II., who "was a lover of the Sciences, especially Chemistry and Mechanics."

Amongst the distinguished men of this epoch were Christopher Wren in Architecture, Robert Hooke in Science—the rival of Newton—T. Sydenham in Medicine, Boyle in Chemistry.

The reaction from the Puritanical manners and laws of the preceding epoch was so strong at the Restoration that Literature and the Drama, when revived, were affected by it. From asceticism all classes fell into licentiousness. The poetry of Dryden and Rochester, the plays of Wycherley and Otway, are striking proofs. The immortal "Hudibras" was written by Butler in Charles's reign; and by exposing the fanaticism and cant of the Parliamentary party of Charles I.'s time, greatly served his son.

THE PAPACY.

THE PAPACY.

It will make the story of the Middle Ages more intelligible if we take a glance at the chequered career of the Papacy. Moreover, the religious history of Europe, though intimately blended with its political transformations, will be more impressive when contemplated apart and disconnected from all extraneous matter. It will be interesting to trace in a general way the slow but steady growth of the Papacy, which century after century marched on from triumph to triumph, till it became the predominant authority of Europe. Kings and Emperors long resisted it. Heretics perished by thousands in assaulting it. In the sixteenth century it reached its zenith, but then received a blow which proved vital. From that date its omnipotence has declined.

With this simple prelude let us turn to its origin.

In 42 A.D., in the reign of the Emperor Claudius, St. Peter, the chief of the twelve Apostles, went to Rome, and made the metropolis of Paganism the head-quarters of the new Religion. From that date the authority of the See of Rome was acknowledged by all the Christian Churches in Europe, and all points in dispute were referred to its decision. When Constantine made Constantinople the new Capital of the Roman Empire, 330, the spiritual supremacy of the Bishops of Rome still continued, and they remained the head of the Christian Church in the East and the West until the Schism of 862, when the Greek Church declared itself independent of the Roman Church, and has ever since remained so.

During the first centuries of Christianity, the Roman Bishops rendered obedience to the various Emperors, or to their delegates in Italy after the seat of the Empire had been removed to Constantinople. Their power was purely spiritual, but as the new doctrines spread their sway over the minds of men high and low continued to increase. The most despotic rulers during the Dark Ages yielded to their counsels and commands. It was not till the eighth century, when the Exarchs, or representatives of the Emperors of the East, were driven out of Italy, and when Pepin the French King, 755, and afterwards Charlemagne, 775, bestowed on them extensive tracts of land, that the Bishops of Rome became territorial rulers. At a much later date, 1077, the Countess Matilda of Tuscany made a gift of her States to the See of Rome, and these various territories received the name of the "Patrimony of St. Peter."

Gregory VII., 1073, was the first Pontiff who assumed the title of Pope.* At first the Bishops of Rome were elected by the people and the Clergy. Then, later, by the Clergy only. The Emperors of Germany often arrogated the right to name the Pope. Finally, from the year 1170, the right of election was given exclusively to the Cardinals † by Pope Alexander III.

The spiritual power of the Popes continued steadily

* The word Pope is derived from the Greek *Páppas*, signifying—father.

† Cardinal is derived from the Latin word *Cardinalis*. At first the name was applied to the priests at the head of the parishes at Rome. They were then below the rank of Bishops of the Church. They gradually rose in importance till they began to be regarded as the Princes of the Church.

to extend over all Christendom, and so great was the credulity of the masses during the greater part of the Middle Ages, so deep was their reverence for the head of the Church, that few Kings or Emperors ventured to resist his mandates. A sentence of Excommunication launched against any Potentate however powerful, impaired his authority over his subjects, who looked on him as accursed of God.

Towards the end of the eleventh century, a Monk named Peter the Hermit came from the Holy Land, and represented to the Pope, Urban II., the outrages suffered by the Christians from the Infidels, and the profanation of the Holy Sepulchre. The Pope authorized Peter to preach a Crusade against the Infidels, and Peter travelled over Europe, his feet bare and a cross in his hand, stirring up the religious zeal of the Christian world. A number of feudal Lords organized an expedition, at the head of which was a French Noble, Godfrey de Bouillon, a man of great capacity. He sold his Duchy to raise funds, and many other Nobles sold or mortgaged their fiefs to follow him. They set out for Asia Minor in 1096, and defeated the Saracens in every battle. Jerusalem was taken, and Godfrey was elected King. The expedition returned in 1100.

The brilliant success of this adventure stimulated other Crusades. The Popes used all their influence to encourage them, as the religious fervor aroused by these pious enterprises served largely to augment their authority. The Second Crusade, 1147, was headed by Louis VII., King of France, and Conrad, Emperor of Germany. It was not so fortunate. The Third, 1189, was led by Richard, *Cœur de Lion*, King of England, by Philip Augustus, King of France, and Frederick

Barbarossa, Emperor of Germany. Europe was greatly excited by this grand array, but the result was not equal to the general expectation. The Emperor of Germany was defeated, and the King of France quarrelled with Richard and returned home.

Five other Crusades followed at different periods. The last, 1270, had Louis IX., King of France, for its chief.

Contemporarily with the Crusades, Italy was distracted by a furious warfare which lasted over three centuries—the wars of the Guelphs and Ghibellines. The quarrel began between two German Princes who aspired to the throne of Germany. At this time the Emperors of Germany ruled over the north of Italy, and the Pope seeing Germany divided by a civil war, thought the occasion a good one to emancipate Italy from the German yoke, and to strengthen the Papacy. His Holiness accordingly joined the Guelph party, which was favorable to the independence of Italy, and the domination of the Church. This sanguinary strife began in 1159, and continued at intervals down to 1495, with no other result than the alternate victory and defeat of either party.

From this may be seen the unhappy condition of Italy during the Middle Ages. France was no better off, for the constant broils of her feudal Lords kept the country in a state of chronic anarchy. Germany was in a similar condition. England suffered less, as the Feudal System was weaker there.

The Papacy, however, flourished and expanded in the midst of the disorder of Europe, which it was often accused of seeking to promote. In every country the Priesthood was composed of the ablest men, who yielded implicit obedience to the orders from Rome. In all matters domestic or foreign of every nation, the Priesthood, through its influence over the minds of men, exercised irresistible sway. The Pope, as the chief of this powerful Hierarchy, was nothing else for several centuries than the Dictator of Europe.

In 1229, a secret ecclesiastical tribunal was organized by Gregory IX. called the Inquisition, before which any person accused of heresy was brought, and often condemned to torture or to death. This odious institution, which sacrificed thousands of lives, was established in most of the States of Europe, and was only abolished in Spain, its last stronghold, when Napoleon entered in 1808.

A few historical facts will illustrate the vast extent of the Papal power during the Middle Ages. In 1200, Innocent III. laid an interdict on France. An interdict declared the whole Nation out of the pale of the Church. In 1208, the same Pope laid an interdict on England. He also pronounced sentences of deposition from the throne against King John of England and Otho IV. of Germany; and to escape the consequences, John acknowledged himself the vassal of the Pope. In 1245, Innocent IV. excommunicated and deposed the Emperor of Germany. In 1294, Boniface VIII. was arbiter between the Kings of France and England. Over two hundred years later, we find Julius II., in 1503, giving permission to Prince Henry of England, afterwards Henry VIII., to marry Catherine of Arragon.

Up to this period Papal domination was so complete that Bishops and Cardinals frequently acted as Ministers of State in the various Kingdoms of Europe, and sometimes appeared at the head of armies. It may be supposed that the Monarchs of Europe, whose absolute power none contested save the Popes, constantly resisted the dictation of Rome, but such was the superstition of all classes that the Monarchs were compelled, however reluctantly, to submit.

At various intervals attempts at rebellion against the Church of Rome were made.

As early as the eleventh century a band of heretics appeared in the south of France called the Albigenses. They had adopted the doctrines of the Manicheans, that is, the opposing principles of good and evil.

Another sect called the Waldenses appeared also in the south of France in the twelfth century. They attacked the morals of the Clergy, and proposed to translate the Scriptures into the current tongue. The Papacy became alarmed at these symptoms of disaffection, and Alexander III. began by excommunicating the disturbers. A little later, 1204, Innocent III. preached a Crusade against these rebels to the Mother-church, and an army was organized, which, under different leaders, committed terrible atrocities, killing thousands of the heretics, and dispersing the rest.

In the beginning of the fourteenth century, Walter Lollard, said to be an Englishman, appeared in Germany. He attacked the doctrines of the Roman Church, and declared that all its ceremonies were the inventions of the Priests. He was arrested, condemned by the Inquisition, and burnt at Cologne, 1322. He left 20,000 followers, called the Lollards.

In the middle of the same century, in England, Wickliffe made a furious onslaught on the Church of Rome. Being deprived of his place as Principal of the College of Canterbury by the Archbishop, he appealed to the Pope, who decided against him. Exasperated at this he made war on the Papal power, assailing in turn all the essential tenets of the Church. He denied the Necessity of Confession; the Damnation of Children who died before Baptism; the Efficacy of Indulgences; the Supremacy of the See of Rome; the Hierarchy; the Right of the Clergy and Monks to Property. The King, Edward III., whom Wickliffe had sustained against the Pope, favored him, but the Pope, Gregory II., ordered the Archbishop of Canterbury to arrest him. Cited before a Council called by the Archbishop, he escaped a condemnation through the influence of one of the Royal Princes, the Duke of Lancaster. A second Council held in London, 1382, condemned ten of his declarations as heresy, but the Clergy could proceed no further, as Wickliffe was under the Royal protection.

In the beginning of the following century, 1409, John Huss, who was the Confessor of the Queen of Bohemia, adopted with great ardor the Anti-Papal opinions of Wickliffe, and began attacking the authority of the Pope, and denouncing the vices of the Clergy; the Excommunications; the Indulgences; the Worship of the Virgin and the Saints. He was excommunicated by the Pope, Alexander V., and summoned before the Council of Constance, where he was condemned as a heretic. Refusing to retract, he was sentenced to be burnt, 1414. He died with intrepidity, persisting in his opposition. His followers were so numerous that they took up arms, and a civil war ensued which lasted many years.

Another rebellious sect called the Moravian Brothers appeared some years later, and increased in spite of great persecution.

LUTHER, CALVIN, AND KNOX.

SIXTEENTH CENTURY.

In the early part of the sixteenth century came Luther, who by his courage and ability succeeded in establishing a Schism in the Roman Church that was destined to be permanent. There is no doubt the success of Luther was facilitated by the efforts of Wickliffe and John Huss. Moreover, the superstition of previous centuries was gradually melting away, and the dread of Papal denunciation was fast disappearing. A spirit of Scepticism united to a hatred of the Papal power had long been fermenting in the German mind; and it only wanted an occasion, above all some resolute man, to evoke it, when it was sure to break forth and assume formidable proportions.

Luther was the son of a poor miner. He joined the Augustine Monks, and then became a Professor of the University. The Pope, Leo X., to raise money* ordered the sale throughout Christendom of Indulgences for Sin, 1517, and gave this privilege to the Dominican Monks of Germany. The Augustine Monks, irritated at this preference, urged Luther to attack this wholesale distribution of Indulgences. He engaged zealously

* This money was at first intended for a Crusade against the Turks, but was employed to finish the church of St. Peter at Rome. Leo X. was a liberal patron of letters, arts, and sciences. During this brilliant epoch flourished Ariosto, Macchiavelli, Michael Angelo, and Raphael.

in the work, and published a powerful denunciation of this Papal scandal, which reverberated through Germany. The chief of the Dominicans publicly burnt Luther's book, and the Pope summoned him to Rome. He refused to go, and the Legate of the Pope at Augsburg demanded a retraction. As he spurned this summons his arrest was ordered, but he escaped, and protected by the Elector of Saxony he launched into a fierce assault on the Church.

He was wonderfully endowed for such a contest. His nature was aggressive and turbulent; his eloquence earnest and soul-stirring; and his industry indefatigable. With the impetuosity of a torrent he wrote and harangued incessantly. Repudiating all authority but the Holy Scriptures, he denounced the Papacy; the Roman Church; Monastic Vows; the Celibacy of Priests; the Ecclesiastical Hierarchy; the Possession of Property by the Clergy. He likewise rejected the Worship of the Saints; the dogmas of Purgatory, of Confession, and the Mass; only recognizing Baptism and the Eucharist of two Kinds.

Leo X. proscribed him by a Bull of Excommunication, 1520, and ordered his writings to be burnt. In return, Luther publicly burnt the Pope's Bull at Wittemberg, with all the decisions of the Holy See. Summoned before the Diet at Worms, 1521, he went there provided with a safe-conduct from the Emperor of Germany, Charles V., and refusing to retract, he was declared under the ban of the Empire. He escaped from Worms, and was concealed for nine months in a Palace of his protector, the Elector of Saxony. He devoted this period, 1522, to a translation of the Bible into the German language.

The extraordinary success of Luther in his efforts to reform the Roman religion showed the earnest desire of a part of the Christian world to escape from the Papal yoke, as well as the awakening of the European intellect to a sense of the spiritual tyranny that had so long oppressed it. The vital principle of the Revolution effected by Luther was the right of "private judgment," as opposed to the assumed infallibility of the Church. He claimed that all had a right to exercise their judgment on the choice of their religion, and were not compelled to accept the doctrines of Rome as infallible—indeed, he took infinite pains to prove that they were not so. This was an audacious heresy in the eyes of the Papacy, but the success of the new doctrine proved that Europe was ripe for a religious revolt, and to Luther must be ascribed the glory of striking the first victorious blow. For though Lollard, Wickliffe, and Huss strained the chain that held the mind and body of man in bondage, yet it was Luther who first broke its links and encouraged humanity to aspire to religious and political independence, which had never been dreamt of before his time.

To Luther's success is due some of the grandest events of Modern history; and it is only logical to regard him as the author of such important results as the English Act of Settlement of 1688, the American Revolution of 1776, and the French Revolution of 1789. If Luther had never lived, these events would have occurred, but possibly not for some hundreds of years. He first attacked with success the religious thraldom that aggrieved the world, and political subjugation was bound to fall in its turn as knowledge spread.

Among the partisans of Luther were numerous Kings

and Princes who longed to throw off the despotism of the Pope. The Sovereigns of Sweden, Denmark, Franconia, Hesse, the Palatinate, Brandenburg, cordially sustained him; and after many struggles a Treaty was signed at Nuremberg, 1532, between the Lutheran Princes and Charles V., Emperor of Germany. Liberty of Conscience, that is, religious independence, was thus formally conceded to the followers of the Reformed religion, who were generally known as the "Protestants," from having *protested* against the decision of the Diet of Spires, in 1529.

The rebellion of Luther against the primitive Church stimulated disaffection far and wide, and numerous other sects of Dissenters sprang up.

Some years before his death, 1546, Luther witnessed the overthrow of the Papacy in England—from causes, however, totally distinct from love of his doctrines.

He also beheld the advent of a new apostle of reform in Calvin, a Frenchman, who embraced Lutheranism, and began preaching in Paris in 1532, whence he was soon obliged to flee to escape arrest. Calvin afterwards became a Professor of Theology at Geneva, where the Reformed religion had been adopted. After various vicissitudes he died there in 1564.

Like most converts to a Revolution, Calvin carried the war against the Roman Church to greater lengths than Luther deemed necessary. He repudiated all external Worship, all pompous Ceremonies, Cathedrals, and Hierarchies; saying Bishops and Priests were no more needed than Popes. Calvin, though a reformer, was fiercely intolerant. He obtained the execution at Geneva of Dr. Servet, a learned man, for professing

Unitarianism, as also of Gentilis, who advocated the same doctrine.

Calvin originated the doctrine of Predestination, declaring that some were predestined to be saved, and others to be damned.

The followers of Calvin spread over Europe. John Knox, a Scotchman, introduced Calvinism—that is, the Reformed religion as further reformed by Calvin—into Scotland in 1547. Knox closely resembled his predecessor Luther in character. He was intrepid, ungovernable, and impassioned. He was twice compelled to flee from Scotland, and was condemned to be burnt as a heretic. He repaired to his friend Calvin at Geneva, where he remained till Elizabeth, a Protestant, ascended the English throne. Returning to Scotland, 1558, he instigated a terrible outbreak against the Catholic Clergy at Perth, and finally influenced the Scotch Parliament to abolish the Roman religion, and adopt Calvinism—there called Presbyterianism. He likewise contributed powerfully to the downfall of Mary, Queen of Scots.

Knox translated the Bible into English. It had previously been translated by Tyndal,* 1526, who was forced for this to escape from England.

In France the partisans of the Reformed religion were known by the name of Huguenots, and underwent great persecution. They were involved in frequent wars with the Government, which adhered to the Roman religion. An attempt was made by Charles IX., 1572, to exterminate them on the night of St. Bartholomew.

* Tyndal went to Germany, and was intimate with Luther; but afterwards, at the demand of Henry VIII. of England, was arrested by he Emperor of Germany, and burnt at Augsburg.

The alliance of the Church with the Throne in France was so close that any attack on its power was dangerous. Still, symptoms of insubordination began to appear. The spirit of Luther was at work.

Towards the middle of this century, Rabelais published a satirical romance, "*Gargantua et Pantagruel*," which adroitly concealed under a mass of buffoonery and indecency a damaging attack on the Clergy.

In 1580, Montaigne ventured to write with less reserve. In his polished Essays on various subjects he revealed the sceptical state of his mind, and his bold query of, *Que sais-je?*—"What do I know?"—was uttered with impunity. Fortunately for himself Montaigne was a favorite at Court.

Twenty years later came Charron with his striking "*Traité de la Sagesse*"—"Treatise on Wisdom"—wherein he dared to discuss the origin of religion itself. "For," says he, "if we look a little deeper we shall see that each of the great religions is built upon that which preceded it. Thus the religion of the Jews is founded on that of the Egyptians; Christianity is the result of Judaism; and from these two last there has naturally sprung Mohammedanism."

The fate of Charron would have been the stake for such language as this had not Henry IV. been on the throne. This great Monarch was a Huguenot, but he readily embraced Catholicism to put an end to civil war. "*Paris*," he said, "*vaut bien une Messe*"—"Paris is well worth a Mass." The grandest act of his reign was the Edict of Nantes, 1598, which guaranteed the religious liberty of the Huguenots. This was the first decisive blow to the Papacy in France.

DESCARTES AND RICHELIEU.

SEVENTEENTH CENTURY.

In the following century, the seventeenth, came Descartes, the greatest intellect France had yet produced. In the variety of his genius he wonderfully resembled Lord Bacon. He was of noble family, and first entered the army, which he abandoned in 1620. He then travelled widely, and returned to Holland to write.

Knowing that all the knowledge of his day was borrowed from the ancient world, and convinced that it was often superficial and erroneous, he resolved to overthrow it and construct a new edifice of science founded on solid proofs.

His books descanting on every known topic electrified Europe. In Mathematics, he applied a new algebraic notation to Geometry, and solved problems before declared insoluble. In Physics, he discovered the true law of the refraction of light, and gave a simple explanation of the rainbow, till then a mystery. In Astronomy and Cosmology, he invented admirable theories of planetary attraction, far beyond any then known. He sustained Galileo's assertion that "the earth moves," which the Papacy pronounced rank blasphemy. Descartes, also, wrote ably on Physiology and Anatomy. He adopted the important discoveries of two of his contemporaries; that of Harvey, who made known the circulation of the blood, and that of Aselli, who detected the lacteal vessels.

The great object of Descartes in his scientific labors was to prove that the learning of his epoch was greater than that of the ancients, and so destroy all reverence for antiquity. He knew the authority of the Church reposed on the *Scholastic Philosophy* that had prevailed from the ninth to the sixteenth centuries. This Scholastic Philosophy simply meant such knowledge as the Church thought it safe to allow, and therefore all knowledge up to the time of Descartes vindicated Theology, that is, the Dogmas of the Church. No one could speak or write to the contrary without incurring the penalty of heresy. To make the Scholastic Philosophy more imposing, the Church had endorsed it with the great name of Aristotle—an outrage upon the Heathen Philosopher. To diminish, then, the respect of France for the Scholastic Philosophy, and thus sap the foundations of the Church's power, Descartes proved by his great discoveries how far the knowledge of his time exceeded that of the ancient world, even including Aristotle.

Antiquity was thus shattered at a blow. The intellect of France arose from its prostration of centuries before the graven image of the Scholastic Philosophy set up by the Church, and began a struggle for emancipation that overwhelmed all opposition. The moment the intellectual basis of the Papacy was thus impaired, its spiritual supremacy was in danger. Descartes had aroused the spirit of doubt, and before it the blind belief that had enveloped the minds of men, as in swaddling clothes, began gradually to fall.

Descartes, however, threw another bomb into the

entrenched camp of the Papacy. He wrote several metaphysical books which founded a New Philosophy. Their purport was simply to establish the supremacy of the Intellect over the traditions and prejudices that had hitherto crushed it. He declared that man was a thinking animal, the incarnation of thought, "For that which constitutes the man is not his bones, nor his flesh, nor his blood. These are the accidents, the incumbrances of his nature. The man himself is the thought. *Je pense, donc je suis*—'I think, therefore I exist.'"

With such bold and novel phrases he sought to build up a pedestal for human Reason, which would rescue it from the ground where it had so long grovelled. After such homage as this to the supremacy of the Intellect, he drew his conclusions. Their design may be seen in the following quotation:—"Hence our religion should not be acquired by the teaching of others, but should be worked out by ourselves; it is not to be borrowed from antiquity, but it is to be discovered by each man's mind. It is not traditional, but personal."

"The mischief," says Buckle, "which these principles must have done to the old theology"—that is, the Papacy—"is very obvious; they were fatal to many of the common dogmas, such as transubstantiation, &c." Of course, it is obvious enough, as that was the aim of Descartes in founding a philosophy which "rejected all authority but the human reason." He was the logical successor of Luther. "He completed what the great German reformer had left undone. He bore to the old systems of philosophy the same relation that Luther bore to the old systems of religion." Yes; these two men, above all others, jointly demolished the intellectual and religious organization of Europe as it had existed for 700 years, from the ninth to the sixteenth century.

The philosophy of Descartes was founded on "Innate Ideas," and was superseded in France fifty years later by the philosophy of Locke, 1690, who, rejecting the theory of Innate Ideas, said the mind was a blank at its birth, and received all its ideas by two channels, "sensation and reflection." It mattered little if Descartes' theory was sound or not. His purpose was to arouse the intellect of his age, and undermine the spiritual despotism of the Papacy, and he succeeded.

All authorities agree that the illustrious Richelieu was in politics what Descartes was in philosophy. Whilst the latter was writing, the bold Cardinal was acting. As chief Minister of Louis XIII., 1624, he did more to weaken the Papacy and humble the French Clergy than all who had preceded him. It astonished all Europe that France should be governed by a Priest who diminished the power of the Ecclesiastics, and who made the interests of the Church subordinate to those of the State.

Richelieu gave many striking proofs that this was his object. It was the clerical law of Europe up to this time that the Clergy could only be taxed by themselves. Consequently the great wealth of the French Clergy never benefited the State. Richelieu said the "State was the first consideration;" and on one occasion he convoked an Assembly of the Clergy at Nantes, and demanded a supply of six millions of francs. There was a cry of sacrilege on the part of some of the dignitaries of the Church, but this he suppressed by banishing four Bishops and two Archbishops. The money was then given. In 1632, in Languedoc, he deprived three Bishops of their places, and seized the temporalities of others. The Papacy was thunderstruck at these outrages from a son of the Church. Richelieu, however, cared more for the glory of France than the satisfaction of the Papacy, and mocked at the thunders of the Vatican.

It is therefore clear that it was by the joint exertions of Descartes and Richelieu that the absolute power of the Papacy was demolished in France.

A rally was made in the reign of Louis XIV. The wonderful eloquence of Bossuet and Massillon shed a temporary lustre over the Roman Church; and the King revoked the Edict of Nantes, 1685, which led to a general emigration of the Huguenots from dread of persecution. In the following reign, that of Louis XV., the Church lost ground rapidly. In 1762, the Order of the Jesuits, which had long been the terror of Europe, was suppressed. In 1787, Louis XVI. issued a new Edict of Toleration, but in 1789 the Revolution swept away the Church itself, and appropriated all its revenues, estimated at two thousand millions of francs.

TREATY OF WESTPHALIA.

SEVENTEENTH CENTURY.

WHILST the Reformed religion was struggling in Switzerland, France, England, and Scotland, it underwent great vicissitudes in Germany. After many minor conflicts a formidable war broke out, in 1618, between the Protestant Princes of the North, and the Catholic Emperor of Southern Germany, which lasted thirty years. The Protestant Kings of Sweden and Denmark joined in it, as did France towards the close. Cardinal Richelieu, to the amazement of Europe, took the Protestant side against his co-religionists; but he thought it a greater object to break down the military power of Austria than to sustain the Catholic religion.

The celebrated Treaty of Westphalia, 1648, put an end to the religious wars of Germany. The parties to this Treaty were France and Sweden, as allies, against the Emperor of Germany. The political and religious state of Europe, as settled by this Treaty, remained undisturbed till 1806, when it was reorganized by Napoleon. This Treaty is memorable, besides, as being the origin of that system of International Law which is now recognized by the civilized world. Buckle thus speaks of it:—"This celebrated Treaty is remarkable as being the first comprehensive attempt to adjust the conflicting interests of the leading European countries. In this important Treaty, ecclesiastical interests were altogether disregarded, and the contracting parties, instead of, as heretofore, depriving each other of their possessions, took the bolder course of indemnifying themselves at the expense of the Church, and did not hesitate to seize her revenues, and secularize several of her bishoprics.* From this grievous insult, which became a precedent in the public law of Europe, the Spiritual Power"—the Papacy—"has never recovered, and since that period diplomatists have in their official acts neglected religious interests, and have preferred the advocacy of matters relating to the commerce and colonies of their respective countries. The truth of this is confirmed by the fact that the Thirty Years' War, to which this same Treaty put an end, is the last great religious war which has ever been waged; no civilized people during two centuries having thought it worth while to peril their own safety in order to disturb the belief of their neighbours."

The Pope was indignant at this Treaty; but he was helpless. Not only had England, Sweden, Denmark, and Northern Germany discarded the Papacy, but even Catholic France under Richelieu had for political motives joined the Protestant League; and the Pope's only ally, the Emperor of Southern Germany, had been defeated.

From this shock the Papacy never fully recovered, but gradually declined in political influence, even in the States that retained the Roman religion.

* By this Treaty France obtanied Metz, Toul, and Verdun, which up to this time had been under the ecclesiastical government of a Bishop, but which were now annexed to France.

Thus we see that up to the beginning of the sixteenth century, the Papacy wielded absolute power over the conscience of Europe, with the exception of Russia, where the Greek religion prevailed. The frequent abuse of this power provoked resistance; and during the sixteenth century the Papacy was successively overthrown in England, North Germany, Sweden, Denmark, and part of Switzerland.

In the seventeenth century, it was successfully defied in France, where, in the eighteenth century, it was temporarily suppressed by the Revolution. Though restored in the nineteenth century, its Ecclesiastical power was limited by a Concordat.

In our own day we have seen the Papacy not only curtailed of some of its sacerdotal immunities in Italy, its birthplace, but utterly stripped of all temporal power. The Roman religion, however, still maintains its hold on the Christian world in spite of the decay of the Papacy.

THE UNITED STATES.

THE UNITED STATES.

COLONIAL EPOCH.

The history of the United States virtually begins with the emigration of the various bands of English settlers who pitched their tents in the forests of North America. The different Colonies which rapidly sprang up one after the other were nothing else than the United States in embryo; and in following, however generally, their growth and development, we shall discover the origin of those traits and institutions which suddenly converted a group of youthful Colonies into a galaxy of sovereign States.

Before entering on any delineation of the incipient States, it may be well to refresh the memory of the general reader with some of the dates connected with the annals of North America.

In 1492, America was discovered by Christopher Columbus.

In 1497, John Cabot, believing he could reach the East Indies by the North-West Passage, induced Henry VII. of England to aid him, and though he failed in his original project, he was the first to discover Newfoundland, Labrador, and Canada. In 1512, Florida was discovered by Ponce de Leon. In 1534, Canada was occupied by the French, and held till 1763. In 1541, the Mississippi river was discovered by De Soto.

In 1584, the English, under Sir Walter Raleigh, landed in Virginia, thus named after the virgin Queen Elizabeth.* In 1608, John Smith founded Jamestown. This was the first permanent settlement in North America. In 1609, Henry Hudson discovered the Hudson river, and Hudson's Bay, both named after him. In 1614, the Dutch founded a Colony on the site afterwards called New York, which they then termed New Amsterdam. In 1620, the Puritans landed at Plymouth. In 1623, the Dutch occupied Delaware, and in 1627, the Swedes followed them, but in 1664, the English dispossessed both. In 1633, Maryland was settled by the English under Leonard Calvert, brother of Lord Baltimore, and Carolina was also inhabited by the English in 1663, the latter having been previously colonized by the Spanish and French. In 1664, the Dutch surrendered New Amsterdam to the English, who then changed its name to New York, after the Duke of York. In 1681, William Penn established a Quaker Colony at Philadelphia. In 1732, an English Colony settled in Georgia, so named after George II. Whilst the coast was thus occupied, Europeans were making their way into the interior. In 1683, Lasalle, starting from Canada, descended the Mississippi, and took possession of Louisiana, named after Louis XIV., where, in 1699, a French Colony was established. In 1717, New Orleans was founded by the French, and in 1735, also Vincennes in Indiana. England, jealous of the French possessions in America, engaged in war with France in 1754, and by the Treaty of Paris, 1763, became owner of all

* For some time after this the whole country was called Virginia, from Florida on the south, belonging to the Spaniards, to Canada on the north, belonging to the French.

North America save a portion of Louisiana. She did not, however, long retain the sovereignty of this vast empire, for in 1776, the English Colonies rose against the Mother-country, which was forced, in 1783, reluctantly to give them up.

So much for dates: now for a glimpse of the colonial epoch of the United States.

THE PURITANS.

SEVENTEENTH CENTURY.

Most of the English settlers of all the Colonies were loyal subjects of their successive Sovereigns, from James I. to George III., for they abandoned the Mother-country purely from a spirit of enterprise, and in hope of wealth.

The first emigrants to Virginia, 1607, were a reckless band of adventurers in search of gold. These were followed later by artisans and agriculturists of the lower class.

This was not the character, however, of another batch of emigrants who, though not insensible to worldly advantages,* entertained projects of a more aspiring description. They were enamored of certain turbulent ideas in religion and politics, for which they were ready to sacrifice everything but their lives. To save these, they fled from England to Holland, 1610, but they saw

* The Rev. Cotton Mather, in his History of New England, copies from a manuscript circulated among the Puritans at the time the various considerations that induced them to emigrate. The following is one of them: "Sixthly: The whole earth is the Lord's garden, and He hath given it to the sons of Adam to be tilled and improved by them. Why then should we stand starving here for places of habitation, and in the meantime suffer whole countries as profitable for the use of man to lie waste without any improvement?" It is plain the Puritans of 1620, with all their "thick-coming fancies" on religion and politics, were a practical people, and their love of theory did not make them indifferent to the ownership of the "Lord's garden" beyond the seas.

little prospect of carrying out their wild schemes among the phlegmatic Dutch, and resolved to embark for the wilderness. They did a wise thing for themselves and posterity those Puritans who embarked at Delfts-Haven, 1620, for nowhere on earth, save in the trackless desert, could such theories as theirs be consummated.

The Puritans were the lineal descendants of Luther's rebellion. No sooner was the Roman Church successfully assailed by the first Reformer, than, as we saw, crop after crop of new rebels sprang up. John Knox's Scotch Presbyterians were the immediate progenitors of these stiff-necked Dissenters south of the Tweed. This new revolutionary Sect proposed to abolish everything but God Himself. Hierarchy, liturgy, music, pontificals, fasting, kneeling, the sign of the cross—all these were abominations borrowed by Rome from Pagan times. They undertook to restore Christianity to its native *purity*, and considered themselves entitled to the novel appellation of Puritans. The religious discussions then raging in England sharpened the wits of men, and the Puritans must have been the keenest of all to start a new Sect. In fact, they were in religion downright levellers, sweeping away everything in doctrine or worship then existing.

It was not likely they would bridle their daring spirit when they had got thus far. Having defied all authority in Church matters, they were sure sooner or later to question authority in State matters. This became so palpable even in Queen Bess's reign, that she and my Lord Burleigh considered them more pestiferous than the Catholics, and launched statute after statute against them.

The Puritans loved their new-fangled notions too well, I repeat, to die for them : they preferred to live and propagate them. Hence their *Exodus* to Holland. Hence their embarkation for the wilds of America. There they found neither Monarchy, nor Aristocracy, nor Catholics, nor Protestants, nor Presbyterians—nothing but the savage and the forest. They attacked one with gunpowder and brandy, and the other with the axe. They soon cleared space enough to erect their temple, and to worship after their own fashion.

No heretic, however, in the shape of a Catholic or Quaker was allowed to approach it.* In England they railed against Church and State for meddling with their conscience, and denying them religious liberty. Once their own masters in America, they forbade any other Sect to enter their boundaries. This was inconsistent, but such is human nature.

Having secured the Church from all rivalry, they next looked sharply after morals. Woe to all sinners against the Decalogue. But even the levities of life were not tolerated. Cotton Mather denounced the drinking of healths at table as Pagan ; proscribed the use of ornaments for the hair by females ; and rebuked the wickedness of leaving their arms and necks uncovered.

These daring innovators clearly meant to construct society anew, and mould human nature after their own pattern. The European mould they considered im-

* By the penal law of Massachusetts, any Catholic Priest who set foot in the Colony after being once driven out of it, was liable to capital punishment. The law against Quakers, 1656, begins, "Whereas an accursed race of heretics called Quakers has sprung up," &c. They were sentenced to be whipped, and imprisoned with hard labor, if found in the Colony. A law in 1644 banished the Anabaptists from the Colony.

perfect, and essayed to break. They ignored the satirical Horace who asserted that, *Naturam expelles furcâ, tamen usque recurret*—"Vain is the attempt to suppress nature, for sooner or later it will vindicate itself."

Religion and morals being now regulated after the Puritan standard, the problem of Government remained. The Puritans who landed at Plymouth, 1620, however they may have differed in intelligence, were otherwise all equals. They represented the Middle Class of England.* "The settlers," says De Tocqueville, "who established themselves on the shores of New England all belonged to the more independent classes of their native country. Their union on the soil of America at once presented the singular phenomenon of a society containing neither *lords nor common people*, neither rich nor poor. These men possessed, in proportion to their number, a greater mass of intelligence† than is to be found in any European nation of our own time. All, without a single exception, had received a good education, and many of them were known in Europe for their talents and acquirements." Without title, privilege, or fortune, it was not likely that such men, at such a time and place, would dream of Monarchy or Aristocracy. Each stood in need of the right arm of the other, and they naturally entered into a Compact to combine themselves into "a civil body politick for our better ordering and preservation," and agreed "to

* A distinguished author remarks that "in England the stronghold of Puritanism was in the middle classes, and it was from the middle classes that the majority of the emigrants came."

† Strange to say, these intelligent men brought to America the absurd delusions existing in England and all Europe on the subject of witchcraft. They seemed to believe that Satan visibly interfered through his agents in the affairs of this world, and frequently condemned to death unfortunate persons accused of "witchcraft."

enact, constitute, and frame such just and equal laws as shall be thought most meet and convenient for the good of the colony." * Had these emigrants come under a leader whose social or intellectual superiority was recognized, then, some one of the old forms of European Government might have been adopted. These Puritans, however, were in condition and intellect so nearly on a level that assumption of authority by any one was impossible, until conferred by the Majority.

In this way was born in the world a Government till then unknown. It is true that thinkers both before and since the Christian era had indulged in visions of a pure Democracy, but out of dreamland it had never existed. Nor was such a scheme possible in Europe, Asia, or Africa, where the superior intellect of the Minority secured for them the Government of the Majority, and the control of the national wealth. It could not be otherwise, as the Majority, from ignorance, were unable to govern, and if at any period in any of these Continents the Minority had chosen to abdicate, anarchy in a thousand forms must have ensued. To have proposed the establishment of a pure Democracy, therefore, in any part of the Old World, that is, the Government of the intellectual few by the ignorant many, would have been an absurdity.

Had the Majority of the English people in the seventeenth century possessed the capacity of the Puritans, there would have been no necessity for the latter to emigrate, as they would have had in their own country the Government of this Majority. But, as such

* This quotation is borrowed from the Compact drawn up by the Puritans in the cabin of the *Mayflower* before landing.

was not the case, these brooding men were dissatisfied. They had religious and political crotchets they were bent on testing. Was it wise to try the experiment in England or elsewhere? Some decided on the former course; others, more practical, chose the latter. The Puritans in England succeeded—1640-1660—in upsetting the rule of the Minority, but the Majority feeling themselves incompetent to govern, restored it at the earliest opportunity.

The band who embarked for *terra incognita* contained a Majority able to make laws and administer them. The 41 men * who began business in December, 1620, on the frozen soil of America at a spot they named Plymouth, voted by a Majority the "just and equal laws" required; and in the same manner appointed "a Governor and seven assistants" to carry them out. They were few enough, at first, to meet together, and make new laws and new Governors by a Majority, as aforesaid. Soon they grew too numerous, and then they chose, by a Majority, Delegates to attend to their Legislative and Executive affairs. This *Representative System* they were obliged to borrow from the Mother-country, which had the honor of inventing it.

This proves that none but English Colonists who understood the political machinery that had been set up in England, and which was meant to supersede the arbitrary will of an individual, or of a single class—it proves, I say, that none but Englishmen of the seventeenth century could have laid the foundation of a pure Democracy. The French and Spaniards who went to America knew nothing of the Representative

* The whole company, including women and children, numbered 101

System. A Government by the Majority of them would only have ended in confusion. They imported the arbitrary rule they had inherited. Even at this day the Majority in France and Spain have not the political knowledge necessary to govern.

The Puritans of Plymouth, however, were the descendants of that Middle Class who, as was shown, in conjunction with the Nobles wrested *Magna Charta* from King John, and members, too, of the same class which was still struggling against the Royal prerogative. These shrewd men doubted the fitness of the Lower Class in England—the Majority—to govern, but they knew what could be accomplished if they once had the *fulcrum* on which to work their lever. In quest of this they came to Plymouth, and planted there the seeds of that Government by a Majority which was sure to prosper so long as the Majority were able to judge if their governmental work was properly done. *The whole secret of Self-government turns on this.* If the Majority of the population can be deluded by their Delegates, then the Republican edifice must crumble. No such danger menaced the intelligent men who colonized New England. The chief function they assigned to Government was to preserve order. They wanted no laws to favor an individual, or a class, at the expense of the rest. They conferred no power on their Delegates, either Executive or Legislative, that could jeopardize their persons or property. They conceded authority only for a time, and renewed it only when satisfied of its proper exercise.*

* Governor Winthrop of Massachusetts was accused on one occasion of arbitrary conduct during his Magistracy. In his reply, he defined the true boundaries of liberty and authority thus:—"Nor would I have you to mistake in the point of your own liberty. There is a liberty of

This outline of the Puritan Fathers has been thought necessary, since their acts will be better understood when their opinions and character are accurately known.

Let us now return to the career of the Colonies. Rapidly springing up north and south, they commenced life in three different modes, or under three different forms of Government, known as the *Charter*, *Royal*, and *Proprietary* Governments. The first was confined to New England. These charters or grants of the Crown conferred on the Colonists the right of the soil; but in fact the New England Settlements started for the most part without sanction from the Mother-country, and organized themselves. It is remarkable that they enjoyed almost complete independence; electing their magistrates, making peace or war, and enacting such "just and equal laws" as they deemed necessary.

In 1628, the Colony of Massachusetts was settled by a company of Puritans from England. In 1631, New Hampshire was colonized. In 1635, Connecticut was occupied by seceders from Massachusetts. At the same period, Roger Williams, a Clergyman at Salem, was expelled from Massachusetts for teaching erroneous

a corrupt nature, which is affected both by men and beasts to do what they list; and this liberty is inconsistent with authority, impatient of all restraint: by this liberty *sumus omnes deteriores*: 'tis the grand enemy of truth and peace, and all the ordinances of God are bent against it. But there is a civil, a moral, a federal liberty, which is the proper end and object of authority; it is a liberty for that only which is just and good; for this liberty you are to stand with the hazard of your very lives, and whatsoever crosses it is not authority, but a distemper thereof. This liberty is maintained by subjection to authority, and the authority set over you will, in all administrations for your good, be quietly submitted unto by all but such as have a disposition to lose their true liberty by murmuring at the honor and power of authority." His clear-sighted audience accepted this straightforward definition, showing when liberty degenerated into license, and when authority distended into tyranny. He was acquitted by acclamation, and repeatedly re-elected Governor.

doctrines, and, with a few followers, established himself at Providence. In 1637, the Colony of New Haven was settled by emigrants from England, and was afterwards united to Connecticut. In 1638, Rhode Island was settled by a Sect of Antinomians,* who were also banished from Massachusetts.

In 1643, a striking event occurred. The Colonies of Massachusetts, Plymouth, Connecticut, and New Haven formed a Confederation under the name of "The United Colonies of New England" for mutual protection against the Indians. By the terms of this Union, the internal concerns of each Colony were left to its own Government. In war, each was to furnish its proportion of men according to its population. The affairs of the Confederacy were to be conducted by a Congress of two Commissioners from each Colony.

It was this League of the infant Colonies of New England for their common defence that led, 133 years later, to the Confederation of the Thirteen Colonies against the Mother-country.

Thus we see these Puritan Colonies exercised almost entire Sovereignty. They established a pure Democracy; but in modelling it they copied from the Parent-land, convinced that there the Supreme Power was sagaciously distributed. The Executive was limited to a single person—the Governor—and the Legislature was divided into two branches—a type of Government corresponding to that of England, by King, Lords, and Commons.

Such was the birth of the Puritan Colonies. To them belongs the renown of originating the *First*

* The Antinomian sect was founded by John Agricola, a contemporary of Luther, who taught that "Evangelical faith was not necessary for salvation."

Republic, if by Republic is meant Government by the Majority. The so-called Republics of Greece, Rome, and the Middle Ages were all Governments by the Minority. *The principle of the Sovereignty of the People* became a reality for the first time when the forty-one Puritans set up at Plymouth a Government by consent of the whole, or the major part of them.

It was plainly the will of Providence that such a Government should rise. The men who undertook it were strikingly adapted to the work. The site selected was unoccupied by civilized men holding contrary opinions. The Mother-country, which alone could have checked the experiment, was engrossed by an intestine feud that diverted her attention from this remote region. Self-government was thus inaugurated. Each New England Colony after the other adopted the first example. All the political institutions that grew out of such a system were successively developed—Universal Suffrage; the Responsibility of Authority; Voting of Taxes; Personal Liberty; Trial by Jury.

These institutions, now the groundwork of several Constitutions in Europe, were utterly unknown two hundred years ago, save in England, where some of them had already budded. Nothing was more natural than Universal Suffrage in the Puritan Colonies, *as all were on a par in condition and sagacity*; nothing more logical than the responsibility of those invested with power, since all authority emanated from the Majority; nothing more equitable than regulating by Vote the expenditure of money for the common good.

It was the ancestors of these men who disputed through centuries the King's right to levy taxes without their consent. But what was easy and just in the deserts of America, where men were all on the same footing in position and knowledge; where, still more important, the political intelligence of all was so great, was simply impossible in the Old World: for there men were arranged in classes according to wealth and capacity, according to poverty and ignorance—an organization which had been maintained for centuries, and the premature overthrow of which would be the beginning of anarchy. For this reason the Puritans broke down in England in the seventeenth century. For this reason the Puritans succeeded in America in the seventeenth century.

It may be useful, and perhaps interesting, to have dwelt so fully on the extraordinary performances of these political Pilgrims to whom belongs for ever the Patent for a New Republic—the first of its kind, and the last of any kind should it unhappily fail.

The second form of Government under which others of the Colonies began was the *Royal* Government, since the Crown named the Governor and a Council, who held their places at its will. The Judges and most of the other public officers were appointed by the King, and subject to his orders. The settlers were allowed the right of representation by electing Burgesses. The Council constituted the Upper House, and the Burgesses the Lower one. The Governor had a *Veto* on the acts of both Houses, but no acts took the form of law until approved by the King.

Virginia was first settled in 1607 under the auspices of the "London Company," who appointed the Governor and Council, but in 1619 the Company instructed the Governor to order the election of a House of Burgesses by "a majority of voices" to assist the Governor and Council in managing the Colony.

James I., displeased at this popular form of Government, dissolved the Company by a writ of *quo warranto*, 1624, and assumed the control of the province. He appointed a Governor and Councillors to govern in his name and under his instructions. They were authorized to levy taxes; to transport the Colonists to England to be tried for crimes committed in Virginia; to ship all tobacco to England to be delivered to agents of the King.

Charles I. for a time maintained the arbitrary system of his father, but afterwards sent a new Governor with instructions to restore the right of representation to the Colony.

These *Royal* Governments existed in Virginia, New York, New Jersey, the Carolinas, and Georgia. The Carolinas and Jersey were at first under *Proprietary* Government, but later they became subject to Royal authority.

Under the third form of Government, known as the *Proprietary*, the right of the soil was conveyed by the Crown to certain individuals called Proprietors, as well as the power to establish a Body Politic. They appointed the Governor and other officials. They organized and convened the Legislature, exercising a *Veto* on its acts. The Proprietors were only responsible to the Crown which created them. Their position in fact greatly resembled that of the feudal Lords in the Middle Ages.

The territory named Pennsylvania was ceded to William Penn by Charles II. in 1681, in lieu of a claim on the Crown.

Penn was a man of culture, integrity, and benevolence.* Montesquieu called him the "Modern Lycurgus." He arrived from England in 1682, with 2,000 emigrants, and founded Philadelphia. He brought with him a form of Government, and a Code of laws prepared by himself. The political structure was similar to that of the other Colonies—a Governor, Council, and an Assembly.

All these Constitutions, *Charter*, *Royal*, *Proprietary*, endured down to the Revolution.

*William Penn was a son of Admiral Sir William Penn. After visiting various countries, he joined the Quaker sect on his return to England, and was disinherited by his father. He continued to write and preach in favor of liberty and conscience, and was twice imprisoned in the Tower. Inheriting a claim on the Crown of £16,000—$80,000—he took in exchange for it the property and sovereignty of the territory "west of the Delaware," which he afterwards colonized. He made it an asylum for all sects; entered into treaties with the Indians which he punctually observed, and abolished slavery. He died in England in 1718, at 74 years of age.

THE MOTHER-COUNTRY RENOUNCED.

THE infant Colonies had scarcely begun to grow before disputes broke out with the Mother-country.

As might have been expected, the Plymouth Colony was the first to make resistance. These spirited men had not left their homes to brave the ordeal they were enduring only to be subject to a political control they had virtually abjured. As early as 1636—the very year that Hampden refused to pay "Ship Money" in England—the men of Plymouth declared through their Legislature that "no taxes should be imposed but by consent of the body of freemen or their representatives." From this date the principle of "no taxation without representation" was established, and Colony after Colony as they matured adopted it. In England, however, it was maintained that Parliament had the power "to bind the Colonies in all cases whatsoever," and consequently the right to tax them.

This was the old quarrel over again with the parties changed. The Nobles and Middle Class in England had long contended that the Crown could impose no taxes without their consent. The Colonies repeated the same constitutional doctrine, and protested that, as British subjects, Parliament had no right to tax them without their consent.

This precipitate outcry against taxation arose from the dread of the Colonies lest England should extend her jurisdiction over their internal affairs, but the Home Government entertained far more practical views. It was not the Administrative control of the Colonies it aimed at, but simply the amount of Revenue it could extract from them. For this object it was sought from the first to monopolize their trade. Even in 1621 it was ordered that "no tobacco or other productions of the Colonies should be carried into any foreign port until first landed in England and the customs paid."

A far more memorable event was the Navigation Act of 1651, which ordained that there should be neither imports nor exports between England and the Colonies, except in English or Colonial vessels. This was meant, of course, to exclude all foreign interference with the trade. It was further enacted that no productions of the Colonies should be exported to any other country than to such as belonged to Great Britain.

It is striking that this sweeping measure, which shut out the Colonies from all the world as to their *exports*, was the work of the Puritan House of Commons under the supremacy of Oliver Cromwell. The King and House of Lords having both disappeared, England was wholly under the sway of the Puritan Politicians and their stern master—another proof that there is little sentiment in politics, for the English Puritans felt no delicacy in fleecing their American brethren to the uttermost.

In 1663, Parliament forbade all *imports* from any part of the world to the Colonies, save in English-built vessels, and shipped from England direct to the said Colonies or Plantations. This monopolizing policy was in such entire harmony with the commercial spirit of that age, that the oppressed Colonies submitted without murmur.

Their internal trade thus far was free, but to obtain more revenue Parliament declared, in 1672, that henceforth Duties must be paid on sugar, tobacco, cotton, &c., transported from one Colony to another. This caused an explosion. Outcries were heard in New England against "these invasions of the rights, liberties, and properties of the subjects of His Majesty, they not being represented in Parliament." This manifest subordination of the interests of the Colonies to those of the Mother-country made a deadly quarrel between them a mere question of time.

These restrictions on their commerce were bad enough, but Colonial manufactures were looming up, and the Mother-country grew alarmed. Forthwith Parliament began enacting that "no wool, yarn, or woollen manufactures of the American colonies should be shipped or transported to any place whatever."

In 1732, another edict appeared forbidding New England to export hats, extensively manufactured there, to Foreign Countries or to the other Colonies.

In 1750, all Colonial manufactures were declared to be "nuisances" which the Governors, under a penalty of £500, were required to abate.

In 1760, regulations still more stringent were issued against the trade of the Colonies.

It may be supposed that the Colonists were exasperated at this grasping policy, but so long as taxation was external, and fell on them in the shape of Duties, they bore it. What they resolved never to tolerate was any attempt to tax them internally. This would be an interference with their domestic Government, which nothing would induce them to brook.

At last the blow came. In 1765, Parliament passed a Law that all obligations in writing, newspapers, pamphlets, &c. in the Colonies must be duly stamped and pay a tax accordingly. This was done in spite of petitions, remonstrances, and protests.

The Colonies immediately organized for resistance. The Legislature of Massachusetts suggested a Congress of Deputies from all the Colonies to meet in New York, October 1765, "to consult on the circumstances of the Colonies, and measures of relief." The Congress promptly assembled, and adopted a Declaration of Rights and Grievances. They called on the King and Parliament to repeal the "Stamp Act," and other abuses, as well as "the other late Acts for the restriction of American Commerce." They prepared an Address to the King, and a Petition to both Houses of Parliament, showing "that Parliament, adhering to the principles of the Constitution, have never hitherto taxed any but those who were actually therein represented." Special agents, of whom Dr. Franklin was one, were sent to England with these manifestoes. The people met in conclave all over the country, and resolved the Stamp Act should never be carried out. The merchants of New York, Philadelphia, and Boston agreed to order no goods from Great Britain, and associations were widely formed against the use of British manufactures, and for the encouragement of domestic fabrics. A phalanx sprung up called the "Sons of Liberty," pledged to go to any part of the country to resist by force the execution of the Stamp Act.

Obviously it was this ill-advised Law of Parliament that was the entering wedge destined at no distant period to sever for ever the connection of the Parentland with her high-spirited Offspring.

A change in the British Cabinet occurred at this

time, and the new Administration declared it was not their intention "to tax the Colonies without their consent." In March, 1766, the Stamp Act was repealed.

This considerate conduct spread joy through the Colonies, but it was soon dampened by a Resolution voted by Parliament asserting their power and right "to make laws of sufficient force and validity to bind the Colonies *in all cases whatsoever*." This was simply a reiteration of the right of taxation, whether the Colonies consented or not.

This foreboded evil, and it soon came. In 1767, an Act was passed imposing Duties on glass, paper, paints, and tea imported into the Colonies from Great Britain, the object of which was declared to be, "to raise a revenue in America."

Hitherto the Colonies had submitted to taxes on their commerce in the form of Duties, not because they considered them just or Constitutional, but because they shrank from a collision with the Mother-country. The unity and courage, however, displayed throughout the Colonies in opposition to the Stamp Act, and its consequent repeal, now emboldened them to repel the new Duties. Massachusetts, whose commerce suffered the most, led off in the fray. Virginia followed her with alacrity. The former tactics were renewed. Petitions and addresses were showered on Parliament. Not only were the Colonies, said these documents, prohibited from importing the commodities and manufactures of Europe, except from Great Britain, but the Colonies were forbidden by Acts of Parliament even from sending their productions to any foreign ports. Both these restrictions were heavy *taxes* on the Colonies.

The Legislatures of Massachusetts and Virginia were

both dissolved by the Royal Governors for their contumacious behaviour. All the Colonies sustained Massachusetts and Virginia, and non-importation agreements became again universal.

Parliament succumbed a second time, and all the proscribed Duties were repealed in 1770, except on tea. An Act was also passed entitling the East India Company to a drawback on teas exported to America, which would make tea cheaper there than in Great Britain.

These concessions failed. The blood of the Colonists was up, and they refused to pay even the Duties on tea. Large shipments of it arrived in Boston, New York, Philadelphia, and other places. The Colonists resolved it should not be landed, lest the Duties might be paid, and the right of Parliament be thereby acknowledged to tax the Colonies without their consent. In New York and Philadelphia the consignees refused to receive the cargoes, which were consequently sent back to England. In Boston the consignee was more pliant, but an enthusiastic meeting at Faneuil Hall voted "that the tea should not be landed." On adjourning, they repaired *en masse* to the wharf, when suddenly a number of men disguised as "Mohawk Indians" boarded the vessels and threw 342 chests of tea into the bay.

This mutinous conduct roused the indignation of Parliament. Instead of further conciliation, Act after Act of repression was fulminated. The "Boston Port Bill" was passed, closing up her harbor to commerce, and removing the Custom House to Salem.* Another

* This Act was loudly condemned in Parliament, but the Minister, Lord North, was able to force it through. In London it excited great

Act followed "for better regulating the government of the Province of Massachusetts Bay." Still another for the "impartial administration of justice in Massachusetts Bay." It was the purpose of Parliament to make the Colony of "Massachusetts Bay" smart for her refractory demeanor. A final Bill was passed for quartering soldiers on the inhabitants of the Colonies.

The time had now come for submission to Parliamentary dictation, or a bold defiance whatever the results.

The Colonists hesitated not a moment. Virginia recommended the 1st of June, on which the Port of Boston was to be closed, as a day of fasting and prayer. It was so observed throughout the Colonies.

A cry was echoed from all quarters for a Congress, and it met in Philadelphia, September, 1774. This body published an emphatic Protest against the right of Great Britain "to tax the Colonies or to interfere with their internal affairs." They also prepared and signed an Agreement for themselves and constituents not to import or use British goods till the Acts complained of should be repealed.

The determination of Parliament not to retreat from its coercive policy rendered appeals and remonstrances alike unavailing. A struggle seemed inevitable, and the Colonies prepared for it. Gunpowder was manufactured, the Militia was trained, and military stores collected.

In April, 1775, the British General, Gage, at Boston, sent troops to destroy a magazine of supplies at Concord.

indignation in the commercial world, and £30,000—$150,000—was subscribed for those who would be thrown out of employment at Boston.

At Lexington the Militia were drawn up to intercept them. A collision ensued, and eight of the militiamen fell.

This incident vibrated like an electric shock through the Colonies. Up to this moment the contest had been political. It suddenly became a conflict of arms.

The Colonies had always hoped to compromise these difficulties with England without violence or separation. This, however, was not the expectation or the purpose of the sagacious Politicians of New England. They were convinced there was no remedy for Colonial wrongs but in complete Independence. It was not merely the commercial oppression of the Mother-country that nerved them to resistance, but still more the determination to establish that Democratic Government which their forefathers had inaugurated at Plymouth in 1620. All New England, therefore, secretly rejoiced at the arrogant policy of England, which was sure to drive the Colonies to revolt.

Massachusetts was active in her preparations for military resistance, and eagerly awaited an opportunity to abandon merely political opposition, and resort to open war. The occasion came when General Gage sent, as stated, a detachment to Concord. Massachusetts rallied her militiamen, and the coveted blow was struck. The struggle for Independence then began.

Astonishment and anger filled the Colonies, but Massachusetts was ready for the emergency. Three days after the affray at Lexington, her Legislature called on New England to raise an army of 30,000 men. Ten days later 20,000 men were encamped around Boston, which was occupied by the King's Governor and army. Soon afterwards volunteer expeditions from Connecticut and Vermont pounced upon the Royal fortresses of Ticonderoga and Crown Point, where cannon and ammunition, greatly needed, were obtained.

This rapid action proves how thoroughly prepared were the political leaders of New England for the crisis they so earnestly desired.

DECLARATION OF INDEPENDENCE.

EIGHTEENTH CENTURY.

IN the midst of the fermentation of these events, the second Colonial Congress met at Philadelphia, May, 1775. Its Members as a matter of policy were disposed to temporize with Great Britain, and voted an Address to the King and Parliament, calling for a redress of grievances, and depicting the evils of separation. At the same time they began to organize for the bloody ordeal that seemed approaching. In the name of the "United Colonies" they set to work to raise an army, equip a navy, and to devise financial resources. The New England forces around Boston were adopted as the Colonial army, and at the suggestion of the New England Delegates, George Washington of Virginia was nominated Commander-in-Chief.

Before he left Philadelphia to take command another decisive event occurred. The British General in Boston decided to seize and fortify Bunker's Hill. To prevent this the Americans threw up a redoubt in the night of the 16th of June, 1775, and the following morning the British troops to the number of 3,000, all veterans, assaulted it. After twice repulsing them, the Americans from want of ammunition retired. The British confessed a loss of over 1,000 men killed and wounded, whilst the American loss was only 449 killed, wounded, and prisoners. Unlike the fight at Lexington, this was a regular pitched battle, and though badly-armed and supplied the Colonists displayed a spirit that augured badly for British supremacy in America. The cannon of Bunker's Hill reverberated from Boston to Georgia.

The cry to arms was loud but not unanimous, though compromise was almost despaired of. Great Britain declared the Colonies "in a state of rebellion," and prepared to reduce them to obedience.

In December, 1775, Parliament interdicted all trade with the Colonies, and ordered the capture of all American vessels and other vessels trading in any port of the Colonies.

At the close of this year the Colonists organized an expedition against Canada under General Montgomery, which was abandoned some months afterwards.

In March, 1776, the British army evacuated Boston and sailed for Halifax. This was a signal triumph for the Colonial cause.

British cruisers repeatedly attacked various points on the coast. In June, they assaulted Charleston, South Carolina, but were driven off with loss.

The war between England and her Colonies was now fully inaugurated. It had been going on for over a year. The Colonies had no alternative but abject submission or desperate resistance. Yet, strange to say, some of the more influential seemed to shrink at a final separation from the Mother-country. When in June, 1776, Richard Henry Lee introduced his Resolution in the Congress at Philadelphia that "the United Colonies are and ought to be free and independent States, and that their political connection with Great Britain is and ought to be dissolved," Pennsylvania and South Carolina voted against the Resolution, Delaware was divided, and New York declined to vote. Nine Colonies, however, sustained it, and a committee was chosen to draft a Declaration of Independence. The firmness of New England, and the ardor of Virginia, finally overcame all doubts and scruples, and the Vote for Independence was passed unanimously by the Thirteen Colonies on July 4th.

It cannot be asserted that all men were unanimous in their desire to renounce the Government of the Mother-country. New England was chiefly eager for Independence: first, because her spirit was always Republican*; and next, because her commerce being the most extensive was the most damaged by the imposts of Great Britain. Many of the leading men of the other Colonies of the political, professional, and mercantile world, also secretly aimed at emancipation, as they believed their prosperity would be thereby promoted. "It was the independent and enlightened classes of society," remarks Guizot, "who had to sustain and invigorate the people in the great struggle in which their country was engaged. The magistrates, the wealthy planters, the great merchants, and the officers of the army, constantly showed themselves the firmest and most ardent adherents of the cause. They gave their example no less than their advice, and the populace instead of urging them on, hardly followed in their track."

This important statement is corroborated by the frequent complaints of Washington of the lukewarmness

* When Charles II. was restored, there was general satisfaction in all the Colonies save New England, which welcomed the regicides Goff and Whalley, and forbade any rejoicings for the return of the King.

and disaffection of the people. In fact, popular opinion was so divided as to the expediency of a Revolution, that the most conspicuous public men considered it prudent not too openly to endorse it. As late as October, 1774, Washington wrote to Captain Mackenzie :—" You are taught to believe that the people of Massachusetts are rebellious—setting up for independence and what not. Give me leave to tell you, my good friend, that you are abused, grossly abused. I think I can announce it as a fact that it is not the wish or interest of that Government—Massachusetts—or any other on this continent, separately or collectively, to set up for independence, but at the same time, you may rely on it that none will ever submit to the loss of those valuable rights and privileges which are essential to the happiness of every free State."

In less than a year from the date of this letter, the writer was commanding the Colonial army before Boston. Had events so utterly outrun the forecast of Washington ; or was he still, in October, 1775, a disbeliever in Independence ; or did he consider it obligatory in 1774 to conceal his real convictions ?

In the beginning of 1775, John Adams publicly declared in Boston :—" That there are any who pant after independence, is the greatest slander on the Provinces." He also asserted on another occasion :— " That there existed a general desire for independence of the Crown in any part of America before the revolution is as far from the truth as the zenith from the nadir. For my own part there was not a moment during the revolution when I would not have given every thing I possessed for a restoration to the state of things before the contest began, provided we could have had a sufficient security for its continuance."

Franklin wrote in March, 1775:—"I have assured Lord Chatham that having travelled more than once almost from one end of the continent to the other, and kept a great variety of company, eating, drinking, and conversing with them freely, I never had heard in any conversation with any person, drunk or sober, the least expression of a wish for a separation, or a hint that such a thing would be advantageous to America."

In November, 1775, five months after the battle of Bunker's Hill, Jefferson wrote:—"Believe me, dear Sir, there is not in the British empire a man who more cordially loves an union with Great Britain than I do. But, by the God that made me, I will cease to exist before I yield to a connexion on such terms as the British Parliament proposes, and in this I think I speak the sentiments of America. We want neither inducement nor power to declare or assert a separation. *It is will alone which is wanting*, and that is growing apace under the fostering hand of our King."*

These significant extracts prove that to the last it was necessary to entice the Colonies to make a Revolution, which might lead to unknown disasters. Guizot alludes to the hesitation which seized on many before taking the final plunge. "It was not for the purpose," he says, "of escaping from the fangs of some atrocious tyranny that the insurrection was begun by the Colonists. They had not, like the Pilgrim-Fathers when they fled the English shores, to recover the first blessings of civil liberty, security for their persons, or liberty for their creed." The Colonists were exasperated, it is true, by

* In February 1776, Tom Paine published in Philadelphia a pamphlet entitled "Common Sense," urging the Colonies in cogent, yet temperate language, to separate from England. He found it necessary to appeal to the reason, rather than the passion of the public.

the vexatious interference of Parliament with their trade, but in the main they were contented and loyal. They knew that all the great Statesmen of England, Chatham, Burke, Fox, were their champions in Parliament. They were aware that the sympathies of the English people were enlisted on their side.*

I think it may be inferred from the foregoing that the Revolution was not the work of the people of the Colonies generally, who had no hatred for the Royal Government, or any preference for a more Democratic organization of which they knew nothing. Of course, I except the New England States, whose Republicanism, and whose commercial interests, as previously remarked, inspired them with a profound craving after Independence. They were the real pioneers of the Revolution. In the other Colonies, Guizot observes that "the upper classes of society chiefly plotted for emancipation, expecting that great material advantages would accrue, and knowing that all political functions would fall into their hands." It may be doubted, therefore, if the Revolution would have occurred for long years if it had not been stimulated by the arrogant obstinacy of a single man, George III., who refusing to yield to the temperate demands of the Colonies for a change of policy, brought on a war which was destined not merely to deprive England of her richest Dependencies, but to create a New Nation, and a New System of Government whose effects on the world defy calculation.

* This was proved when the British Government found themselves obliged to hire troops in Germany, especially in Hesse, since the English people generally refused to enlist in the war against the Colonies.

THE WAR.

Some months before the Declaration of Independence the Royal Governors of the Colonies began to withdraw, and the Colonists proceeded to construct anew their Local Governments. Legislatures were elected consisting, as before, of two branches, and these in turn elected the Governor of the State. The Thirteen Colonies were now suddenly transformed into so many Sovereign States. They were not only independent of Great Britain, but independent of each other.

This condition of things soon filled the political leaders of the Revolution with the utmost alarm.

The young States were so proud of their Sovereignty that no one would be advised by the other. They began to think only of their individual interest, and to ignore the common good of all. To be sure, they were engaged in a war that threatened all alike. The general danger demanded harmonious action. Yet jealousies broke out and mistrust of each other began to spread.

What was to be the fate of these infant States? Were they destined to imitate the ancient States of Greece, and waste themselves in fratricidal conflicts till swallowed up by a modern Philip of Macedon? Europe contemplated the result with interest, if not anxiety.

Such was the general dislike of England, that every nation of Europe was pleased at the probable loss of her Colonies. France and Spain more especially, enraged at their expulsion from the American Continent, 1763, were eager to aid the rebellious States and only waited for a favorable opportunity. Various maritime Powers, as Holland, Genoa, Naples, and Tuscany, from jealousy of the commercial ascendency of England, sympathized with the Revolutionists. Even Prussia and Russia, from envy of England, affected to condemn her deportment to her Colonies.

If the Statesmen of Europe could have possibly divined the astounding political results fated to spring from the Revolution they were patting so complacently on the back, it is hardly to be doubted that they would have been more eager than England herself to crush it in the bud. If the ghost of George III. takes any interest in passing events, it must be consoled at the havoc that the Democratic principles hatched in the American Revolution are making in the countries that plotted against him.

For more than a year after the Declaration of Independence, the Revolution was in constant danger of failure. Washington left Boston a victor, and brought his army to New York. In June, 1776, General Howe landed at Staten Island with a considerable force, which was soon augmented to 30,000 men. Washington's raw and ill-supplied levies were no match for such an army. In August, the campaign began with a battle on Long Island which the Americans lost. Washington then began a retreat which he was obliged to continue, until in December he found himself on the south side of the Delaware river at the head of less than 4,000 men, without tents, blankets, clothing, or food. So desperate had become the prospects of the Revolution, that great numbers abandoned it and accepted the British General's offer of pardon and amnesty. Despondency seized the most confident, and the Rebellion seemed on the verge of utter discomfiture.

Worst of all, the Congress that was still sitting at Philadelphia could do nothing. It was composed of Delegates from the thirteen new States, but they had no authority to enforce their opinions. They could do no act without orders from their respective States: their only mission was to vote piteous appeals to the various Legislatures to furnish men and money to carry on the war.

The States were now all Sovereign, as said before, and independent of each other. There were rivalry of interests, and suspicion of motives. Many of them, too, were alarmed at raising a large army that might subjugate them again.

In this grave situation the difficulty was to induce them to act in concert. The political leaders saw it was imperatively necessary that the States should give their Delegates in Congress powers of some sort to sustain the war, and provide for the common welfare. The States hesitated to do this, lest Congress might obtain an ascendency over them. They were so jealous of their new Sovereignty, that they shrank from parting with the least portion of it. They feared lest Congress might become a sort of Central Authority, a kind of National Government, which might act contrary to their wishes and interests.

This was the gloomy condition of the rebellious States at the end of 1776. The helpless Members of Congress must have often fancied the halter round their necks. All they could do was to encourage Washington, and to implore their States to save the cause.

A gleam of hope suddenly lit up the horizon. The British army, consisting in part of Hessian mercenaries, was encamped at Trenton, New Jersey. On the opposite bank of the river, which was choked with ice, were posted Washington and his half-starved followers. The British and their German allies devoted the Christmas of 1776 to feasting and festivity. Plunged at night in the stupor of drunken sleep, the opportunity was irresistible. Washington embarked his dispirited Militia, and pushed over the river during the darkness in the face of a snowstorm. At daylight he fell on the stupefied enemy, put them to flight, and captured 1,000 Hessians. He followed them to Princeton, and two days later, January, 1777, defeated them again.

This double success rescued the sinking Revolution, and Washington was able to recruit his army to 7,000 men. The British General made every effort to bring on a general engagement, but the wary Washington skilfully eluded his purpose, knowing his ill-trained Militia was unfit to cope with an enemy so superior in discipline and numbers.

General Howe then withdrew from New Jersey, sailed with 16,000 men for Chesapeake Bay, and landing on Elk river, threatened Philadelphia. To protect the Capital, Washington made his way to Delaware, where he was defeated in the battle of Brandywine, September, 1777. The British then marched on Philadelphia, and Congress made a precipitate retreat to York, a town in the interior.

Hoping to retrieve himself Washington attacked the British army at Germantown near Philadelphia, in October, and was again repulsed.

The gloom of these disasters was relieved by a grand

event. A British army, nearly 10,000 strong, led by General Burgoyne, entered the State of New York from Canada, and met at Saratoga an American force under General Gates. Two battles ensued which led to the capitulation of Burgoyne and his army.

This brilliant result decided the fortunes of the war. It turned despondency into exultation at home, while the effect abroad was momentous. France was now encouraged openly to assist the American Rebellion, and to agree to a Treaty of Alliance.

In November of this year, 1777, the States were induced to venture on a more cordial co-operation, and consented to enter into a "Confederation" with each other. Articles were drawn up and signed, July, 1778, by which they agreed to concede to their Delegates in Congress certain powers which were designated. They refused, however, to grant the only two rights that were essential. They would not allow Congress to assess and collect taxes: each State reserved to itself this privilege. Congress might vote money, but it belonged to the States to raise it through their own Legislatures. Congress therefore was always on its knees supplicating the States to furnish means which came slowly, or not at all. If it had not been for the loans made to Congress by Holland and France, the Revolution must have collapsed. The second right, as indispensable to Congress as levying and collecting taxes, was to regulate trade and commerce by imposing a uniform scale of Duties. The States would not listen to such a proposition. To give up the right to regulate their own trade according to their interests was tantamount, they said, to abdicating their Sovereignty altogether. Each insisted on imposing its own Duties, not only on foreign goods, but on the productions of the sister States. The Thirteen Independent States entrenched themselves behind their respective custom-houses, and trade was as much or more harassed than when they were in a Colonial condition. The consequences were rivalries and resentments sure to lead sooner or later to serious results.

Nevertheless, the leaders of the Revolution thought it wise to unite the States in a Confederation, however defective, in order to accustom them to act together. They hoped a better knowledge of their interests would induce them some day to create a Central Authority or National Government with the requisite powers to promote the common welfare.

The sagacity and moderation of the Statesmen of the Revolution surmounted stupendous difficulties. If the leaders in Congress had not acted in perfect accord, all would have been lost. To be sure, their lives depended on success, and this enforced the utmost forbearance.

A proof that the new Confederation of the States did little for the situation may be seen in the following statement of Washington. He was encamped the winter of 1777–78 at Valley Forge, twenty miles from Philadelphia, and in a touching application for aid to the President of Congress he wrote :—" We have by a field-return, this day made, no less than 2,898 men now in camp unfit for duty, because they are barefoot and otherwise naked. We find gentlemen, without knowing whether the army was really going into winter-quarters or not, reprobating the measure as much as if they thought the soldiers were made of stocks and stones, and equally insensible to frost and snow; and moreover, as if they conceived it easily practicable for an inferior army, under the disadvantages which I have described ours to be, and which are by no means exaggerated, to confine a superior one—in all respects well appointed and provided for a winter campaign—within the city of Philadelphia, and to cover from depredation and waste the States of Pennsylvania and Jersey. I can assure those gentlemen that it is a much easier and less distressing thing to draw remonstrances in a comfortable room by a good fireside, than to occupy a cold, bleak hill, and sleep under frost and snow without clothes or blankets. However, although they seem to have little feeling for the naked and distressed soldiers, I feel superabundantly for them, and from my soul I pity those miseries which it is neither in my power to relieve or prevent."

Congress could make no other response to such an appeal than to invoke the Thirteen States to come to the General's rescue, and to authorize him to obtain all the assistance he could from the various local Governments.

The want of men and money at this dreary juncture was not Washington's sole embarrassment. The only hope of Congress and the country was in the army, and its condition may be seen in the following graphic sketch:—

"In the army itself, which was the object of so much distrust to the States, the strongest spirit of insubordination and democracy prevailed. Every order was disputed. Every detachment aspired to act on its own account, and to consult its own convenience. The troops of the different States would obey no generals but their own, and the soldiers no officers not directly chosen or appointed by themselves. The day after a defeat which was to be repaired, or a victory to be followed up, whole regiments disbanded themselves, and retired without even consenting to wait a few days until their successors arrived."

Thus, with discord between the States, insubordination in the army, disaffection among the people, trade paralyzed, a depreciated paper-currency,* the most sanguine might well despair of the Revolution.

It was not alone the firmness or ability of the leaders in Congress from the North and the South which carried the Revolution through such tremendous obstacles. To Washington more than to anyone else was due the final success. Nor was it achieved merely by his superior intellect or military skill, but rather by a marvellous combination of qualities which imparted to his character a moral grandeur that inspired respect and commanded esteem. His patience, prudence, disinterestedness, firmness, and forbearance never failed, although these traits were daily put to the severest tests. A tranquil dignity and strict decorum uniformly characterized his deportment and language. Through all his actions and his utterances written or verbal might be discerned the steady light of a conscientiousness that never flickered nor waned. Since the days of Socrates no character so perfectly proportioned and happily blended had appeared; and it may be doubted if the Athenian philosopher, who accepted death to prove his deference for law, underwent a more cruel ordeal than did Washington, who from an equally exalted motive contended serenely for years with trials almost superhuman. The admirable balance of his mind and character is happily portrayed in the lines of Shakespeare:—

* From June, 1775, to November, 1779, Congress authorized the issue of 246 millions of dollars in paper, generally known as "Continen money."

"And the elements
So mixed in him that Nature might stand up,
And say to all the world, *This was a man.*"

In the spring of 1778 came the intelligence that France had signed a Treaty of Alliance, and would despatch a fleet to aid the struggling States. No wonder the wretched soldiers of "Valley Forge" fired off their cannon and joyfully shouted in honor of the French King, Louis XVI.

The French Alliance startled George III., and Parliament hastened to repeal all the obnoxious Acts against their late Colonies. Commissioners were sent out to negotiate a reconciliation, but Congress refused to treat except on the basis of Independence.

In June, 1778, the British evacuated Philadelphia, and marched for New York. Washington followed them across New Jersey, and on the 28th of the same month a battle ensued at Monmouth. The Americans remained masters of the field, and the enemy fell back on New York. A French fleet under Count d'Estaing had arrived, and in August co-operated in an attack on the British forces in Rhode Island, which failed.

The war was carried on principally at the South during 1779, and by the middle of the summer, Georgia was occupied by the British. During this year also, Spain declared war against England. French and American cruisers at this period were inflicting heavy losses on English commerce. In September of this year, Paul Jones, a Scotchman, who was in the American service, captured two English frigates with his single ship in one battle.

The war was actively pursued at the South during 1780. Charleston surrendered to the British in May, and South Carolina was subsequently overrun.

An important event happened in July of this year. A second French fleet, under the Count de Rochambeau, arrived at Newport, R. I., bringing 6,000 trained soldiers. In September, Washington went to Hartford to devise a plan of operations with the French Commander. It was at this period that the treason of Benedict Arnold was discovered. He had agreed to deliver the fortress of West Point to the British General at New York.

At the close of this year England declared war against Holland, which was negotiating a Treaty of Alliance with the United States.

The chief military operations of 1781 were still at the South. Various conflicts occurred in both the Carolinas, in which the Americans had the advantage.

The grand event of this campaign, however, was the siege of Yorktown. The American army of the North under Washington, and the French army under Count de Rochambeau, had agreed on a junction ostensibly to attack the British in New York, but instead, the Allies, about 12,000 strong, made their way to Virginia, and besieged Lord Cornwallis in Yorktown. The attack began September 28th, and on October 19th, Cornwallis capitulated with all his force, some 7,000 men.

This was the crowning victory, for its effect in England forced Lord North, the tool of the King, to retire from the Government; and the new Cabinet, of which Fox was the leading Minister, ordered hostilities against the United States to cease, April, 1782. Congress then appointed Commissioners to negotiate for peace, and in November, 1782, a Preliminary Treaty was signed in Paris, and in September, 1783, a Definitive Treaty followed in which Great Britain acknowledged the United States to be Free, Sovereign, and Independent.

In November, 1783, New York, the last stronghold of the British, was evacuated.

The younger Pitt spoke of this war as "a detested and impious quarrel, conceived in injustice, and nurtured in folly, and whose footsteps were marked with slaughter and devastation."

In the six years of active warfare, from the conflict at Lexington to the surrender at Yorktown, Great Britain sent to America 112,000 soldiers and some 22,000 seamen. The troops raised by the United States during the same period consisted of 230,000 continental soldiers, and 56,000 militia.*

In November, 1783, Washington issued a Farewell Address to the army of the United States, and in December resigned his Commission.

* These figures are copied from an able and comprehensive article on the United States in the "New American Encyclopedia," Vol. XV.

FAILURE OF THE CONFEDERATION.

The state of things which followed the peace by no means responded to the expectations of the leaders of the Revolution, or the hopes of the people. The States were overwhelmed with debts contracted in the Old World and the New. The taxes which were to meet these liabilities had not been levied by the States. The only circulating medium was a depreciated paper-currency. Gold and silver were scarcely known. Some of the States passed laws which conflicted with those of other States; some levied Duties detrimental to their neighbours; and adjacent ports in different States competed with each other by lowering the rate of imposts. The various States yielded more and more to animosities, mistrust, and selfish views. Congress under the "Articles of Confederation" was powerless, as it had no right to legislate for the whole country, to reconcile discordant interests, or mitigate the dissensions of the jealous States.

A continuance of these evils involved civil war and ultimate anarchy. In Massachusetts an Insurrection known as "Shay's Rebellion" broke out against the State Government. When this news reached Washington, he exclaimed:—"What, gracious God, is man, that there should be such inconsistency and perfidiousness in his conduct! It was but the other day that we were shedding our blood to obtain the Constitutions under which we live; Constitutions of our own choice and making; and now we are unsheathing the sword to overturn them." Deep discontent was universal. Manufactures drooped; agriculture declined; trade decayed. In Europe the reputation of the United States was rapidly sinking. It was doubted if the United States as a Nation would ever exist at all. "I think often of our situation," wrote Washington, "and view it with alarm. From the high ground we stood upon, from the plain path which invited our footsteps, to be so fallen, so lost, is really mortifying. I feel infinitely more than I can express the disorders which have arisen in these States. Good God, who besides a Tory could have foreseen, or a Briton have predicted them?"

It was plain to all that unless some strong and better organization than the "Articles of Confederation" could be found; unless some Central Power, some General Government could be devised that would superintend the interests of all the States, and legislate for their mutual benefit; then, all hope of these clashing States being moulded into a great and prosperous Nation must be abandoned. "We have probably had," declared Washington, "too good an opinion of human nature in forming our Confederation. Experience has taught us that men will not adopt, and carry into execution, measures the best calculated for their own good, without the intervention of a *coercive power*. I do not conceive we can long exist as a Nation without having lodged somewhere a power which will pervade the whole Union in as energetic a manner as the authority of the State Governments extends over the several States."

Amid all his anxiety and alarm Washington seemed

never to despair. "I do not believe," he wrote to Lafayette in 1788, "that Providence has done so much for nothing. It has always been my creed that we should not be left as a monument to prove that mankind, under the most favorable circumstances for civil liberty and happiness, are unequal to the task of governing themselves, and therefore made for a master." Again he wrote:—"No country upon earth ever had it more in its power than United America to establish good order and government, and to render the nation happy at home, and respectable abroad. Wondrously strange and sad would it be were we to neglect the means, and depart from the road which Providence has pointed out to us so plainly. I cannot believe it will ever come to pass. The Great Governor of the Universe has led us too long and too far on the road of happiness and glory to forsake us in the midst of it."

Finally, the exhortations of Washington, the influence of the leading public men, love of country, dread of the pity or the derision of Europe, the necessity of order, the salvation of their interests—all contributed to induce and compel the people of the States to abandon their abortive Confederation, and establish a new bond of union in the shape of a Federal Government with the necessary vitality to remedy past evils and provide against future dangers.

It was under this pressure that a Convention of Delegates from all the States met in Philadelphia, May, 1787, and began their constitutional alchemy. Their task was indeed a solemn one. If the new political structure were no better than the last, then the Thirteen Independent States would surely live to regret the loss of the Mother-Government.

The Convention elected Washington their President, and for four months sat every day with closed doors. It was a short gestation for so marvellous a product. The danger was that the sticklers for State Sovereignty would refuse as before to create a General Government that might control or hamper the independence of the various States. The influence of Washington, the wisdom of the political leaders, and, beyond doubt, the pressure of popular opinion removed this stumbling block; and the result was a piece of political mechanism such as had never issued from the hand of man. Profound thinkers in their philosophic reveries have conjured up a political phenomenon like the American Constitution, but never yet had it taken shape or become a reality in the history of mankind.

Before calling attention to its striking merits and pointing out its marked originality, I will briefly state that it remedied the glaring defects of the old Confederation by giving to the new Federal Government the right to collect revenue for national purposes, and the right to regulate commerce by imposing uniform duties for all the States. The *coercive power*, which Washington remarked the State Governments possessed in order to maintain their authority, was also conferred on the new Central Government, so that it might, if needs were, compel a contumacious State to live in harmony with its brethren.

These were important concessions to the augmented spirit of union, but an object of far higher value than these was secured. The last Union was only an Union of the States—independent and sovereign States; a League of the various State Governments, and nothing more. This was just the crying faultof the recent Confederation;

whereas now the purpose was to create an Union, not of the States, but of the *people* of the States. The new Constitution began, "We, the people of the United States," whilst the late Confederation was signed by its framers "as Delegates of the States." A protest was made by Patrick Henry, and those of his political creed, against this innovation. "Who authorized them, the Members of the Federal Convention," he demanded, "to speak the language of, 'We, the people,' instead of 'We, the States'? If the States be not the agents of this compact, it must be one great consolidated national government of the people of all the States."

This interpretation was true. Yet how strange that such men as Patrick Henry, Jefferson, and other good patriots should still cling to State Sovereignty, when it had been so clearly demonstrated that unless the States gave up enough of their independence to constitute a National Government invested with a *coercive power*, they would surely drift into collision ending in anarchy.

The majority of the framers of the new Constitution knew that the people of all the States comprehended the perils of their position, and demanded such a reform of the General Government as would secure order and protect their common interests, whilst it left the authority of the States unrestricted within their own borders. In deference to popular sentiment the minority of crotchety Politicians, both in the Federal and State Conventions, gradually abandoned their opposition and the new Constitution was adopted.

THE NEW CONSTITUTION.

THE National Government established by this instrument was fashioned after the various State Governments, which consisted of an Executive, and a Legislature divided into two branches — a political organization which had been imported, as shown, by the Colonists from the Mother-country, where an Executive, and a Legislature in two branches, had long existed under the style and title of King, Lords, and Commons.

This theory of dividing the Supreme Power between an Executive, and a Legislature representing the Upper and Lower Classes, grew out of the history of England, as heretofore described. It is the only theory on which durable Government can be based in modern times. In the ancient world no such Government was possible, for though the Executive or Monarch, and the Upper Class or Aristocracy existed, yet the Lower Class or People had no legal being. It was not until the House of Commons rose in England that the People were politically born.

These three ingredients of all society are eternal. In the ancient, as in the modern world, we find in all communities the *Monos*,* the natural Monarch,

* The familiar Greek words *Monos* meaning — single or alone; *Aristoi*, the plural of *Aristos*, signifying—the best; and *Demos* expressing —the mass, are used in the text as best adapted to explain my meaning. From a compound of *Monos* with *Archo*—I rule, is derived the English word, Monarchy; and from compounds of *Aristos* and *Demos* with *Krateo*—I govern, we have the English words, Aristocracy and Democracy.

the dominant intellect, the "one man-power," as familiarly styled in the United States. Next in universality come the *Aristoi*, the natural Aristocracy, the governing intellects, the class of higher intelligences. Finally, follow the *Demos*, the Democracy, the mass, the sovereignty of number.

As just stated, this third element was not known in Government till events in English history gave it a voice over its own destiny. We saw in the ancient Asiatic, African, and European civilizations, that the masses were regarded simply as "hewers of wood, and drawers of water"; and in this condition they continued down to the thirteenth century, 1265 of our era, without rights, power, or security.

The Rebellion of the American Colonies transferred the Supreme Power from the English Government to the Mass. At this juncture arose the *Monos*, the natural Monarch, in the person of Washington; at the same moment appeared the *Aristoi*, the intellectual Aristocracy, in the form of a Congress; and both conceded its just share in the Government to the *Demos*, or Mass. The ignorance of the Mass had up to this time always entailed upon them the loss of their part in the Supreme Power.

It was these three elements combined that carried the Revolution to victory, in spite of the clumsy structure of the "Articles of Confederation," which assigned no constitutional sphere of action to the Monarchical and Democratic elements. The Congress of that day simply represented the Aristocratic class of the Colonies, the leading intellects. Such a Body long governed the various so-called Italian Republics of the Middle Ages, but could not permanently survive amid a Democracy so enlightened as that of the American Colonies.

Down to this period history presented but two forms of Government—that of Monarchy, where the Supreme Power was wielded by a single ruler; or that of Aristocracy, where the Supreme Power was vested in the hands of a few. Under either of these original forms, if beneficently administered, the welfare of the governed would be secured.

The experience of ages, however, has proved that *unlimited power* in the hands of either a single man, or a group of men, is sure to be abused; such is the inherent weakness of human nature. The Plantagenet Kings of England obeying these natural instincts, tyrannized just as other Monarchs of all ages had done, but by the combination of circumstances already described * their despotism was curbed, and the political advent of the People was the result. Since that day these three constituent elements—the *Monos*, the *Aristoi*, and the *Demos*—have not only co-existed in England, but have struggled with each other for the possession of the Supreme Power.

It is renown enough for England to have given a *legal birth-right to the People* by associating her Commons in the Government with the Aristocracy and Monarchy. If she has not yet succeeded in providing by skilful machinery against the rival pretensions of these naturally antagonistic elements, she is, nevertheless, entitled to the gratitude of the masses throughout the world.

* It was shown in the chapters on England how the Democracy in alliance with the Aristocracy—and this never occurred before—raise its head in the reign of John, and, later, obtained a legal sphere action of its own in the House of Commons.

It was reserved, however, for her progeny in another Hemisphere to accomplish this marvel by the ingenious combination of the antagonistic forces in question, and to realize in the American Constitution of 1787 the dreamy speculations of Cicero and Tacitus. No civilizations that had preceded the epoch of these great thinkers * had furnished an instance of the Popular element being admitted to any participation in Government, yet their profound reflections brought them to the conclusion that the best Government was that composed of the three elements. Cicero declared that "the best constituted government is that which in moderation is composed of the three original elements —the Monarchical, the Aristocratic, and the Popular." Tacitus endorsed this opinion :—"All nations and cities," said he, "must be governed either by the People; the First Men—*primores*; or a Single Ruler. A Government compounded of these three it is easier to admire than to believe possible. If it should ever exist, it will be of short duration." The doubt of Tacitus had reference to the difficulty of combining the three elements naturally inimical so as to ensure harmonious action. The political mechanicians of 1787 essayed this arduous task. Will their work falsify the prediction of Tacitus; or, have they only constructed an *Ideal Government* irreconcilable with the passions of men?

In November, 1775, John Adams in a letter to R. Henry Lee, sketched a plan for a New Government, founded on the English model. He spoke of "a House

* The first instance, as already stated, of the popular element—that is, the majority of the population—being *represented* in Government was by the creation of the House of Commons in England, 1265. Previously to this, the minority alone were *represented* in Government; the majority—never.

of Commons, a Council, and a Governor." Here were the three elements, but he displayed rare sagacity in the following comments :—" It is by *balancing* each of these powers against the other two that the effort in human nature towards tyranny can alone be checked and restrained, and any degree of freedom preserved in the Constitution."

The Federal fabric of 1787 not only brought the three elements together, but gave to each an orbit of its own, with distinct action, and perfect independence. To the Monarchical element, styled President, it assigned certain functions. The same was done with the Aristocratic element or Senate, and with the Democratic element or House of Representatives.

Each had special powers, but they were all defined, and therefore *limited.* This is what Cicero meant by speaking of " a Government composed in *moderation* of the three elements." It is this Limitation of Power which is expressed by the familiar term of " Checks."

An additional Check was applied by fixing the duration of these powers. The Monarchical element was limited to four years, the Aristocratic to six years, and the Democratic to two years.

Each was endowed with a separate vitality or independence. For example, the Democratic branch alone could originate financial measures; the Aristocratic united Executive to its Legislative duties, since it confirmed or rejected all nominations to office; whilst to the Monarchical element was accorded a *Veto* over all the acts of its rivals, and, also, the power of removal from office.

The Supreme Power was in this manner divided between the competing elements, and they were thus "balanced against each other" in the sense of the astute John Adams.

Their harmonious action was secured by rendering their *joint* concurrence necessary to any complete result. No law was valid till all assented, though on this vital point an union of two-thirds of the Legislative branches —that is, of the Aristocratic and Democratic elements —could make a law without the co-operation of the Executive or Monarchical element.

In a country where the Supreme Power is in the hands of the *Demos*—that is, where Universal Suffrage exists—there is no way of maintaining stability unless constitutional spheres are provided for the *Monos* and the *Aristoi* in which to exercise their natural authority. This has been sufficiently illustrated in the analysis given of the Constitution of the United States, where the *Monos* and the *Aristoi* have their respective orbits assigned and their intrinsic merits fully recognized, but where both are so sagaciously restricted as not to endanger the safety of the *Demos* or Mass.

This is true not only of the Constitution of the Nation, but equally so of those of every State and town. In these, likewise, the *Monos* and the *Aristoi* have their legal areas of action ; and so long as they are confined within them the security of the *Demos* is guaranteed, and the harmony of society is preserved.

The simple fact that the same feature is common to all the political organizations of the United States is a recognition of the universal truth that in all societies of men—in all communities the smallest as well as the largest—in the village as in the nation—are to be found for ever co-existent the *dominant*, the *superior*, and the *ordinary* intellect.

As civilization advances, and the intelligence of the multitude expands, the problem of Government can only be solved by political organizations similar to those of the United States, where the three elements in question are united, but so *checked* and *balanced* as to work in harmony. Whilst the balance is preserved the Constitution is imperishable. This is just what Tacitus distrusted: this is just what John Adams sought. The balance of the Federal Constitution was in danger but the other day, when the Aristocratic and Democratic elements conspired to overthrow their Monarchical rival. One vote only saved Andrew Johnson from Deposition.*

One single remark more. In the United States, for the first time, circumstances favored the tranquil combination of these three elements. A new Society sprang up there, where neither the Monarchical nor Aristocratic elements had taken root, as in the Old World. No Revolutions, no prolonged struggles for years were necessary before the claim of the Democratic element was recognized. There, the Democracy was politically so intelligent that its fitness to share in the Government was incontestable.†

* In 1868, the President of the United States was impeached by the House of Representatives, and tried by the Senate. A single vote prevented his removal.

† It is curious to note that some of the framers of the Federal Constitution doubted the capacity of the people to wield political power, notwithstanding the people of the American Colonies were more experienced and better educated in politics than any people before or since. In the debate on this point, Messrs. Roger Sherman and Gerry, as well as some of the Southern Delegates, contested the expediency of "trusting the people with a direct exercise of power in the general government." Messrs. Madison, Mason, and Wilson thought "no republican government could be permanent in which the people were denied a direct participation." Surely to have excluded the Democratic element from the Constitution would have been a fatal error.

Up to that time in Europe, no Nation save England offered any parallel to this. Everywhere the People were not only rudimentally ignorant, but without the faintest conception of the Science of Government. To admit the Democratic element into Government before it is competent to assume such a responsibility is sure to lead to confusion, and to jeopardize the interests of all. What progress towards this consummation has been made in the various Nations of Europe since the birth of the United States, is one of the topics I propose to treat in the work already referred to, "The History of my Times."

Above all, the political organization of England will be interesting to examine, and though the three original elements are not there balanced as in the Constitution of the United States, since the Monarchical and Aristocratic elements have by usage become subordinate to their rival, yet the Administration is so judiciously conducted, and so exactly corresponds to the condition of the community, that any premature modification of the Constitution might be alike inexpedient and dangerous.

To return from this somewhat prolonged digression to the history of the United States.

It is perhaps worthy of remark that the framers of the National Constitution scarcely appreciated their own workmanship, since none were entirely pleased with it. In the State Conventions which were called to ratify it, opinions as to its merits were greatly divided. In Massachusetts, New York, and Virginia, the opposition was protracted and obstinate. During 1788, however, it was accepted by nine States, which made it the Supreme Law of the land.

PRESIDENCY OF WASHINGTON.

In accordance with the Constitution, Washington was chosen President of the United States, in February, 1789, and John Adams, Vice-President. In April following, the first Congress elected under its provisions assembled in New York, where the oath of office was taken by the President, and he entered upon his duties. Congress immediately created the necessary Executive Offices, namely, those of Foreign Affairs, Treasury, and War. The President named Thomas Jefferson, Secretary for Foreign Affairs, Alexander Hamilton, Secretary for the Treasury, and General Knox, Secretary for War.

Two political parties had already sprung up in the country out of the differences of opinion respecting the Constitution. Those who desired a vigorous administration of the General Government were known as "Federalists," whilst those who clung to State Sovereignty, and dreaded the preponderance of the Central Authority, called themselves "Anti-Federalists." The latter accused their adversaries of inclining to Monarchy, whilst the Federalists charged the Anti-Federalists with seeking to weaken, if not to break up the Union.

These were not mere party cries, but had their origin in sectional feelings and sectional interests. The Northern and Southern States were both peopled by British settlers, but of very different character, as was seen. The Puritans who occupied the North came there to realize their doctrines in religion and politics undisturbed. The first inhabitants of Virginia, on the other hand, were a band of adventurers of whom Captain Smith spoke somewhat disparagingly thus :—"Unruly sparks packed off by their friends to escape worse destinies at home." Those who followed in Maryland, the Carolinas, and Georgia, were of a better order, but all came in hope of aggrandizement.

To these causes of difference must be added those of climate and soil: the North, bleak and unfruitful, imparting industry and perseverance to its inhabitants; and the South, genial and fertile, developing habits of indolence and luxury. The early introduction of slavery, 1619, into the South rapidly tended to widen the dissimilarities already existing.

The interests of the two sections were likewise different, if not opposed. The North was commercial and manufacturing, whilst the South was wholly agricultural. To be sure, the people of both were united by the strong ties of a common descent, with similar language, laws, and customs. In spite of their prejudices and jealousies, they had joined in throwing off the yoke of the Mother-country, but the great danger was apprehended of their separating into rival, perhaps hostile communities. This risk was immense during the anarchical period that followed the Peace of 1783, but the efforts of the patriotic leaders of both sections succeeded, as described, in enticing North and South to enter into the covenant of the Constitution, which both were pledged to maintain for better for worse.*

* During the debates on the Constitution in the Convention at Phila

No sooner, however, was the Constitution set to work, than the two political parties mentioned, the Federalists and Anti-Federalists, representing the North and South, arose. The North insisted on an energetic Federal Government, whilst the South, fearing that the North from its greater population would control it, proclaimed their adhesion to State Sovereignty, and a strict limitation of the Federal power.

These parties found champions in two able and distinguished men, Alexander Hamilton of New York, and Thomas Jefferson of Virginia. Washington dreading the effects of their political antagonism, induced them both to enter his Cabinet, where by his influence and impartiality he endeavored to secure their joint support for the various measures of his policy.

Throughout his Presidency the greatest solicitude of Washington was to check political excitement, and restrain the passions of the people. His object was to give time for the new institutions to settle down, and to acquire a hold on the respect and affections of the country that had of late years undergone so many vicissitudes, and where disorder had become almost chronic. To establish the Constitution, born of yesterday, and distrusted by a formidable party; to reconcile the State Governments to the preponderance of the Federal Government, and prevent any clash of jurisdiction; in a word, to set the wheels of the new political machine in motion, and regulate their orderly revolution—this was the mighty task that Washington undertook when he accepted the Presidency, and it

delphia, C. Pinckney of South Carolina declared on one occasion: "I had prejudices against the Eastern States before I came here, but cheerfully acknowledge I have found their representatives as candid and liberal as any men whatever."

may be doubted if any man less conscientious, less experienced, less firm, and less respected, could have succeeded in his patriotic object.

The first Law of the new Congress was moved by Mr. Madison of Virginia, to the effect that Duties be levied on "goods, wares, and merchandise imported," with a view to obtain revenue, and promote manufactures. An Act was also passed to favor American tonnage. It was regarded as patriotic and generous in a Representative of the South to recommend laws favorable to manufactures and navigation—both Northern interests.

In the second Session of Congress, January, 1790, a violent struggle ensued between the Federalists and Anti-Federalists, the North and the South, on the subject of the Debts contracted by the late Confederation as well as by the States during the Revolution. Some eleven millions of dollars were owing to France and Holland, and a much larger sum at home. The Secretary of the Treasury, Hamilton, proposed in an able Report that the United States should assume both these Debts, and provide for their liquidation. Both parties agreed on the discharge of the foreign Debt, but to pay the large domestic obligations of the Confederation and the States would involve a National Debt. This the South resisted, as it would tend to consolidate the General Government. After a heated contest the South withdrew all opposition, and the necessary Acts were passed.

The North on this occasion disarmed the South by agreeing to establish the permanent seat of the Government on the Potomac.*

* The Potomac River is the conventional dividing-line between North and South.

In 1791, Congress created a *Bank of the United States*, with a view to facilitate the financial operations of the Government and the country. The South opposed it from the same apprehension of putting another lever in the hands of the Federal Government.

As the close of Washington's first term of office approached, he had the satisfaction to see the country he had found in such confusion gradually returning to order and confidence. The financial system he had established not only relieved the States from a crushing mass of debt, but afforded such facilities to trade and industry as to promote general prosperity. Under his guidance the Constitution was daily becoming more stable, and its popularity, even at the South, was spreading so rapidly that the Opposition dropped the name of "Anti-Federalists," and assumed that of "Republicans." Washington contemplated with patriotic joy the buoyant prospects of the Nation. On returning from one of his excursions to various parts of the Union, he wrote:—"The country appears to me in a very improving state, and industry and frugality are becoming more common than hitherto. Tranquillity reigns among the people, with that disposition towards the general government which is likely to preserve it. They begin to feel the good effects of equal laws and equal protection. The farmer finds a ready market for his produce, and the merchant calculates with more certainty on his payments. Each day's experience of the Government of the United States seems to confirm its establishment, and to render it more popular. A ready acquiescence in the laws made under it shows in a strong light the confidence the people have in their representatives, and in the upright views of those who administer the Government."

Almost at the same period, Jefferson felt constrained to bear similar testimony to the thriving condition of the country. Though a member of Washington's Cabinet, he was the acknowledged leader of the party which, in the first place, took exception to the Constitution as likely to confer too much authority on the Central Government; which, next, opposed the funding of the Debts of the Confederation and the States; and which, finally, resisted the creation of the Bank of the United States that rendered at the time to every class the most efficient service. Yet he was forced to admit the incontestable success of Washington's sagacious policy. He thus wrote:—"In general, our affairs are proceeding in a train of unexampled prosperity. This arises from the real improvement in our government; from the unbounded confidence reposed in it by the people, their zeal to support it, and their conviction that a solid union is the best rock of their safety; from the favorable seasons also, which for some years have increased the productions of agriculture, and from the growth of industry, economy, and domestic manufactures. So that I believe I may say with truth, that there is not a nation under the sun enjoying more present prosperity, nor with more in prospect."

Under these favorable circumstances it is no wonder that Washington regarding his mission as complete, should express his earnest desire to retire from the harassing cares of office, and seek needed repose in the calm of "Mount Vernon." A protest resounded throughout the land. An instinctive dread seemed to seize on the people. The loss of his sound judgment, his firm character, and disinterested patriotism, filled them with apprehension. His Cabinet, Congress, and the Nation united to solicit his re-election. Washington hesitated. He knew that the Constitution, though in a less precarious condition than when he began to administer it, had hardly yet settled down on a firm foundation. His anxiety, too, was awakened by the increasing virulence of the two great parties which, under the leadership of Hamilton and Jefferson, grew daily more bitter in their strife. Worse than all, he was alarmed at the effect in the United States of the recent French Revolution, which had deeply aroused the sympathies of the Nation for their old Ally. He felt that he alone of all men could avert under Providence the dangers that loomed in the horizon. He consented, therefore, to a re-election in 1792.

His apprehensions were speedily realized. No sooner had a Coalition been formed in Europe against the French Revolution, with England at its head, than an universal shout was raised to succor France and declare war on England. Washington's attachment to France was sincere, but he considered the intervention of the United States in her wars as Quixotic, since little service could be rendered to France, whilst immense losses would be incurred. With his usual foresight, Washington seemed to anticipate the failure of the French Revolution. He wrote to Henry Lee, 1793, in these words :—"The affairs of France would seem to me in the highest paroxysm of disorder, not so much from the presence of foreign enemies, for in the cause of liberty this ought to be fuel to the fire of the patriot soldier, but because those in whose hands the government is entrusted are ready to tear each other to pieces, and will more than probably prove the worst foes the country has."

His determination was soon taken as to the policy

that prudence suggested, and he consulted his Cabinet on the expediency of issuing a Proclamation of Neutrality. His Cabinet were then unanimous, and in April, 1793, the President in an able document declared the neutrality of the United States in the war then prevailing between France and an European Coalition. The following is an extract:—"My policy has been, and will continue to be while I have the honor to remain in the Administration, to maintain friendly terms with, but to be independent of all the nations of the earth; to share in the broils of none, to fulfil our own engagements. * * * Nothing short of self-respect, and that justice which is essential to a national character, ought to involve us in war; for sure I am, if this country is preserved in tranquillity twenty years longer, it may bid defiance in a just cause to any Power whatever, such in that time will be its wealth, power, and resources." This, and many other declarations, showed that Washington was resolved to adhere inflexibly to neutrality, and for a time his influence calmed the country.

The "Republican" or Democratic party of that day, however, determined with the sanction of their champion, Jefferson, to raise the banner of France, and appeal to the passions of the people.

At the same moment arrived in the United States, the new Minister of the French Republic, "Citizen Genet," and he set to work with reckless zeal to embroil the country in a war with Great Britain. In defiance of the Proclamation of Neutrality he began enlisting recruits; fitting out privateers; establishing prize courts in various ports of the Union; organizing expeditions against the Spanish rule in Florida; issuing inflammatory addresses to the people. His language to the Government was frequently not only disrespectful, but insolent. He accused it of "a cowardly abandonment of its friends," and of acting against "the intention of the people of America, whose fraternal voice resounded from every quarter around him."

Unfortunately his obnoxious conduct received cordial support from the "Republican" party which had espoused the cause of France, and daily assailed the policy of neutrality. Two of its organs in Philadelphia, then the seat of Government, and where Genet resided, violently attacked the Government, and ventured to decry Washington himself. *Freneau's Gazette* * thus encouraged Genet:—"The Minister of France I hope will act with firmness and spirit. The people are his friends, or the friends of France, and he will have nothing to apprehend, for, as yet, the people are sovereign in the United States. * * * If one of the leading features of our Government is pusillanimity when the British Lion shows his teeth, let France and her minister act as becomes the dignity and justice of her cause." *Bache's Advertiser* used the following language:—"It is no longer possible to doubt that the intention of the Executive of the United States is to look upon the Treaty of Amity and Commerce between France and America as a nullity, and that they are prepared to join the league of Kings against France."

To stimulate popular enthusiasm still further Associations were formed called "Democratic Societies," the object of which was declared to be to protect American liberty against an "European Confederacy"

* Freneau was a Frenchman, and employed in the State Department by the Secretary, Mr. Jefferson, as a translator.

and "the pride of wealth and arrogance of power" at home.*

Doubtless Washington was shocked at the frenzy of party spirit which sought to plunge the country anew into war, and he must secretly have deplored the infatuation of a portion of the people. Whatever were his reflections or emotions, his composure was unruffled by all this clamor. He lost no time, however, in vindicating the dignity of the Government and the supremacy of the laws. He called on the Governors of Pennsylvania and South Carolina to put a peremptory stop to the illegal conduct of the French Envoy,† and also demanded of his Government to order his prompt recall. A new Minister succeeded him in February, 1794.

The difficulties of the situation were aggravated by the conduct of the British Government, which seized all American vessels laden with bread-stuffs for France as contraband, and frequently impressed American seamen. The exasperation caused by these acts in the United States was zealously heightened by the Republican party, and the chances of war increased so rapidly that the President sent John Jay on a mission to England, May, 1794, to put an end if possible to the grievances complained of. Mr. Jay succeeded in making a new Treaty with the British Cabinet conceding most of the demands of the American Government. The Senate ratified the Treaty, with certain modifications, and the President finally signed it. This removed all

* These events are described in detail in Young's "American Statesman."

† It was stated that some fifty British vessels were captured—some within the jurisdiction of the United States—by privateers fitted out under the authority of Genet.

danger of hostilities, and the anger of the Republican party knew no bounds.

It can hardly be credited that the party of Mr. Jefferson * seriously contemplated a war with England. Their real object was, doubtless, to obtain possession of the Government by inducing a majority of the people to adopt their party cries. Already they had secured the control of the House of Representatives, and elected their Speaker, December, 1793, by a majority of 10 over the candidate of the Federalist party. They felt sure, therefore, that by keeping alive the popular sympathies for France, they would raise Jefferson to the Presidency at the next election. The Treaty with England, as well as the horrors of the French Revolution, had both tended to allay political excitement, and the Republican Politicians dreading defeat gave way to the most intemperate conduct. They called public meetings all over the country to denounce the Treaty; the negotiator, Mr. Jay, was burned in effigy in different places; a copy of the Treaty was burned before the houses of the British Minister and Consul in Philadelphia. The Senators who ratified it were denounced. Nor did they stop here, but indulged in flagrant abuse of Washington; disparaged him as Soldier and Statesman; demanded his Impeachment for ordering the negotiation of the Treaty; and finally published forged letters purporting to have been written by him in 1776, favorable to Great Britain and opposed to the cause of Independence.

The unscrupulous attacks of the Republican leaders

* Mr. Jefferson's opposition to the peace policy of Washington constrained him to retire from his Cabinet, December, 1793. He was succeeded by Edmund Randolph of Virginia.

and their party journals on Washington greatly shocked the country, and caused a reaction in favor of the Federalists. Party feeling ran so high that an attempt was made in the House of Representatives, March, 1796, to invalidate the Treaty with Great Britain. Edward Livingston of New York, a leader of the Republican party, moved that the President be called on to lay the Instructions to Mr. Jay, with the Correspondence, before the House of Representatives. After a prolonged debate the motion was adopted by 62 to 37. This demand was a direct violation of the Constitution which had confided the treaty-making power to the President and the Senate. Washington declined to comply with the call of the House, as it would be conceding a right the Constitution had not conferred on it, and establishing a dangerous precedent. He declared that "the power of making Treaties is exclusively vested in the President, by and with the advice and consent of the Senate, provided two-thirds of the Senate concur, and that every Treaty so made and promulgated is thenceforward the law of the land. . . . . In this construction of the Constitution, every House of Representatives has heretofore acquiesced, and until the present time not a doubt or suspicion has appeared to my knowledge that this construction was not the true one."

The determination of Washington to maintain the Constitution in its integrity awed the Opposition, and they abandoned their untenable position.

The Revolutionary Government of France was more incensed at the "Jay Treaty," which had settled all difficulties with Great Britain, than even the Jefferson party, for they hoped to see the United States at war with their enemy. In a spirit of hostility they issued decrees damaging to American commerce, and in violation of Treaties. Finally, they refused to receive Mr. Pinckney, the American Minister, whom they threatened to arrest on his arrival in Paris.

The conscientious and patriotic efforts of Washington to promote the welfare of the country, though cordially sustained by the mass of the people, did not protect him from the persistent diatribes of the Opposition organs.

On one occasion Mr. Jefferson was suspected of being connected with these insidious attacks, and he wrote to Washington to exonerate himself. The President thus replied:—" As you have mentioned the subject yourself, it would not be frank, candid, or friendly, to conceal that your conduct has been represented as derogating from that opinion I conceived you entertained of me; that to your particular friends and connections you have described, and they have denounced me, as a person under a dangerous influence; and that if I would listen more to some other opinions, all would be well. My answer has invariably been, that I had never discovered anything in the conduct of Mr. Jefferson to raise suspicions in my mind of his sincerity; that if he would retrace my conduct whilst he was in the Administration, abundant proof would occur to him that truth and upright decisions were the sole objects of my pursuit; that there were many instances within his own knowledge of my having decided against, as in favor of the person alluded to (Hamilton); and, moreover, that I was no believer in the infallibility of the politics or measures of any man living. In short, that I was no party-man myself, and that the first wish of my heart was, if parties did exist, to reconcile them. To this I may add, that until the last year or two I had no conception that parties would, or even could, go the lengths I have been witness to; nor did I believe until lately, that it was within the bounds of probability —hardly within those of possibility—that while I was using my utmost exertions to establish a national character of our own, independent, as far as our obligations and justice would permit, of every nation of the earth, and wished, by steering a steady course, to preserve this country from the horrors of a desolating war, I should be accused of being the enemy of one nation, and subject to the influence of another, and to prove it, that every act of my administration would be tortured, and the grossest and most insidious misrepresentations would be made, by giving one side only of a subject, and that, too, in such exaggerated and indecent terms, as would scarcely be applied to a Nero, to a notorious defaulter, or, even, to a common pick-pocket. But enough of this. I have already gone further in the expression of my feelings than I intended." *

It was not the outrages of faction alone that Washington had to endure during his second term of

* Notwithstanding Washington's confidence in the sincerity of Jefferson, it would seem he was a determined opponent of the President's policy. A letter written by Jefferson to P. Mazzei, a foreigner, in April, 1796, was published the following year in the United States. This curious epistle is given in the "American Statesman," p. 150, whose author makes the following comment:—"Such a letter from one with whom he (Washington) had long sustained the most intimate and friendly relations, private and official, accusing him of antagonism to republican principles, and of co-operating with a monarchical party to change the government—characterizing his administration as 'the calm of despotism,' and representing its measures as 'contrivances invented for the purposes of corruption'—gave Washington great pain, and marred, if it did not terminate, the friendship which had so long subsisted between these two eminent and esteemed individuals."

office, but trials of far greater magnitude. An Insurrection broke out in Western Pennsylvania against the tax on whisky in the summer of 1794. Finding his Proclamation set at defiance, Washington ordered out 15,000 of the Militia of the adjoining States, and of Eastern Pennsylvania, and was preparing to take the command in person when the Insurgents broke up and dispersed. A sanguinary war with the Indians on the North-Western frontier, which began at the end of 1791, was carried on for two years. One of the armies sent against them under General St. Clair was defeated by disobeying Washington's instructions. They were finally overpowered by General Wayne.

In September, 1796, Washington issued his Farewell Address to the United States; modestly but firmly declining a re-election for a third term. This memorable document conveying in solemn language his parting injunctions to the Nation is always regarded by his country with veneration.

In December he met Congress for the last time, when he had the satisfaction to announce that all difficulties with Foreign Nations had been adjusted, and that the prosperity of the country was steadily augmenting. These were the closing words of his Address:—"The situation in which I now stand for the last time, in the midst of the representatives of the people of the United States, naturally recalls the period when the administration of the present form of Government commenced, and I cannot omit the occasion to congratulate you, and my country, on the success of the experiment, or to repeat my fervent supplications to the Supreme Ruler of the Universe, that his Providential care may still be extended to the United States;

that the virtue and happiness of the people may be preserved; and that the Government which they have instituted for the protection of their liberties may be perpetuated." Both Houses of Congress on this occasion voted complimentary Addresses. That of the House of Representatives stated amongst other clauses:—"We entertain a grateful conviction that your wise, firm, and patriotic administration has been signally conducive to the success of the present form of government." The Address of the Senate was voted unanimously; but that of the House was opposed by twelve of its Members; among whom were Edward Livingston, and Andrew Jackson, both prominent leaders of the Republican or Jefferson party.

An astonishing instance of the frenzy of party may be found in the following paragraph from the *Aurora*, published in Philadelphia, and which appeared a few days after the Addresses voted by Congress:—"If ever a nation was debauched by a man, the American nation has been debauched by Washington. If ever a nation has been deceived by a man, the American nation has been deceived by Washington. Let his conduct then be an example to future ages. Let it serve as a warning that no man may be an idol. Let the history of the Federal government instruct mankind that the mask of patriotism may be worn to conceal the foulest designs against the liberties of the people." This senseless ebullition against a man who in his own time was regarded as a model of uprightness in public and private life, is only worth citing as a proof that party spirit defies alike the bounds of reason, truth and decency. To the honor of his country let it be said, that such sentiments as the above were simply the effusions of some distempered Politicians. The mass of his countrymen entertained for Washington the respect and veneration his conduct and services were calculated to inspire.

On March 3rd, 1797, the Administration of the first President ended.

During this period all disputes with Foreign Nations except France were terminated; Credit was restored; the payment of the Public Debt provided for; Commerce, Manufactures, and Agriculture prospered; the Exports and Imports nearly trebled; and the Public Revenues augmented beyond all expectation. Far more assuring than this, however, was the stability which Washington's Administration had given to the young Constitution. "My predominant motive has been," said Washington in his Farewell Address, "to endeavor to gain time to our country to settle and mature its yet recent institutions."

In commenting on the career of Washington, Guizot thus writes:—"The trials of public life were painful to him; he preferred the independence and repose of a private position to the exercise of power. But he accepted without hesitation the task his country imposed on him, and in fulfilling it he made neither with the nation nor himself any compromises that might have lightened the burden. Born for government, although it afforded him little satisfaction, he spoke to the American people what he believed true, and maintained what he believed wise, with a firmness as inflexible as it was simple, and often at a sacrifice of popularity, the more meritorious as it was not compensated by the mere love of domination. The servant of an infant Republic when the Democratic spirit was in the ascendant, he obtained its confidence, and assured its triumph by defending its interests against its passions, and by persisting in a policy at once modest and severe, reserved and independent—a rare success, alike honorable to Washington and his country." "Of all great men," says this eloquent writer, "Washington was the most virtuous and the most fortunate. God has in this world no higher favors to bestow."

Washington was beyond question the foremost of the remarkable men that figured in the American Revolution. *Quorum pars magna fuit.*

PRESIDENCY OF JOHN ADAMS.

WHEN Washington positively declined a re-election, the two rival parties selected their candidates for the Presidency. The Federalists united on John Adams, one of the ablest Statesmen of the Revolution, and the Republicans upon their leader, Thomas Jefferson, who had retired from the Cabinet of Washington, December, 1793, condemning his policy of neutrality.

In the Presidential election of 1796, the Republican Politicians made strong appeals to the popular prejudices against Great Britain. The French Minister, Adet, took an active part in the canvass. He published in the *Aurora*, the organ of the Republican party, a letter ostensibly written to the Secretary of State, denouncing the "bad faith and ingratitude" of Washington's Administration to France. Adet also published in the *Aurora* an order to all Frenchmen in the United States to wear during the election the tri-colored cockade, which was generally assumed as a badge by the Republican party. All these intrigues, however, failed, for John Adams, the champion of the neutrality doctrine, was elected, and the peace policy of Washington was sustained by the country.

The Administration of the second President began on March 4th, 1797. He retained the Cabinet of Washington—Timothy Pickering, Secretary of State; Oliver Wolcott, Secretary of the Treasury; and James McHenry, Secretary of War.

The relations of the country with France were at that time very critical. The French Government incensed at the United States for persisting in their neutral policy resorted to the most hostile measures against her commerce. They ordered all American vessels carrying any productions of Great Britain to be captured. This was in violation of neutral rights, as well as of the Treaty between France and the United States. Under these circumstances President Adams called an extra Session of Congress, May, 1797. There was a majority in both Houses in favor of the Administration. Active preparations were made for the probable contingency of war.

The President dreading this alternative sent three Commissioners to France to negotiate a pacific adjustment of all difficulties. Talleyrand, the Minister of the French Government, demanded large sums of money as the price of peace. The American Government refused these terms, and broke off negotiations. The Congress of 1798 passed an Act suspending all commercial intercourse with France. It created at the same time the Navy Department, and B. Stoddart of Maryland was nominated as Secretary.

As the chances of war were imminent, Washington was solicited to take the command of the armies of the United States. He consented with great reluctance. "With sorrow I should quit," he wrote, "the shades of my peaceful abode to encounter anew the turmoils of war, to which, possibly, my strength and powers might be found incompetent." He was nominated to the chief command, with the rank of Lieutenant-General, even before his answer was received.

Fortunately in November, 1799, the French Government fell into the hands of General Bonaparte, and he directed at once that all disputes with the United States should be settled, and consequently a new Treaty was made in September, 1800, which restored the old relations of amity between the two countries.

During the Session which closed in July, 1798, Congress passed two Acts which obtained great notoriety. These were the famous "Alien" and "Sedition" laws.

The Act concerning aliens empowered the President to order any foreigner he considered "dangerous to the peace and safety of the United States, or suspected of being engaged in any treasonable machinations against the Government thereof, to depart out of the country." The motive of this Act was the notorious fact that not only Foreign Ministers, more especially those of France, but a herd of political writers both French and English were actively engaged in traducing the Government and policy of the United States, and seeking to sow discord among its citizens. This abuse Congress deemed it necessary to check.

This enactment was followed up by another called the "Sedition Law," which was levelled at any one, foreign or native, who should either endeavor to stir up riots and insurrections; or who should "write, print, utter, and publish any false, scandalous, or malicious writing," against the Government, Congress, or President of the United States.

These laws were meant to restrain the truculence of party writers, the most unscrupulous of whom were foreigners: * laws which had the sanction of Washing-

* Among the most conspicuous of these literary adventurers were Freneau, of the *National Gazette*, Philadelphia,—a Frenchman; J. Duane, of the *Aurora*, Philadelphia,—an Irishman; T. Callender, of the

ton, Patrick Henry, and many eminent patriots. The "Alien Act" was never enforced, as its passage induced the most obnoxious foreigners to quit the country at once. Several prosecutions took place under the "Sedition Law." Fine and imprisonment were imposed by both these laws.

Whatever the necessity for these enactments, the shrewd leaders of the Republican party thought them admirably adapted for political agitation, and the signal was given to begin a relentless war against them. It was declared by them that the "Alien" and "Sedition" laws were "palpable and alarming infractions of the Constitution," and their party organs all over the country taking up the cry resounded with the loudest denunciations of the Federalist party which had passed them.

With a view to give more effect to this political onslaught on their rivals, Mr. Madison, at the request of Mr. Jefferson, introduced into the Legislature of Virginia, December, 1798, a series of Resolutions solemnly declaring "the Alien and Sedition laws to be in violation of the Constitution." These Resolutions were ordered to be transmitted to the Governors of the other States to be laid before their respective Legislatures.

Not content with this broadside against the peccant Federalists, Mr. Jefferson, the head and front of the

Examiner, Richmond,—a Scotchman. This latter was an instrument of Jefferson, who refused, when he became President, to make him postmaster at Richmond. In anger, Callender published numerous letters of Jefferson, proving he had been his political tool. William Cobbett, of the *Porcupine Gazette*, Philadelphia, was an Englishman. Being condemned to $5,000 damages in a libel suit, he left the country in 1800.

Republican party, drew up with his own hand another set of Resolutions which were laid by his allies before the Legislature of Kentucky, and were passed before those of Virginia, November, 1798. These Kentucky Resolutions of Mr. Jefferson turned out another Pandora's box, for they contained the germ of that political heresy since so sadly known as the doctrine of *Nullification.*

These Resolutions declared :—"That the Union was a compact between the States, as *States*, instead of *the people* of the several States."

This was in contradiction to the preamble of the Constitution, which begins, "We, the people of the United States."

They further declared :—"That, as in other cases of compact between parties having no common judge, *each party has an equal right to judge for itself*, as well of the infractions, as of the mode and measure of redress."

This denied the jurisdiction of the Supreme Court, whose prerogative it is to pronounce on the constitutionality of any Federal law.

In conformity to these views of State-rights, the Resolutions affirmed "the Alien and Sedition Acts to be, *not law, but altogether void and of no force.*" It was further asserted :—"That when powers are assumed which have not been delegated, a *Nullification of the Act is the right remedy*, and that every State has a natural right to *nullify of its own authority* all assumptions of power by others within its limits."

As Mr. Jefferson was the author of these Kentucky Resolutions, he must be regarded as the father of the doctrine of *Nullification*, which from that time became the favourite dogma of many Politicians of the Southern States. It may be that Mr. Jefferson entertained an honest dread of the undue supremacy of the Federal Government over the States, but the failure of the first Union known as the "Confederation" proved that if the States retained their complete independence, anarchy and civil war were inevitable. To obviate this, as we saw, a new Union was organized which gave the Federal Government a preponderance over the States, and furnished it with the necessary *coercive power* to enforce its supremacy. The powers delegated to the Federal Government by the framers of the Constitution of 1789 show that it was their intention to limit the Sovereignty of the States, and to make the Federal authority Supreme. In case of dispute between the Federal and State Governments as to the constitutionality of any Federal law, a High Court was created to pronounce its solemn fiat thereon. Yet in the face of these recent and undeniable facts Mr. Jefferson in 1798 was guilty of the flat heresy recorded in the above Resolutions. He was too clear-headed not to know he was setting up a false idol, but his zeal as a Politician overcame his reason and his patriotism.

The Virginia and Kentucky Resolutions were duly communicated to the other States, but met with no response. The Legislatures of Delaware, New York, and New England disclaimed them.

The real object of the Republican leaders, however, was achieved. They inflamed the popular mind against the Alien and Sedition Acts, and the chances of Mr. Jefferson in the next election were increased.

Another event still more serious rendered the reelection of Mr. Adams doubtful. In his negotiations with France, he acted in opposition to the views of the majority of his Cabinet, and of several influential Federalists, notably General Hamilton and Gouverneur Morris. This led to a schism in his party. In May, 1800, the President demanded the resignation of the Secretaries of State and War. John Marshall of Virginia, and S. Dexter of Massachusetts, were called to succeed them. This only made the breach more irreparable. As the Presidential election of 1800 approached, the Federalist leaders opposed to Mr. Adams plotted to obtain the majority of the electoral votes for C. C. Pinckney, the Federalist candidate for the Vice-Presidency. The manœuvre failed. The Republican candidates, Jefferson and Burr, received each 73 votes; the Federalist candidates, Adams and Pinckney, 65 and 64 votes. As there was a tie between Jefferson and Burr, the election of President devolved by the Constitution on the House of Representatives.

It was during the Presidency of Mr. Adams, in the summer of 1800, that the seat of Government was transferred from Philadelphia to the city of Washington.

PRESIDENCY OF THOMAS JEFFERSON.

It must have been a source of mortification to Mr. Jefferson that he, the author of the "Declaration of Independence," and perhaps the ablest Statesman of the Revolution, should find himself on a par in the estimation of the country with such a man as Aaron Burr, in every way his inferior. Doubtless his political course during the Administrations of Washington and Adams had lowered him in the respect of his fellow-citizens.

In the balloting for the President in the House of Representatives, the opposition to Jefferson was prolonged. As there were then sixteen States in the Union, nine were necessary to a choice, each State giving but one vote. The Federalist party from its dislike of Jefferson was mostly disposed to vote for Burr, whom it could have elected, but many eminent Federalists considered Burr unworthy of the position. General Hamilton exerted all his influence with his party against him. He denounced Burr in a private letter which soon became public in the following terms:—"There is no doubt that upon every prudent and virtuous calculation Jefferson is to be preferred. He is by far not so dangerous a man, and he has pretensions to character. As to Burr he has nothing in his favor. His private character is not defended by his most partial friends. His public principles have no other spring or aim than his own aggrandizement. If he can, he will certainly disturb our institutions to secure himself permanent power, and with it wealth. * * * To accomplish his ends, he must lean upon unprincipled men, and will continue to adhere to the myrmidons who have hitherto surrounded him. To these he will no doubt add able rogues of the Federal party; but he will employ the rogues of all parties to overrule the good men of all parties, and to promote projects which wise men of every description will disapprove."*

The struggle between the partisans of Jefferson and Burr in the House of Representatives continued for a week, but at last some members of the Federalist party agreed to withdraw their opposition if Mr. Jefferson would consent when elected, first, to support the public credit; second, to maintain the navy; third, not to remove subordinate public officers for political motives. These terms were accepted, and on the thirty-sixth ballot Thomas Jefferson was chosen President.

In his Inaugural Address, March, 1801, he dropped the *rôle* of a sectional Politician that he had hitherto played, and assumed a tone more becoming his exalted position. He used conciliatory language towards the Federalist or Northern party, which he had previously assailed with bitterness. "We have called," said his Inaugural, "by different names brethren of the same principle. We are all Republicans—we are all Federalists. If there be any among us who would wish to dissolve this Union, or to change its Republican form, let them stand undisturbed as monuments of the safety

* General Hamilton's strenuous efforts tended to prevent Burr's election. Treasuring up this wrong, he abided his opportunity, and in 1804, near the close of his term as Vice-President of the United States, he demanded reparation of General Hamilton in a duel, in which the latter was killed.

with which error of opinion may be tolerated when reason is left free to combat it."

The new President made Madison of Virginia, Secretary of State; Dearborn of Massachusetts, Secretary of War. He retained at the head of the Treasury and Navy the Secretaries appointed by his predecessor.*

The Republican or Southern party was in a majority in both Houses of Congress, and the influence of President Jefferson over its legislation was therefore unbounded.

Most of the office-holders had been appointed by President Washington, and represented the Federalist party, now in minority. It was feared they would be generally removed for members of the dominant side On this point the President showed more regard for the interests of the country than of his party. Yet he did not think it fair that the "monopoly of office was to be continued in the hands of the minority," but his desire was to remove only the least worthy. He recorded his opinion that the only questions concerning a candidate for office should be, "Is he honest, is he capable, is he faithful to the Constitution?" The whole of the removals during his Administration numbered less than forty.

The great sensation of 1801 was the rumor that Spain had secretly ceded her territory of Louisiana to France. This, of course, invalidated the treaties between Spain and the United States, securing to the latter the navigation of the Mississippi river. The western

* The *National Intelligencer*, one of the most reputable journals ever published in the United States, was established at this period in Washington, and became the official organ of the Government, and of the Republican or Southern party.

country was up in arms at this news, and insisted on the Government taking effectual means in their behalf. The French Government for over a year denied the reported cession, but finally admitted that it had occurred in October, 1801. Such was the agitation on this subject that President Jefferson resolved by every possible means to nullify the effects of this unexpected event. The Minister to France, Robert R. Livingston, was instructed to employ all the efforts of diplomacy to effect a satisfactory solution of the difficulty. The chances of a breach between the two countries were suddenly averted by an offer of the First Consul—Bonaparte—to sell the territory in question to the United States. This led to a new perplexity. What authority had the Government under the Constitution to undertake such a purchase? The advantages of the acquisition, however, were so immense that our Minister to France, supported by Mr. Monroe who had been sent out for this purpose, ventured to enter on the negotiation, and without instructions they assumed the responsibility of striking a bargain by which the United States were to become the owners of this immense domain for some fifteen millions of dollars. They signed a Treaty to that effect and sent it to the President. It is not to be presumed that the Ministers to France would have taken a step so far transcending their powers without some secret instructions from their Government. This was proved by the action of the President who endorsed the unauthorized Treaty, and called an extra Session of Congress in October, 1803, to ratify it, which was promptly done. By means of this diplomatic manœuvre Louisiana became the property of the United States.

At the close of his first term of office Jefferson was

re-elected in 1804, and entered on his second Administration the ensuing March. His popularity had greatly increased, for his re-election was almost unanimous.

The second term of Mr. Jefferson was seriously disturbed by the war raging between England and France. In their eagerness to injure each other the infuriated combatants set the interests of all neutral Nations at defiance. They interpreted the Law of Nations as they pleased, and made new regulations to suit their purpose. Under these circumstances the commerce of the States suffered great damage, and, worse still, Great Britain to recruit her navy frequently *impressed* seamen in the American service on the ground that they were British subjects, which, indeed, was often the case. The Secretary of State reported in March, 1806, that the number of seamen seized during the European war amounted to 2,273.

Though deeply incensed at the outrages of both England and France, the United States did not deem it expedient to resort to war; but the Government resolved on retaliatory measures. Congress, consequently, passed an Act, 1806, prohibiting the importation of manufactures from Great Britain and her Colonies.

In December of this year, a Treaty was negotiated with England by Monroe and Pinkney, the American Ministers in London, which guaranteed the commercial intercourse of both Nations; but the question of *impressment* was reserved for future negotiation. The British Government, however, gave assurances which satisfied the American Ministers that the utmost care should be taken not to molest any citizens of the United States, and that prompt reparation should be made for any injury.

This important Treaty, as it was regarded by the commercial community as well as by the negotiators —the confidential friends of the President—was rejected by Mr. Jefferson without submitting it to the Senate. His motive was never fully disclosed. The Federalist party attributed its rejection to his well-known partiality for France. The British Cabinet regarded it as a proof of his desire to embroil the relations of the two countries. There is no doubt the President's refusal to submit this Treaty to the Senate was one of the causes which finally led to war.

Comformably to Art. I., Sec. 9th, of the Constitution, Congress, in the Session of 1806–7, passed an Act, at the suggestion of the President, abolishing the Slave Trade after January 1st, 1808.

The spoliations committed on the commerce of neutral Nations in the beginning of the conflict between Great Britain and France were greatly aggravated, in 1806, by new measures of hostility. In May of that year England, by Orders in Council, declared the west coast of Europe under blockade "from the River Elbe to Brest inclusive." In November of the same year Napoleon retaliated by his Berlin Decree, which declared the British Islands in a state of blockade, and "all commerce and correspondence with them prohibited."

In disregard of the Treaties between France and the United States, the American Minister at Paris was informed that the Decree was applicable to American commerce.

In November, 1807, England, by new Orders in Council, declared that "all ports and places belonging to France and her Allies were under blockade, and all trade in the produce or manufactures of these countries and their colonies prohibited." In December of the same year Napoleon retorted by his Milan Decree, of a still more sweeping character than that of Berlin.

Amongst other clauses was one especially levelled at the United States, to the effect "that every ship of whatever nation which had submitted to search by an English ship, or had made a voyage to England, or paid any tax to that Government, was thereby *denationalized* and lawful prize." In consequence of these Orders and Decrees, violating both Treaties and the Law of Nations, a vast number of American vessels with their cargoes were captured by the cruisers of the two belligerents. Exasperated by these wholesale depredations, sensible that remonstrance or menace was alike useless, and knowing that the country was unable to cope with both England and France, Congress passed in December, 1807, on the recommendation of the President, the famous "Embargo Law," by which all vessels within the jurisdiction of the United States bound to a foreign port were prohibited from sailing. Thus American commerce, with the exception of the coasting trade, was utterly suppressed.

It was supposed that the effect of the Embargo, by stopping the exportation of cotton and grain, would coerce the belligerents to show more respect to American commerce, but such was not the case. General Armstrong, United States Minister in France, wrote in August, 1808 :—" Here the Embargo is not felt, whilst in England, amid the exciting scenes of the day, it is forgotten."

Very different, however, was the result in the United States, where the stoppage of all foreign trade led to wide-spread disaster. In New England, especially, wl ere capital was largely invested in commercial pursuits, ruin was universal. So loud was the outcry all over the country against this baneful Law that it was repealed, March 1st, 1809, and a new Act was substituted by Congress called the "Non-Intercourse Law," by which foreign trade was restored, except with England and France.

Political passions were running high when Jefferson retired from office. The Federalist or Northern party accused him of the destruction of American trade and commerce by wantonly rejecting the Treaty with England through his undoubted sympathies with France. "Our agriculture," they declared, "is discouraged; the fisheries abandoned; navigation forbidden; the revenue extinguished; the navy sold and dismantled;* the nation weakened by internal animosities and divisions." On the other hand, the Southern, or Democratic party as it now was generally called, pointed with exultation to the acquisition of Louisiana, with its million of square miles of territory, and the free navigation of the Mississippi river.

* This had reference to a whim of Mr. Jefferson, who said that gunboats or cutters were all that was required for the coast defences of the United States, and that a navy was an unnecessary expense.

PRESIDENCY OF JAMES MADISON.

In spite of the "Embargo Law" and its consequences, the Democratic party retained its hold on the country, and raised James Madison to the Presidency in 1808. He received 122 electoral votes, whilst his Federalist opponent obtained but 47.

The new Administration found itself immediately engaged in angry discussions with England and France for their constant aggressions on American commerce. Napoleon resented the "Non-Intercourse Law" of the United States, by issuing his Rambouillet Decree in March, 1810, which, in the words of Mr. Monroe, "made a sweep of all American property within the reach of the French power."

In May, 1810, Congress passed an Act proposing to revoke the "Non-Intercourse Law," if England or France would within the year agree to revoke their edicts against American commerce. Napoleon, who sought every opportunity to involve his adversary England in disputes with the United States, seized the new occasion that offered. He told the United States Minister at Paris that "his Berlin and Milan Decrees were revoked," and the President by proclamation revoked the "Non-Intercourse Law," as regarded France, without requiring any proof beyond the Emperor's mere declaration. England refused to recall her Orders in Council until satisfied that France was not deluding the

United States, which turned out afterwards to be the case.

Napoleon's artifice succeeded, for the Administration believing that France was disposed to respect neutral rights demanded with energy that England should do the same. The correspondence between the two Governments became more animated than ever, and the prospect of a final rupture steadily increased. A war faction sprang up in the United States led on by the youthful Politicans of the Southern party, of whom Calhoun, Clay, and Lowndes were the most ardent.

In the summer of 1811, the Indian tribes north of the Ohio river, under the lead of Tecumseh, a Chief of great reputation, made war on the United States. It was asserted that British emissaries had stimulated them to this act. They were completely routed by General W. H. Harrison.

In March, 1812, the President communicated to Congress certain documents which went to show the existence of a British plot to dismember the Union by seducing the Eastern States to retire from the Confederacy. It appeared that a John Henry had been employed by the Governor-General of Canada to visit secretly the United States to ascertain "the state of public opinion as to the probability of a war with Great Britain; the strength of the two leading parties, and which was most likely to prevail." Henry was recalled "without having had any conversation with any person in the country on the subject of his mission." Dissatisfied with the recognition of his services by the British Government, he offered to sell his information to the United States Government, and was paid $50,000 by the Secretary of State, Mr. Monroe. The

British Cabinet denied all knowledge of the transaction in open Parliament.

Hostility to England now ran so high that the Democratic or Southern party refused to renominate Mr. Madison for the Presidency, unless he pledged himself "to go for war." He considered a war inexpedient, as did his Secretary of the Treasury, Mr. Gallatin, but he yielded, at length, to political pressure, and was made a candidate for re-election.

Various Acts were passed by Congress as "preliminary war measures;" amongst others a new Embargo Law, and an Act forbidding the exportation of specie. In June, 1812, the President sent a Message to Congress recommending war with Great Britain. The reasons assigned were, first, the *impressment* of American seamen; next, the British doctrines and system of blockade; and finally, the depredations committed by English subjects on the commerce of the United States. A vehement debate ensued, which was carried on with *closed doors*, against the protest of the minority. Both Houses of Congress voted for war—19 to 13 in the Senate, and 79 to 49 in the House.

The anti-war party was composed of the Northern Members, or Federalists. They drew up an emphatic remonstrance against the war as unnecessary and inexpedient. They declared that, as to the point of *impressment,* all the Governments of Europe maintained the right to the services of their citizens in time of war. With regard to England, they showed by the Correspondence of the United States Minister in London, that she had renounced her prescriptive right on the "high seas," still claiming it on the "narrow seas." The Minister, Mr. King, however, stated "that with more time than was left him for the negotiation, this restriction could be overcome."

After showing that all the causes of war alleged were insufficient, they wound up their appeal to their countrymen in this strain:—"If honor demands a war with England, what opiate lulls that honor to sleep over the wrongs done us by France? On land, robberies, seizures, and imprisonments by French authorities; at sea, pillage, sinkings, and burnings under French orders. These are notorious. Is any alleviation to be found in the correspondence and humiliations of the present United States Minister at the French Court? In his communication to our Government, now before the public, where is the cause for selecting France as the friend, and England as the enemy of our country?"*

The Act declaring war was signed by the President, June 18th, 1812. The British Government ignorant of this voluntarily revoked the Orders in Council on June 23rd.†

James Madison was elected again to the Presidency in 1812, by the Southern or Democratic party, receiving 128 electoral votes against 89 for the rival candidate—all of which were given by States North of the Potomac, save South Carolina.

The United States Government had made very inadequate preparations for the war it had undertaken. The Treasury was nearly empty in consequence of the various Embargo Acts. The army numbered less than

* This document showed that the exports from the United States for 1811 amounted to 45 millions of dollars, of which 1 million only went to France.

† Had the Atlantic Cable existed in those days, the transmission of this fact would have averted the war.

10,000 men, the half of them mere recruits. The navy consisted of 8 frigates, 2 sloops, and 5 brigs. Congress voted a new army of 25,000 regulars, and 50,000 volunteers. General Dearborn was appointed Commander-in-Chief.

Hostilities began by an invasion of Canada from Detroit, under General Hull. His forces were wholly insufficient, and he was compelled to surrender, in August, to the British General, Brock. A second invasion of Canada on the Niagara frontier was equally unfortunate. On the ocean, however, the navy, small as it was, acquired great renown. In August, the *Constitution*, Capt. Hull, captured the *Guerrière*; in October, the *Wasp*, Capt. Jones, captured the *Frolic*; in October, also, the *United States*, Capt. Decatur, captured the *Macedonia*; and in December, the *Constitution*, Capt. Bainbridge now commanding, captured the *Java*. Besides these successes in regular warfare, the privateers which covered the sea captured during the year some 300 British merchant vessels.

Thus ended the campaign of 1812.

For the following year, three armies were raised to operate on the Canadian frontier. Numerous engagements occurred with alternate successes and reverses. The campaign closed on land with no decided result. The navy was again more fortunate than the army. In September, on Lake Erie, a British fleet of six vessels was taken by Commodore Perry. On the ocean, in February, the *Hornet*, Capt. Lawrence, captured the *Peacock*; and in September, the *Enterprise*, Lieut. Burrows, captured the *Boxer*. In June, however, Capt. Lawrence of the *Chesapeake* was forced to surrender to Capt. Broke of the English frigate *Shannon*, who was knighted for this feat.

The succeeding campaign of 1814 was conducted with more spirit on both sides. In July, the British were defeated at Chippewa by General Brown; and again, in the same month, at Lundy's Lane by Generals Brown and Scott. In August, a British fleet arrived in the Chesapeake with an army of 5,000 men, under General Ross, who landed and marched on Washington. The Federal city had been left without defence, and was easily taken. The President and his Cabinet had abandoned it, and the British General burned the Capitol and other public buildings. In September, the same army made an attack on Baltimore, but was routed, and General [illegible] killed. In September, on Lake Champlain, a British fleet was vanquished by Commodore MacDonough; and on the same day, an English army of 14,000 men, under General Prevost, besieging Plattsburg, was repulsed by General Macomb. On the ocean this year the British lost six vessels of war, and the Americans two, the frigates *Essex* and *President.*

In January, 1815, a British army under General Pakenham, 12,000 strong, landed to make an attack on New Orleans, which was defended by General Jackson with 5,000 men, chiefly militia. The attack was repulsed, January 8th, with a loss to the British of 2,000 killed and wounded.*

In 1813, the Emperor of Russia had offered to mediate between the United States and Great Britain, which the first accepted, but the latter declined. In 1814, negotiations for peace at the instance of Great

* This action was fought before the news of Peace, signed December 24th, 1814, reached the United States — another instance where an Atlantic Cable would have changed the history of men and things.

Britain were renewed, and Commissioners were appointed by both Governments, who met at Ghent, where a Treaty of Peace was signed in December, 1814. The Treaty provided for the restoration of all territory taken during the war, and the settlement of the northern boundary of the United States.

It is a striking fact that nothing was said of the *impressment* of American seamen, one of the main causes of the war. The President had instructed the United States Commissioners, "if peace could not be had on other terms, to waive the question of *impressment*, and leave it for future negotiation." "The inquiry naturally presents itself," says the author of the "American Statesman," "that as *impressment* was the only grievance to be redressed by war, after the revocation of the British Orders in Council, and as this point was waived by our Government in the negotiation, *what was gained by the war?*" He also remarks that the elder Statesmen and leading men of the Administration were opposed to the war party, but yielded to the impulsive young Politicians, Calhoun, Clay, and others, who, it was suspected, were seeking simply to turn "the prejudice against Great Britain to their own political advantage." "Whether," continues this author, "the nation has ever obtained an equivalent for the 30,000 lives and the hundred millions of money expended, for the loss of property and several years of prosperous commerce, for the depravation of public morals, and other evils consequent on war, is a question which, at least, admits of a reasonable doubt."*

* If the insinuation is just that the "impulsive young politicians," Calhoun and Clay, urged on the war from ambitious motives, they were doomed to disappointment, as they never reached the Presidential

In connection with the hostilities of 1812 should be mentioned the discontent of the Eastern States, whose commercial interests were much damaged by the Embargo Acts, and wholly prostrated by the war. With a view to mitigate these evils, and if possible to terminate the war, a Convention of Delegates from several of the New England States met at Hartford, in December, 1814. It is this body that afterwards became so notorious as the *Hartford Convention.* They sat with closed doors, but from the published Report of their proceedings it would appear they proposed to amend the Federal Constitution rather than to effect a dissolution of the Union, as was alleged. One of the Amendments passed was "to prohibit Congress from laying an Embargo for more than sixty days;" and another, "requiring the concurrence of two-thirds of both Houses to declare war." The Southern Politicians adroitly seized on this incident to raise the cry of Treason against their Northern rivals. The truth of the accusation was so generally suspected, if not believed, that the Federalist party, of whose members the *Hartford Convention* was composed, lost its hold on the country and rapidly broke up.

It is worthy of notice that the *Protective System* was introduced into the United States by the Southern States. The reason was obvious. Great Britain blunderingly imposed a Duty on cotton, which made the cotton-growing States naturally anxious to manufacture that important staple at home. Consequently President Madison, the candidate of the Southern States, in his Message to Congress, December, 1815, recommended a

chair, but were only instrumental in raising to it Jackson and Harrison, two Generals who acquired distinction in the war.

Tariff on imports, not merely with a view to revenue, but to afford encouragement to certain branches of native manufactures. The leading Representatives of the South, Calhoun, Lowndes, Clay, earnestly advocated this Protective policy. On the other hand the New England States, with Webster as their chief exponent, energetically opposed it, for their interests being commercial, they were desirous to give extension to the carrying trade, which a Protective Tariff with its restrictions on foreign goods would hamper. In consequence of the suggestions of the President, the Southern or Democratic party passed a Law imposing a scale of Duties on imports ranging from twenty to thirty-five per cent.

At the close of the war, the financial condition of the country was in utter disorder. All the Banks save those of New England, had suspended specie payments, and the want of an uniform solvent currency was pressingly felt. There seemed no hope of rescue from the general confusion but in a National Bank. In Congress and out of it, the majority believed that such an institution could alone restore the currency, and enable the Government to ride over its financial difficulties.

The first *Bank of the United States* was chartered by Congress in 1791, and approved by President Washington. It was incorporated for twenty years and rendered eminent services to the trade and commerce of the country. The charter expired in 1811.

It is noteworthy that this first Bank of the United States was ardently opposed by the South in Congress, and as ardently supported by the North.

In 1816, when another Government Bank became a national necessity, it is singular to find the South taking a strong stand for its immediate incorporation, whilst the North was as decided in opposition. The Bill to create the Bank was reported by J. C. Calhoun, the leader of the Southern or Democratic party, and Daniel Webster, the head of the Northern party, argued ably against it. It passed the Lower House by 80 to 71 and the Senate by 22 to 12.

The Bank was chartered for twenty years with a capital of thirty-five millions of dollars, of which one-fifth was to be paid in specie, and one-fifth to be subscribed for by the Government. It was to be entitled to the deposit of the public funds, which it was required to disburse without charge. A bonus of a million and a-half dollars was demanded for its charter. The Government was to appoint five of the twenty-five Directors.

The South and the North voted almost in a body against each other on this Bill.

On both these questions of a Protective Tariff, and of a Bank of the United States, the South and the North completely changed sides in the lapse of a few years, which simply proves that these great sections took at different periods a different view of their interests. The consequence was that the Politicians of the South assailed the Politicians of the North, in 1791, for sustaining a Government Bank, and, in 1816, the former again attacked the latter for *not* sustaining it. So, in 1816, the Politicians of the North fell upon the Politicians of the South for advocating a Protective System, and, in 1828, the former again denounced the latter for *not* advocating it. In short, the Politicians of the North and South were compelled to exchange arguments with each other, and to take positions on these two questions directly opposite to those first assumed.

PRESIDENCY OF JAMES MONROE.

James Monroe of Virginia, the candidate of the Southern party, was elected President in 1816, by 183 electoral votes to 43 given to the opposing candidate.

He was inaugurated March 4th, 1817, and selected his Cabinet from the members of the Democratic party. J. Q. Adams was made Secretary of State; J. C. Calhoun, Secretary of War; W. H. Crawford, Secretary of the Treasury; and B. W. Crowinshield, Secretary of the Navy.

Mr. Monroe had the good fortune to begin his Administration without any party opposition. The resistance made to the war by the Federalist party of the North compromised its standing with the country, and the uproar raised by its rival, the Democratic party of the South, about the *Hartford Convention* gave the quietus to all its hopes of future success at the polls. The conciliatory tone of the President to his late political opponents, the Federalists, afforded them the coveted opportunity, and they promptly tendered their support to his Administration.

For the greater part of President Monroe's first term the Politicians of the two sections, North and South, were united in joint support of such measures as came up. The political sea was unruffled. It was the first complete calm the country had witnessed. As far as the eye could reach no cloud of disagreement could be descried. "It is gratifying to witness," wrote the President, "the increased harmony of opinion which pervades the Union. Discord does not belong to our system." For some three years this "era of good feeling" continued.

During this interval there was little of national interest occurred save an Indian war—the Seminole—in Florida. It led in the end to the cession of all this territory to the United States by a Treaty with Spain in February, 1819, wherein the United States Government bound itself to pay five millions of dollars in lieu of all claims for spoliations committed by Spain against citizens of the United States.

The political lull which had so happily prevailed was suddenly dispelled by an incident which occurred in the House of Representatives in the beginning of 1819. The territory of Missouri applied for admission as a State of the Union, when a New York Member, James Tallmadge, got up and moved an Amendment prohibiting the further introduction of slavery within the said territory. Thereupon the Southern Members passionately exclaimed that this was a violation of the Constitution. The Northern Members responded as warmly that the assertion was unfounded. Cobb of Georgia said, "a fire had been kindled which only seas of blood could extinguish." Tallmadge of New York replied, "if blood was necessary to extinguish any fire he had kindled, he was ready to contribute his own."

The North and South were again at loggerheads, but this time the split was serious indeed. Hitherto, they had quarrelled on points of policy on which sometimes the North was divided against itself, and sometimes the same occurred at the South. But this time the whole North—Federalists and Democrats—were united against the South, which was equally unanimous. On the part of the North it was a question of sentiment, but on the part of the South it was one of material interest.

Strange to say the North and the South had changed sides on this subject as they had done on nearly all others.

At a very early date the New England Colonies, following the example of the Mother-country,* were actively engaged in the African Slave Trade. New England ships made the voyage to England with tobacco and rice; there took in British manufactures for the Guinea Coast, which exchanging for blacks, they returned to the Southern Colonies, sold them, and reloading with tobacco and rice for Europe, as before, completed the round voyage.

The South finding themselves inundated with a black population, began to remonstrate against its further increase. In 1777, Mr. Jefferson introduced a Bill into the Virginia Legislature which became a Law "to prevent the importation of slaves." In 1784, Mr. Jefferson

*In 1561, a Sir John Hawkins sailed for the Guinea Coast with English merchandise, which he exchanged for a cargo of negroes. These he carried to Hispaniola, sold for sugar and ginger, and then returned to England. Similar expeditions followed. In 1689, the British Government entered into a convention with Spain by which she agreed to provide her West India Colonies with African slaves. In 1713, the "South Sea Company" entered into a similar agreement, and furnished the Spanish Colonies with 4,800 slaves per annum for thirty years. In 1760, General O'Hara, Governor of Senegambia, reported that in the "previous fifty years no less than 70,000 blacks had been deported per annum from that country alone." In the development of this commerce there were three great interests that especially prospered: the manufacturers, the shippers, and the merchants. The venture of Sir John Hawkins was the commencement of the trade in African blacks, which was carried on by England with immense profits for the period of 246 years.

proposed in the Congress of the Confederation, a Bill to prohibit slavery in all the territory held by the United States, and in all that might be afterwards acquired. This did not succeed at the time, but in 1787 a Bill was passed prohibiting slavery in the territory north-west of the Ohio. In the Convention which framed the Federal Constitution, the South insisted on the abolition of the Slave Trade in the United States, which the North consented to at the expiration of nineteen years, 1808, on condition of receiving as compensation for this "thriving trade," the monopoly of the coasting trade against all foreign tonnage.

But when 1808 arrived, a complete change of opinion had occurred in the North and South relative to slavery. The invention of the cotton-gin* which increased the production of that staple, and the acquisition of Louisiana with its almost tropical soil, had greatly enhanced the demand for slave labor. Consequently, instead of a grievance, slavery had become a profit to the South, which vindicated it strongly, whilst the North on the other hand having washed its hands of all connection with the blacks, began to take a more philanthropic view of the matter. In this reversed position affairs stood for a few years, the North merely exacting that a Free State should enter the Union for every Slave State. Accordingly, Vermont was followed by Kentucky; Tennessee by Ohio; Louisiana by Indiana; Mississippi by Illinois; Alabama by Maine.

When, however, it was proposed in Congress, as related, to admit Missouri as a Slave State in 1819, the North

* The cotton-gin, invented by Eli Whitney of Massachusetts, was an ingenious machine for separating the seed from the cotton with extreme celerity.

in the person of a New York Member objected. Then occurred the scene alluded to in which the South fulminated threats, and the North shouted its defiance.

After the adjournment of Congress in 1819, a tremendous agitation on the slavery question broke out in the North. Public meetings were called in all the towns and villages; the Legislatures of the middle States drew up memorials to Congress; the New England States joined in the general chorus: all vociferating that it was "the right and duty of Congress to prohibit slavery in the Territories."

When Congress met, its halls rang with angry echoes, and the excited Politicians gave free vent to their sectional feelings. At last, reason in a measure recovered its sway, and a compromise was agreed on. It was settled that Missouri should be admitted to the Union as a Slave State, but for ever after slavery was to be prohibited north of 36° 30′ north latitude. This was the famous "Missouri Compromise," which for a time put an end to the slavery agitation, but as events proved it was only "scotched not killed."

Without discussing the arguments of the various orators, Northern and Southern, as to the constitutionality of slavery, or the right of Congress to interfere with it—much less stopping to consider slavery in the abstract—it is worth while to mention the taunt of the South as to the motives which had stirred up this alarming perturbation. The Southern Politicians insinuated that their rivals of the North had been beaten at the game of politics; that they had lost their hold on the National Government since the Administration of John Adams; and that in the hope of recovering it they were seeking to inflame the imagination of the people on the subject of slavery reckless of the consequences, amongst which might be civil war and a dissolution of the Union. However this may have been, the words of the Georgia Member were indeed prophetic, that "a fire had been kindled which only seas of blood could extinguish."

The only other striking event which distinguished the Administration of President Monroe was the recognition in 1822 of the South American Colonies of Spain as independent Republics. In his Message to Congress preceding this event, he protested with moderation against the intervention of any European power in the affairs of the American Continent. He declared that "as a principle the American continents, by the free and independent position which they have assumed and maintained, are henceforth not to be considered as subjects for future colonization by any European power." This declaration has since been christened as the "Monroe Doctrine," and is often quoted.

Monroe was the last to occupy the Presidential chair of the Statesmen who figured in the Revolutionary struggle.

PRESIDENCY OF JOHN QUINCY ADAMS.

In the Presidential election for 1824, the North presented no candidate. The Southern or Democratic party failed to unite on any candidate, and in consequence the electoral colleges gave their votes to various prominent individuals of that party. General Jackson received 99 votes; J. Q. Adams, 84; W. H. Crawford, 41; and Henry Clay, 37. As none had a majority, the election for President vested in the House of Representatives, where, in February, 1825, J. Q. Adams received the vote of 13 States; General Jackson, of 7; and W. H. Crawford, of 4. Mr. Adams was therefore, by a majority of the States, elected President.

Being convinced of the impossibility of his election, Mr. Clay had withdrawn his name from the canvass, and desired the States who were ready to support him to record their votes for Mr. Adams.

On the accession to office of President Adams, he tendered the Secretaryship of State to Mr. Clay. Upon this a loud outcry was raised by the partisans of the defeated candidates of a bargain having been made between Mr. Adams and Mr. Clay. It was baptized as the "Coalition," and led to a vast amount of personal altercation. The only thing certain was that Mr. Clay retired from the contest when he saw no chance of success, and as he preferred Mr. Adams' nomination to that of General Jackson, he naturally used his influence to secure it. Mr. Adams, on the other hand, selected him for his chief Secretary, as the best qualified for the post, but no doubt felt grateful to Mr. Clay for giving his claims the preference over those of his rival, General Jackson. The partisans of the latter, however, made an immense clamor over the alleged "Coalition," and manœuvred skilfully to ensure General Jackson's elevation to the Presidency at the next election.

There was little in the foreign or domestic policy of President Adams which requires special notice. "His administration was remarkable for order, method, and economy, though party spirit springing from quarrels generated by the election was higher and more rancorous than it had been for many years." *

The most interesting event of this Administration was the passing of a new Act by Congress, May, 1828, further increasing the Duties on the importation of wool and woollen goods, with a view to encourage American manufactures. In the last year of President Monroe's Administration, 1824, the Tariff had been raised in conformity to suggestions in his last Message, but it was complained by the manufacturers that the Duties in question had been evaded, and in the last year of the Administration of President Adams, 1828, it was proposed in their interest to remodel them. An acrimonious debate ensued, and the greatest diversity of opinion prevailed. The Southern States vehemently opposed any augmentation of the Tariff as detrimental to the agricultural interest, whilst some of the Northern States advocated it zealously for the reason that it was beneficial to that interest. The South, also, was disposed to deny the constitutionality of a Tariff to

* "New American Cyclopædia."

protect home manufactures, but it was shown that in the first Congress which met after the adoption of the Constitution, and where so many of its framers were present, no one questioned the power of Congress to adopt a Protective policy under the clause which authorized it to "levy and collect taxes, duties, imports, and excises—to regulate commerce with foreign nations."

A conclusive proof of the change of opinion on the subject of a Protective Tariff at the North and South may be found in the fact that, in 1824, Mr. Webster of Massachusetts was the ablest opponent of such a measure, used all his talents and influence against it, and brought a formidable array of facts and figures to show its inexpediency; whereas, in 1828, he was discovered on the opposite side of the same question, and displayed just as much ability in vindicating the efficiency of higher imposts to develope manufacturing prosperity. Within this short interval the State he represented in Congress had begun to invest her capital in manufactures, and, of course, he was obliged to change his ground and express different views.

The Tariff Bill of 1828 passed the House of Representatives by 105 to 94, and the Senate by 26 to 21, which shows that the division of opinion was nearly equal. The eccentric John Randolph of Virginia declared in the House that "the Bill, if it had its true name, should be called a Bill to rob and plunder nearly one half the Union for the benefit of the residue." Mr. Drayton of South Carolina moved to amend the title of the Bill, and insert, "to increase the Duties upon certain imports for the purpose of increasing the profits of certain manufacturers."

I shall here close the retrospect of the political

history of the United States. In 1828, General Jackson was elected President, but as I was a spectator of most of the events connected with his Administration, I shall treat of them in the volume already referred to,—"The History of my Times."

SUMMARY.

SUMMARY.

The following summary will comprise an impartial estimate of the historical facts recorded rather than a mere recapitulation. It may be that the general reader will obtain in this way a clearer perception of the purport of this volume, which is chiefly designed to show that, from the Christian era, a single principle, which then first appeared, has by its gradual development shaped the history of the world and the destiny of mankind.

First Civilization.

Asia was the seat of the first civilization, and its salient features were the concentration of all the power, wealth, and knowledge in the hands of the Upper Classes, whilst ignorance, poverty, and slavery were the lot of the Lower Class, which constituted three-fourths of the population. This state of society has been invariably upheld by the Laws and Religions of Asia, and endures to this day essentially the same as it was some three thousand years before the Christian era.

The solution of this phenomenon is to be found in physical causes.

Second Civilization.

Africa was the seat of the second civilization, where similar physical causes produced a state of society in all respects analagous to that in Asia.

A Mystery.

History affords no clue to the civilization found existing in America in the fifteenth century. The features, political and social, were identical with those of Asia and Africa. As the climate of Mexico and Peru resembles that of the Eastern countries mentioned, it is another proof that physical causes alone explain the peculiar condition of all these countries.

Third Civilization.

Europe was the seat of the third civilization, which, intellectually, far surpassed those preceding it; but, in other respects, the organization of society was the same. Power, wealth, and knowledge were still monopolized by the Upper Classes, whilst ignorance, poverty, and slavery, were still the heritage of the Lower Class. The intellectual superiority of the third civilization is attributed to physical conditions different from those of Asia, Africa, and America.

Fourth Civilization.

The fourth civilization followed the advent of the Messiah, and was founded on the doctrines of the New Religion. The most conspicuous among these was the dogma that all men were equal in the sight of God. This principle of *Equality* was till then unknown in the world, and its religious and moral effect on the masses was so great that it led, first, to the extinction of the Pagan Religion, and, next, to the fall of the Roman Empire—both based on the religious and moral inequality of mankind.

Dark Ages.

The successful invasion of Roman Europe by the barbarous tribes of Germany was due to the New Religion, which indisposed the masses to sustain a religious and political fabric founded on their permanent enslavement. The chaotic condition of the world known as the "Dark Ages" was marked by the conflict between Christianity and brute force, in which the former triumphed. The rise of Charlemagne in the eighth century may be regarded as the period when the new ideas predominated. Material order, moral culture, and religious instruction, in harmony with the New Revelation, then began to prevail.

The New Polity.

The confusion and lawlessness which characterized the Dark Ages received their first check under the Empire of Charlemagne. It was only after his death when Europe, consolidated for a time by his genius, broke up into various Nationalities that the New Polity began to reveal itself. It was at this period, the dawn of the Middle Ages, that the authority of Christianity was strong enough over the greater part of Europe to influence Government. This may, therefore, be called the Inauguration of the New Polity, for from the fall of the Roman Empire in the fifth century to the rise of Charlemagne in the eighth nothing deserving the name of Government existed in Europe. The political organizations which then successively arose were all Christian, but the doctrines of the New Religion were interpreted to accord with tyrannical instincts, and their beneficent effects on the condition of the masses were destined for long ages to be ignored. Yet it is none the less memorable that with the close of the Dark Ages the old civilizations lost their hold on Europe. It was then the fourth civilization—the New Polity—obtained its ascendency; it was then that moral power derived from the teachings of Christianity began its career; and it was then that mere physical force in the government of men was put on its trial. The doctrine of the inequality of men, which was the corner-stone of the ancient civilizations, was undermined when the New Polities were set up—when Governments under the sway of the Christian religion began their ministration. It can hardly be regarded as less than marvellous that in a period of scarcely four centuries, the fourth or Christian civilization had made such progress that Royal Power, then regarded as of divine origin, should be compelled to acknowledge that the masses had rights. When King John of England, in 1215, bound himself not to "deny or delay to any man right or justice," it proved that truly a New Polity had appeared in the world, and that the Ancient Polities which taught the hereditary inequality of men, and the permanent subjection of the many to the moral, legal, and political authority of the few, were doomed to decay.

France.

The first permanent organization of society which sprang up in Europe under the fourth civilization is known as the Feudal System. It was totally unlike anything that had appeared before the Christian era. It is true that during its sway power and wealth still remained in the hands of the Upper Class, but they were no longer monopolized. It is true that slavery was still the lot of the Lower Class, but it was no longer regarded as a final condition. It was in France that the Feudal System was first developed, where it was better organized and more vigorously maintained than in other parts of Europe. In spite, however, of its great power, it was steadily invaded by the subtle influence of that irresistible doctrine brought into existence by Christianity, and during the whole of the Middle Ages *Equality* continued to expand and acquire new strength. *Vires acquirit eundo.* Various events, as related, combined with this new and restless principle to sap the basis of the Feudal system, and it fell to pieces in the seventeenth century. It was superseded by Absolute Monarchy, which reached its zenith in the reign of Louis XIV. In the eighteenth century, the fermentation engendered by the fourth civilization—which had been working for so many centuries, and for which no legitimate channel had been provided—burst forth and deluged the land. In ancient or modern history no similar event to the French Revolution had occurred. The multitude rose in their might, and, under the inspiration of the Christian dogma of the *Equality* of all men before God, demanded emancipation for mind and body under legal guarantees. It was obtained, and can never be lost. Since then power, wealth, and knowledge are monopolized by no Class; and ignorance, poverty, and slavery are no longer the bequest of unequal laws.

England.

In England, the withdrawal of the Romans was followed, as elsewhere, by the irruption of German tribes, which gradually fell under the influence of Christianity. Towards the end of the eighth century—the epoch of Charlemagne—order, morality, and religion began to glimmer in England. Under the Saxon régime the power and wealth were in the possession of the Upper Class, but, as in all parts of Christianized Europe, no longer monopolized. So far from that, members of the free Middle Class in England constantly ascended into the Nobility, and the slaves or Lower Class were constantly obtaining freedom. The regular development of Saxon society was disturbed by the Norman Conquest, which led to the Saxon Upper Class being superseded by the Norman Upper Class. This singular conjunction of a Norman Upper Class, a Saxon Middle Class, and a native Lower Class on the same soil, is a peculiar feature of English history. A compromise between the interests of all ensued, and hence the origin of *Magna Charta* and the House of Commons. The prerogatives of the Upper Class, power and wealth, were shared with the Middle Class, which in its turn opened its ranks to the aspiring of the Lower Class. Thus it happened that the Christian dogma of *Equality* which in France was excluded or dammed up, as it were, was in England favored by accidental circumstances, and found natural and easy outlets. Consequently no hurricane like the French Revolution was needed in England to effect an organization of society in harmony with the fourth civilization. There the power, wealth, and knowledge, which in the ancient world were engrossed by the Upper Class, became more and more accessible to all who sought them, or whose intelligence commanded them.

The Papacy.

The establishment at Rome in 42 A.D. of a spiritual Head for the young Church, was one of the most potent means of securing its advancement, by giving unity to the efforts, and encouragement to the zeal of the Christian Priesthood. So long as the See of Rome was solely occupied with the interests of the Church, and the propagation of the primitive doctrines, its influence was beneficial, and constantly augmented. In the progress of centuries the spiritual power of the Papacy became so vast that it grew insensible to its true mission; and instead of occupying itself with the religious and moral welfare of mankind, it began to interest itself in the temporal concerns of the world.

Worse than this, the Papacy, forgetful of its origin, and disregarding the interests of the masses, on which Christianity was founded, allied itself wholly with the Upper Classes, and thereby strengthened and prolonged their power. These derelictions from its early and true *rôle* weakened its hold on the Lower Class, and have in the process of time exposed it not only to damaging vicissitudes, but have greatly impaired its spiritual influence. Stripped in our day of its temporal power, and chastened by the ordeal it has undergone, the Papacy may yet return to the pious discharge of those purely spiritual offices which were once its only care, and which laid the foundation of its supremacy.

The United States.

It was shown in the preceding pages of this volume, that under the three civilizations of the ancient world Society was substantially divided into two great classes, the Upper and the Lower. The fourth civilization introduced a novel and disturbing principle when it announced the *Equality* of all men before God. Since then, the Lower Class in Europe has struggled through the Dark Ages, the Middle Ages, and Modern Times to obtain its emancipation, and to occupy in the framework of society its just and natural position. The repugnance of the Upper Class, and the perseverance of the Lower towards this consummation, explain in great part the convulsions of the European world for centuries past. The deliberate abandonment of their native land by the Puritans in the seventeenth century, like the retreat of the Roman Lower Class to *Mons Sacer*, gave a new phase to this protracted conflict. These men of the popular class, clinging to their Christian dogma of *Equality*, and despairing of its recognition at home, carried it off to the wilderness where there were none to dispute it. This was the first instance of a Society established on the basis of absolute equality before God and before the Law. This was the culmination of the fourth civilization, and the very antithesis of the three civilizations of the ancient world. In the latter, all power, wealth, and knowledge were absorbed by the Upper Class, whilst the Lower Class was consigned to perpetual exclusion; but in the wilds of North America a Society sprang up consisting of but one Class, all and equally entitled to whatever share of power, wealth, and knowledge its members could through intelligence and industry obtain. What inequalities exist in the United States are of God's making, and not of man's. He has decreed to His creatures different degrees of intelligence; and it is in harmony with this that we find in the new Society the distribution of men in Upper, Middle, and Lower Classes, but to none is given any privilege, monopoly, or advantage, save such as can be obtained by the exercise of his intellect. If one man is more influential, or richer, or wiser than another, it is the guerdon of a superior capacity, and none contest this natural preponderance. For all the rest, Religion is free, Law is equal, and Government the choice of the Majority. Whether a country so constituted is a final solution, or simply a *beau idéal* not compatible with the passions of men, remains to be seen.

In closing this Summary, may I venture a comment on the Present, and a glance at the Future.

In denoting the perturbations of European society for so many centuries, I have assigned as their principal cause the efforts of the Lower Class of inferior intelligence to obtain from the Upper Class of superior intelligence an exemption from unjust oppression, and the recognition of their *Equality* before God and the Law. I have shown that this *ground-swell*, so to speak, dates from the Christian era; and it may now be said to have nearly exhausted itself in three of the leading countries of the world.

In the United States is seen a Society constructed on the basis of absolute equality, religious, legal, and political. Such social distinctions as exist flow from the inherent differences between men, and are accepted as inevitable. All that remains to be tested is the fitness of the Mass for self-government, which must be solved by the example of the United States. Everything has favored the experiment in that country: and if it be proved that the popular control exercised there over Government cannot preserve it from corruption, folly, and crime—then all hope must be abandoned of arriving at *perfect* Government. But happen what may—be it the fate of the American Union to republicanize the world, or be it its fate to establish beyond all question that the laborious Majority is unable to curb the more intelligent Minority—yet it cannot be doubted that never again will it be possible to restore the ancient civilizations which gave all to the Upper Class and nothing to the multitude. No Government, hereafter, will be durable or strong which does not promote the interests of the masses, who, if not able to guide it, know they have the strength to overturn it.

In England a state of society virtually similar exists, since no obstacles are interposed to the claims of genuine intelligence. The Upper Class enjoys no privilege beyond the reach of any. Merit ascends by regular gradation to its natural level. As in the United States, Religion is practically free, Law equal, and the Government, though not the choice of the Majority, is administered in its interest. To give the Majority the control of Government before it is competent by education and experience to exercise it, would be, as has been said, to involve society in confusion.

In France, at the present day, the Lower Class is in plenary possession of the absolute equality prevailing in the United States. Nay more, not content with this, there are fanatics, called Communists, who would despoil superior intelligence of its acquisitions, to bestow them on those without claim. Though it is true that the Lower Class has achieved its complete emancipation in France; though it is true that power, wealth, and knowledge, as in the United States, are denied to none; yet society is unsettled, and frequently falls into disorder. The reason is to be ascribed to the fact that the Lower Class having, through the blind arrogance of the Upper Class, obtained sudden Independence by revolution, is unfitted by education and experience—which the United States possess—to preserve it. In consequence, the people abandon it at one time in despair, and at another seize upon it with fury. Time, with its discipline, can alone provide a remedy and ensure ultimate stability.

It is plain that all Europe is drifting in the direction of the fourth civilization. The abolition of serfdom in Russia; the resurrection of Italy; the consolidation of Germany; the anarchy of Spain: all attest it.

But the renovation of society on a more equal basis is not limited to Europe and America. Already has the fourth or Christian civilization with its wonderful results—its telegraphs, railways, finance, and trade—penetrated into the long stagnant reservoirs of the ancient civilizations. The Missionary armed with the New Testament is but a Pioneer. In his train follow legislation, science, enterprise—in a word, the moral and material progeny which, after the gestation of centuries, the fourth civilization has brought forth, confirming its Divine origin and confounding scepticism. For who can deny that Christianity by emancipating the mind of the Mass is the parent of all the prodigies enumerated? It is through the stimulus of England, France, and the United States, that the heathen lands of Asia and Africa are awakening to the new influences. The Religions and Laws which have there so long guaranteed the supremacy of the Upper Classes are being constantly modified; and the burdens and exactions imposed on the masses for ages are being constantly diminished and removed.* To what extent

* Sir Bartle Frere, in his speech to the working men at Bath, October 10th, 1873, stated that "the working men, almost universally throughout the two hundred and odd millions inhabiting India, were everywhere trodden down by the strictest possible system of *caste*; but Christianity had been silently and imperceptibly breaking down the bonds of *caste*. He believed there were 33 societies of different denominations which were actively engaged in preaching the Gospel, through missionaries, to the people, and the effect had been to permeate the whole of Indian society more or less with the spirit of Christianity. Through the spirit of Christianity, through railways, through legislation, and through the hundred influences of the Central Government, power had been communicated to the people, which was gradually and imperceptibly, but surely, breaking down the power of *caste*: and he believed that if, by the blessing of God, the empire of England over that country was perpetuated, before very many generations had passed, they would find that *caste* had melted away before the influences of Christianity."

As an additional proof of the progress of the fourth civilization, it may be stated that active efforts are being made by English capitalists these ancient communities can be remodelled on the Christian basis, it is impossible to foresee. It will be remembered that the political and social organizations so long existing in these tropical lands, were shown to be chiefly due to physical causes. How far these may be eluded or tampered with by human laws is an enigma which the Future must disclose.

to introduce railways and telegraphs into China. In spite of the firm opposition of the Government, it would appear by the last advices that a line of telegraph of some ten miles has been erected, which may be regarded as the entering wedge.

It is unnecessary to remind the reader that Japan has opened wide its gates, and welcomed the coming of the Christian civilization.

INDEX.

THE END.

PRESCOTT'S WORKS.

CROWN OCTAVO EDITION.

COMPLETE IN FIFTEEN UNIFORM VOLUMES.

EACH VOLUME WITH PORTRAIT ON STEEL.

Prescott's History of the Reign of Ferdinand and Isabella the Catholic. Three vols. 8vo.

Prescott's Biographical and Critical Miscellanies. With a finely engraved steel Portrait of the Author. One vol. 8vo.

Prescott's History of the Conquest of Mexico, with a Preliminary View of the Ancient Mexican Civilization, and the Life of the Conqueror, Fernando Cortez. In three vols. 8vo.

Prescott's History of the Reign of Philip the Second, King of Spain. In three vols. 8vo.

Prescott's History of the Conquest of Peru, with a Preliminary View of the Civilization of the Incas. In two vols. 8vo.

Prescott's Robertson's History of the Reign of the Emperor Charles the Fifth. With an account of the Emperor's Life after his Abdication. In three vols. 8vo.

Each work sold separately. Price per vol., cloth, $2.50; half calf, neat, $3.75; half calf, gilt extra, marble edges, $4.25; half Turkey, gilt top, $4.50. Complete sets, printed on tinted paper, handsomely bound in green or claret-colored cloth, gilt top, beveled boards. Price, $40.

CHAMBERS'S BOOK OF DAYS.

The Book of Days: A Miscellany of Popular Antiquities in connection with the Calendar, including Anecdote, Biography and History, Curiosities of Literature, and Oddities of Human Life and Character. In two vols. royal 8vo. Price per set, cloth, $9; sheep, $10; half Turkey, $11. Edited under the supervision of ROBERT CHAMBERS.

This work consists of

I.—Matters connected with the Church Calendar, including the Popular Festivals, Saints' Days, and other Holidays, with illustrations of Christian Antiquities in general.

II.—Phenomena connected with the Seasonal Changes.

III.—Folk-Lore of the United Kingdom: namely, Popular Notions and Observances connected with Times and Seasons.

IV.—Notable Events, Biographies and Anecdotes connected with the Days of the Year.

V.—Articles of Popular Archæology, of an entertaining character tending to illustrate the progress of Civilization, Manners, Literature and Ideas in those kingdoms.

VI.—Curious, Fugitive and Inedited Pieces.

The work is printed in a new, elegant and readable type and illustrated with an abundance of Wood Engravings.

THE

Works of Washington Irving.

EDITIONS OF IRVING'S WORKS.

I. The Knickerbocker Edition.—Large 12*mo, on* superfine laid, tinted paper. Profusely Illustrated with Steel Plates and Wood-cuts, elegantly printed from new stereotype plates. Complete in 27 vols. Bound in extra cloth, gilt top. Per vol. $2.50. Half calf, gilt extra. Per vol. $4.

II. The Riverside Edition.—16*mo, on fine white* paper; from new stereotype plates. With Steel Plates. Complete in 26 vols. Green crape cloth, gilt top, beveled edges. Per vol. $1.75. Half calf, gilt extra. Per vol. $3.25.

*III. The People's Edition.—From the same stereo-*type plates as above, but printed on cheaper paper. Complete in 26 vols. 16mo. With Steel Vignette Titles. Neatly bound in cloth. Per vol. $1.25. Half calf neat. Per vol. $2.50.

IV. The Sunnyside Edition.—12*mo, on fine toned* paper. With Steel Plates. Complete in 28 vols. Handsomely bound in dark-green cloth. Per vol. $2.25. Half calf, gilt extra. Per vol. $4.

Embracing the following:

Bracebridge Hall,
Wolfert's Roost.
Sketch Book,
Traveler,
Knickerbocker,
Crayon Miscellany,
Goldsmith,
Alhambra,
Columbus, 3 vols.,
Astoria,
Bonneville,
Mahomet, 2 vols.,
Granada,
Salmagundi,
Spanish Papers, 2 vols.
Washington, 5 vols.,
Life and Letters, 4 vols.

The reissue of these works in their several forms is unusually elegant. The plates are new, the paper superior, the printing handsome, and each, in proportion to price, combining good taste with economy.

☞ **EACH WORK SOLD SEPARATELY.** ☜

www.ingramcontent.com/pod-product-compliance
Lightning Source LLC
LaVergne TN
LVHW021149110826
845150LV00005B/1168

* 9 7 8 1 4 2 5 5 4 7 2 9 5 *